KRISTALLNACHT

Other books by Martin Gilbert

KRISTALLNACHT

Prelude to Destruction

Martin Gilbert

HarperCollins*Publishers*

Published in Great Britain in 2006 by HarperCollins Publishers.

ISBN-13: 978-0-7394-7590-4

CONTENTS

ILLUSTRATIONS

MAPS

INTRODUCTION

Starting in the early hours of 10 November 1938, and continuing until nightfall, violence against the Jews of Germany was unleashed in a whirlwind of destruction. Within a few hours more than a thousand synagogues were set on fire and destroyed. Where it was thought that fire might endanger nearby non-Jewish buildings, the rioters smashed the synagogues with hammers and axes. This was no spontaneous outburst of destruction, but a coordinated, comprehensive rampage.

In hundreds of Jewish neighbourhoods, paramilitary stormtroopers of the SA 'Sturmabteilung', or Storm Division – some in their Brownshirt uniforms, others in civilian clothes – lit bonfires and threw furniture and books from synagogues and private homes into the flames. In the streets, Jews were chased, reviled and beaten up. Tens of thousands of Jewish shops and homes were ransacked. Jews were attacked in every German town, from the capital, Berlin, to the smallest towns and villages in which Jews lived throughout Hitler's Reich. In twenty-four hours of violence, ninety-one Jews were killed.

Within those twenty-four hours, more than 30,000 Jewish men between the ages of sixteen and sixty – a quarter of all Jewish men still in Germany – were arrested and sent to concentration camps. There they were tortured and tormented for several months. More than a thousand died in these camps.

The name given to the night and day of terror was 'Kristallnacht':

the Night of Broken Glass. For the perpetrators of the destruction, the name reflected their sense of both triumph and contempt: triumph at what they had destroyed, laughter at the thought of the sound of breaking glass. Yet fear and distress were inflicted on every German Jew that night.

No event in the history of the fate of German Jews between 1933 and 1945 was so widely covered by the newspapers while it was taking place. There were several hundred foreign journalists in Germany, including those from the main international news agencies, who reported freely on what they saw and heard. This was not wartime. Five weeks earlier Germany had negotiated an agreement with Britain and France to annex the Sudetenland region of Czechoslovakia; an agreement, in the words of the British Prime Minister Neville Chamberlain, which had inaugurated 'peace in our time'.

The detailed accounts of the scale and virulence of the attacks on Jews and Jewish property during Kristallnacht created shock waves in all democratic countries and effectively ended whatever attractions Nazism had earlier held for ordinary people and their governments. Kristallnacht was a dramatic turning point in the way Nazism was perceived.

This book begins with the origins and events of the night itself, a night still vivid to those who lived through it. It then looks at the six years leading up to that upsurge of terror. It goes on to trace the response of the Jews of Germany, of the German government and of the world to the events of Kristallnacht.

Almost four hundred years earlier, in 1543, Martin Luther, in his pastoral letter *On the Jews and Their Lies*, advised that the synagogues of the Jews 'should be set on fire, and whatever does not burn up should be covered or spread over with dirt so that no one may be able to see a cinder or stone of it. And this ought to be done for the honour of God . . .' Hitler and his acolytes followed this advice for their own destructive purposes.

There are in these pages accounts of Germans of goodwill, as well as foreign diplomats, who tried to help. Their courage should not be forgotten. But nothing can lessen the suffering of those who were the victims of that night of terror, or mitigate the terrible consequences for the Jews of Germany, and for the human condition. Kristallnacht was the prelude to the destruction of a whole people, and an indication of what happens when a society falls victim to its baser instincts.

MARTIN GILBERT
25 September 2005

ACKNOWLEDGEMENTS

I am grateful above all to the following eye-witnesses of Kristall-nacht, who sent me their previously unpublished recollections: Esther Adler (Breslau), Reiner Auman (Frankfurt-on-Main), Susan Ben Yosef (Vienna), Gertrude Bibring (Vienna), Hans Biglajzer (Cologne), Jerry Bocian (Berlin), Lassar Brueckheimer (Marktbreit-on-Main), Chava Cohn (Berlin and Ratibor), Janet Ettelman (Mannheim), Ruth Fluss (Danzig), Zerem Freier (Berlin), Herbert Friedman (Vienna), Fred Garfunkel (Vienna), Marianne Geernaert (Bad Kreuznach), Edgar Gold (Hamburg), Fred Gottlieb (Siegburg), Ruth Gutmann (Hanover), Gary Himler (Vienna), Renie Inow (Wuppertal), Elsa Kissel (Mainz), Adina Koor (Hamburg), Max Kopfstein (Berlin), Charlotte Lapian (Würzburg), Helga Leib (Berlin), Ruth Lewin (Glatz), Miriam Litke (Berlin), Ilse Loeb (Vienna), Walter Loeb (Karlsruhe), Martin Lowenberg (Fulda), Laurie Lowenthal (Aschaffenburg), the late Eric Lucas (Hoengen), Lucy Mandelstam (Vienna), Hans Benjamin Marx (Frankfurt-on-Main), Gerhard Maschkowski (Elbing), Helga Milberg (Vienna), Ruben Moller (Bochum), Rita Newell (Cologne), Lore Oppenheimer (Hanover), Oskar Prager (Furth), Batya Rabin (Frankfurt-on-Main), Esther Reisz (Leipzig), Felix Rinde (Vienna), Edith Rogers (Stuttgart), Inge Sadan (Munich), Pesach Schindler (Munich), Joseph Schwarzberg (Leipzig), Stephanie Segerman (Leipzig), Felix Seiler (Vienna), Bronia Sonnenschein (Vienna), Miriam Spira (Berlin), Henry

Stern (Stuttgart), Frank Wachsner (Breslau), Hans Waizner (Vienna), Lea Weems (Ladenburg), Naftali Kurt Wertheim (Fulda), Margot Wilde (Horb), Joseph Wohlfarth (Frankfurt-on-Main) and Margot Wohlman-Wertheim (Fulda).

Accounts of Kristallnacht were also sent to me by children and grandchildren of those who witnessed it, and spoke about it in their family circle. I am grateful to David Bier (recollections of his mother Vera Bier), Benjamin Gutman (Ilse Wertheimer, Kippenheim), Joel Hess (David Hess, Würzburg), Joan Lessing (Willy Lessing, Bamberg) and Ted Shealy (Ernst Gerstenfeld, Dachau).

Many other people have answered my queries about Kristallnacht, its prelude and its aftermath, or given me documents and personal recollections. I am particularly grateful to Dr Richard A. Baker (United States Senate Historian), Dvir Bar-Gal, Dov Bar-Ner, Michael Bienefeld, Naomi Blake, Anna Charin (Librarian, *Jewish Chronicle*), John David, the late Lord Egremont (John Wyndham), Alexander Fagelson, Pal Foti, Anne Fox, Elie Freud (Professor Arthur Freud), Professor Alain Goldschläger, Professor Richard Griffiths, Dr Ruth Gruber, Arieh and Henny Handler, Chris Havern (United States Coast Guard Historian), Hannelore Headley, Gerda Hoffer, Professor Otto Hutter, Rabbi Harry Jacobi, Seth E. Jacobson, Peter Joy, Arno Klarsfeld, Adaire J. Klein (Director of Library and Archival Services, Simon Wiesenthal Centre, Los Angeles), James Klein, Dr Robert Krell, Joan Lessing, Rachel Man, Marianne Meyer, Judy Montagu (Letters Editor, the *Jerusalem Post*), Professor Peter Neary, Fori Nehru, Dr Stephen Nicholls, Yoni Ozdana, Ze'ev Padan, Mordecai Paldiel, Alan Palmer, Dr Arnold Reisman, Bozenna Rotman, Eric Saul, His Excellency Pavel Seifter, Margaret Shannon (Senior Research Historian, Washington Historical Research), Renée Silberman, Frederick Taylor, Jacqui Wasilewsky (Sydney Jewish Museum), Serena

Woolrich (Allgenerations, Washington DC), Pauline Worner and Enid Wurtman. Dorothea Shefer-Vanson sent me Fraenze Hirsch's letter of 15 March 1939 (Sprottau).

In the course of my work, Esther Goldberg was a font of wise suggestions. Kay Thomson undertook the onerous tasks involved in coordinating an author's work. Robert Lacey and his team at HarperCollins have been supportive throughout, as have been Caradoc King and all those at A. P. Watt, my literary agents.

As with all my books during the past twenty years, the British cartographer Tim Aspden has turned my rough drafts and ideas into maps of the highest quality. Through them, in this book, the reader can follow the events and consequences of Kristallnacht, and see the locations of the many towns and villages in which synagogues were set on fire or destroyed.

KRISTALLNACHT

1

The Night of Broken Glass

ON 18 OCTOBER 1938, on Hitler's orders, more than 12,000 Jews were expelled from Germany. They were Polish-born Jews who had been living in Germany, legally, for many years. They were ordered to leave their homes in a single night, and were allowed to take with them only one suitcase each. As these Jews were taken away, everything they had earned and accumulated in Germany during ten, twenty, even thirty years, their furniture, cutlery, linen, beds, stoves, books, was seized as booty, both by the Nazi authorities and, in hundreds of recorded instances, by their neighbours.

The 12,000 expellees were taken from their homes under the guns and bayonets of the Gestapo to the nearest railway stations, where they were put on trains to the Polish border. Four thousand were accepted by Poland. But 8,000, denied entry into Poland, were forced to stay at the border, at least 7,000 of them on the cold stone floors of the Polish border station of Zbaszyn, and in nearby stables. There, in harsh conditions, they waited for the Polish government to agree to take them in. Hundreds more, one British newspaper told its readers, 'are reported to be lying about, penniless and deserted, in little villages along the frontier near where they had been driven out by the Gestapo and left'.[1]

---

1 'Expelled Jews' Dark Outlook', *The Times*, 1 November 1938.

'I have in my notebook,' wrote a British journalist from Zbaszyn, 'the name of a ninety-three-year-old woman who was among those driven into Poland, and also that of a blind man of seventy-six from Hanover, who was not allowed to take even a handkerchief with him.'[2]

While the authorities in Poland hesitated to give entry permits, the expellees at Zbaszyn waited, hungry, distressed, confused and angry. At least five committed suicide. One expelled couple, who had been living in Hanover for more than twenty-seven years, had a seventeen-year-old son, Herschel Grynszpan, living in Paris. From the border his sister Berta sent him a postcard describing their expulsion: 'No one told us what was up, but we realised this was going to be the end.' Her final appeal: 'We haven't a penny. Could you send us something . . . ?'

Herschel Grynszpan received his sister's short but anguished message on November 3. On the following day he read a graphic account of the deportations in a Paris Yiddish newspaper, which reported a number of instances of insanity and suicide among the expellees. Grynszpan was outraged. On the morning of Sunday, November 6 he bought a pistol, loaded it with five bullets, and on the following day went by Metro to the German Embassy. His plan was to kill the Ambassador. After telling the doorman that he had 'an important document' to deliver, he was sent to the room of the Third Secretary, Ernst vom Rath. 'Did you have an important document to give me?' vom Rath asked. Drawing his pistol, Grynszpan called out: 'You are a filthy Boche and here, in the name of 12,000 persecuted Jews, is your document.'[3]

Grynszpan fired five shots. Two of them hit vom Rath but did

2 '7,000 Jews Still at Frontier', News Chronicle, 1 November 1938.
3 German State Archives, Potsdam, quoted in Rita Thalmann and Emmanuel Feinermann, Crystal Night, 9–10 November 1938, pages 33, 42.

not kill him. One of the diplomat's injuries, however, was grave in the extreme, and he was rushed to the nearest clinic. As soon as Hitler learned of the shooting he ordered his personal physician, Dr Brandt, to fly to Paris, together with the director of the clinic of Munich University. The two physicians left shortly after midnight on November 7. In Germany, the morning newspapers on November 8 denounced the Jewish people as murderers. They pointed out, as proof of an ongoing Jewish campaign against Nazi Germany, that three years earlier a German Jew, David Frankfurter, had shot and killed Wilhelm Gustloff, head of the Nazi organisation of Germans resident in Switzerland.

The German morning newspapers also drew attention to the fact that eleven years before Gustloff's assassination, in the same Paris where Grynszpan had shot vom Rath, a Polish Jew, Samuel Schwarzbart, had shot and killed the Ukrainian Simon Petliura, whose soldiers had murdered tens of thousands of Jews in the Ukraine immediately after the First World War.

During November 8 the first collective punitive measures were announced. All Jewish newspapers and magazines must cease publication forthwith. This ban cut off the Jews from their most accessible contact with their leadership, whose task was to advise and guide them, especially on matters of emigration. It was a measure, one British newspaper explained, 'intended to disrupt the Jewish community and rob it of the last frail ties which hold it together'. There were at that time three German Jewish newspapers with a national circulation, four cultural papers, several sports papers, and several dozen community bulletins, of which the one in Berlin had a circulation of 40,000.

Also on November 8 it was announced that Jewish children could no longer attend 'Aryan' state elementary schools, something that had hitherto been allowed where there were not sufficient Jewish elementary schools. At the same time all Jewish cultural activities were suspended 'indefinitely'.[4]

A violent mass action against the Jews had been in the minds of the Nazi leaders for some time. As vom Rath lay gravely wounded, the moment seemed to have come to bring existing plans into instant readiness. Reinhard Heydrich, one of the leading Jew-haters of the Third Reich – deputy head under Heinrich Himmler of the Gestapo and the SS, with responsibility for the concentration camps – was about to have a moment of glory.

November 8 saw a number of outbursts of what the Minister of Propaganda, Dr Josef Goebbels, a Jew-hater in the Heydrich mould, called 'spontaneous demonstrations' against the Jews of Germany. In London it was reported that a synagogue had been 'burned to the ground' at Hersfeld in Hesse, 'the second to be destroyed in that region in twenty-four hours'.[5] Another British newspaper wrote of reports that night from both Kassel and Vienna 'that the windows of Jewish shops have been broken', and that there had been 'demonstrations against synagogues, and damage done to the interior of at least one of them by the crowd which broke in'. There were fears, the paper added, that demonstrations and 'window-smashing' would take place in Berlin that night, 'but so far as can be ascertained there have been no anti-Jewish disturbances to a late hour'.[6]

It was learned a week later that on the night of November 8, and into the early hours of November 9, the execution had begun of Jews who had been incarcerated months earlier in Buchenwald

4 'Nazis Planning Revenge on Jews', *News Chronicle*, 9 November 1938.
5 'Synagogue Set on Fire', *The Times*, 10 November 1938.
6 'Germany Begins Reprisals Against the Jews', *Manchester Guardian*, 9 November 1938.

concentration camp.[7] The number of Jews murdered on the night of November 8–9 was later said by a 'sure source' to have reached seventy.[8] Also that night, Jews were attacked in the province of Hesse and driven from their homes. Fleeing to Frankfurt, they arrived 'bruised and bleeding'.[9]

During November 9 the British Consul General in the Free City of Danzig, Gerald Shepherd, reported an 'intensification of the anti-Jewish campaign' in the city, which had been nominally under League of Nations control since 1920. The walls and windows of Jewish-owned shops had been 'disfigured with derogatory slogans, and, in at least one case, their windows broken'. A Jewish-owned chocolate factory had been transferred under pressure to 'a prominent National Socialist'. Several Jews, 'as well as the Aryan women with whom they have had intimate relations have been taken into protective custody, although there is no legal justification for such action'.[10]

On the evening of Wednesday, November 9, news reached Berlin that vom Rath had died of his wounds. German radio stations observed a two-minute silence. What the consequences of vom Rath's death would be was unknown. 'Messages from Germany tonight,' one British newspaper reported, 'do not indicate any immediate extension of official reprisals against the Jews, but unofficial demonstrations are said to be becoming more intense. Several synagogues were set on fire by angry mobs . . .'

In the fashionable Unter den Linden in Berlin, crowds converged

---

7 Diplomatic correspondent, *Manchester Guardian*, 15 November 1938.
8 Diplomatic correspondent, *Manchester Guardian*, 18 November 1938.
9 'Extent of German Pogrom', *Manchester Guardian*, 18 November 1938.
10 Gerald Shepherd, report of 9 November 1938: Foreign Office papers, FO 371/21637.

on the French tourist office, where a number of Jews were waiting in line, as they did every day, for the timetables and travel details that they would need in order to emigrate. The crowd forced the tourist office to close, while chanting: 'Down with the Jews! They are going to Paris to join the murderer!'[11] One Berlin newspaper described Grynszpan as 'only one of a gang of bandits'.[12]

A British newspaper noted that there were many German Jews who had been incarcerated in concentration camps for some time, and commented on the 'great barbarities' to which they had been subjected. The mortality among those Jews was so high – 'they perish of ill-treatment or are driven to suicide' in the camps – that one who had recently been released stated that 'even in normal times' in the concentration camps the Jews 'die off like flies in autumn'. The newspaper added: 'It is to be feared that ill-treatment will be intensified as a reprisal for the assassination of a German diplomat. The German press and wireless accuse the Jews as a whole of responsibility for the deed.'[13]

While vom Rath had lain gravely wounded in Paris, Hitler was in Munich at a gathering of Nazi Party leaders and uniformed SA men, the Brownshirts, for the annual celebration of the Beer Hall Putsch of 1923, when he had tried to seize power in the Bavarian capital. On the evening of November 9 he was told that vom Rath was dead. Hitler's Minister of Propaganda, Dr Goebbels, who was with him in Munich, told him that violence against Jews had

11 'Diplomat Dies: Nazi Rage', *Daily Herald*, 10 November 1938.
12 *Lokalanzeiger*, 9 November 1938, quoted in the *Manchester Guardian*, 10 November 1938.
13 'Death of Shot Diplomatist, Reprisals Likely', *Manchester Guardian*, 10 November 1938.

already broken out in several German cities. Goebbels recorded Hitler's response in his diary: 'He decides: demonstrations should be allowed to continue. The police should be withdrawn. For once the Jews should get the feel of popular anger.' Goebbels added: 'I immediately give the necessary instructions to the police and the Party. Then I briefly speak in that vein to the Party leadership. Stormy applause. All are instantly at the phones. Now people will act.'[14]

That action was swift and furious. 'The orgy began in the early hours of this morning,' one British newspaper correspondent reported from Berlin, 'with almost simultaneous outbreaks of fire in nine of the eleven synagogues . . .'[15] 'The trouble began,' another British newspaper reported, 'when half-drunk mobs armed with crow bars and bricks began window-smashing in the West End, mishandling Jews and placarding shops with handbills . . .' The handbills read: 'Führer! Free us from the Jewish plague!' In the course of an hour and a half, at least two hundred Jewish-owned shops were wrecked.[16]

Goebbels was delighted, writing in his diary: 'As was to be expected, the entire nation is in uproar. This is one dead man who is costing the Jews dear. Our darling Jews will think twice in future before simply gunning down German diplomats.'[17]

The senior British diplomat in Germany, Sir George Ogilvie Forbes, the Counsellor of Embassy in Berlin, who witnessed the destruction in the capital, wrote in his first full report: 'I especially noted the demeanour of the groups which followed each band

14 Goebbels diary, quoted in Saul Friedländer, *Nazi Germany and the Jews: The Years of Persecution, 1933–1939*, page 272.
15 'Nazi Attacks on Jews', *The Times*, 11 November 1938.
16 'Streets in Ruins', *Evening Standard*, 10 November 1938.
17 Goebbels diary, Elke Frohlich (editor), *Die Tagebücher von Joseph Goebbels*, diary entry for 10 November 1938.

of marauders. I heard no expression of shame or disgust, but in spite of the complete passiveness of many of the onlookers I did notice the inane grin which often inadvertently betrays the guilty conscience.'[18]

Berlin was only one of more than a thousand cities, towns and villages throughout Germany in which terrible events took place while it was still dark. 'In the middle of the night,' wrote Laurie Lowenthal, who was then fourteen, recalling the events in the town of Aschaffenburg, 'we were woken by the sound of shooting. My father's cousin, Ludwig Lowenthal, and his partner in business, lived on the first floor of our house with his family. Two men broke down their front door and shot him point blank while he was in bed. The ambulance took him to hospital. Meanwhile, his brother-in-law, Alfons Vogel, was kidnapped, taken to the nearby woods, tied to a tree and used as target practice and killed.'[19]

The Jews of Germany were a long-established community, dating back 2,000 years to Roman times. Two years before Kristallnacht, Laurie Lowenthal had won a prize at school for tracing his own family tree back to their arrival in Germany almost three hundred years earlier. The Jews were also German patriots. Twelve thousand had been killed in action fighting for Germany in the First World War. One of Laurie Lowenthal's uncles, an officer in a German Guards regiment, had been killed in action within three months of the outbreak of the First World War. One of his cousins had been killed at the front in October

18 Sir George Ogilvie Forbes, Despatch No. 1224 of 16 November 1938: Foreign Office papers, FO 371/21637.
19 Laurie Lowenthal, 'My Childhood in Germany' (typescript), sent to the author 6 June 2005.

1916. His own father had won the Iron Cross for bravery during the war.

Dawn brought scenes of appalling destruction throughout Germany. That evening Reuters news agency reported that among the towns in which synagogues had been burned down were Stettin on the Baltic, Konstanz near the Swiss border, Essen and Düsseldorf in the industrial Ruhr, as well as Krefeld, Cottbus, Brandenburg, Offenburg and Eberswalde.[20] The synagogue in Essen, built in 1913, was considered one of the finest in Germany. In Mainz, six synagogues were destroyed, as were the Jewish religious school, the Jewish museum and the Jewish library, and the ancient Jewish cemetery, the oldest gravestones in which went back more than nine hundred years. One thousand and thirty-two years before Kristallnacht, a Church Council in Mainz had ruled that a person who killed a Jew out of malice must make amends like any other murderer.

In Aschaffenburg, Laurie Lowenthal saw flames coming from the direction of the synagogue, hurried to the scene, but found his way blocked by Brownshirts.[21] In the Austrian town of Graz, whose rabbi was the leading Jewish historian David Herzog, and where the Nobel Prize laureate Otto Loewi, a distinguished Austrian Jew, had taught pharmacology at the university until the German annexation, the magnificent synagogue and adjoining Jewish school, each standing proudly on the banks of the river, were both destroyed.[22] Sometimes synagogues were destroyed in

20 See the map on page 273 for the places mentioned in this chapter in which synagogues were destroyed.
21 Laurie Lowenthal, 'My Childhood in Germany' (typescript).
22 Meir Lamed, 'Graz', *Encyclopaedia Judaica*, Volume 7, column 864, with photograph of the synagogue and school before destruction.

towns where there were no Jews. The Jews of Eisenstadt, in Austria, had been expelled immediately after the German annexation in March. This did not stop the mob destroying the interior of the synagogue. The building was then demolished.[23]

The British Consul General in Munich, Donald St Clair Gainer, reported similar destruction throughout Austria: a synagogue in Linz 'was burned to the ground'; the synagogue in Salzburg 'was wrecked and its contents thrown into the street'; at the resort towns of Bad Hallein and Bad Gastein 'the Jewish hotels and pensions were sacked'.

Gainer noted that in Vienna the attacks were carried out 'by the Austrian SA, most of whom were in full uniform, and the police had obviously received instructions not to intervene'. Nineteen synagogues were said to have been 'completely destroyed by fire'. All the fire brigades of Vienna 'were fully employed' preventing the fires spreading, 'as at one time there seemed to be a grave danger of a serious and widespread conflagration involving large sections of the city.' The Vienna correspondent of *The Times* told Gainer that on being taken under arrest to the police station, and before being released, 'he observed a number of Jews cowering in corners so terrified that they were unable even to remember their names, while an old Jew with white hair and beard was lying on the floor being brutally kicked by an SA man while the regular police looked on'.

That night, in Gainer's bitter words, 'Vienna presented an extraordinary spectacle, with fires raging all over the city and Jews being hustled along the streets, cursed at and assaulted by crowds of hooligans whose pride is to belong to one of the greatest and

23 Aharon Fuerst and Yehouda Marton, 'Eisenstadt', *Encyclopaedia Judaica*, Volume 6, column 548.

civilised nations of the world.'[24] In all, ninety-five synagogues and houses of prayer were destroyed in Vienna on Kristallnacht.

From Munich, a British newspaper correspondent sent a list of four towns in southern Germany where 'shops were smashed and synagogues burned'. These were Munich itself, Nuremberg, Bamberg and Bayreuth.[25] The Bayreuth synagogue had been consecrated in 1760. Reports from Nuremberg on November 10 told of a day of terror. 'Brownshirts smashed their way into Jewish houses, tore down the curtains, slashed carpets and upholstery with knives, and broke up the furniture,' one British newspaper reported. 'Terrified children were turned sobbing out of their beds, which were then smashed to pieces.' The paper added: 'Many of the wreckers were youths in their teens.'[26]

An American newspaper reported that in the Friedrichstrasse 'in downtown Berlin, crowds pushed police aside in their hunt for plunder'. The paper also reported that in Cologne 'crowds broke windows in nearly every Jewish shop, forced entrance into a synagogue, overturned its seats and smashed the windows'. In Salzburg the synagogue was destroyed and Jewish-owned shops 'looted'. In Vienna, where twenty-two Jews were reported to have committed suicide, 'truckloads of Jews were taken by Storm Troopers to Doliner Street and put to work tearing down a synagogue'. Synagogues were also reported 'raided, demolished or burned' in Potsdam, Treuchtlingen, Bamberg, Brandenburg, Eberswalde and Cottbus.[27] The Treuchtlingen synagogue dated back to 1730.

24 D. St Clair Gainer, Report of 11 November 1938: Foreign Office papers, FO 371/21637.
25 'Special Reports of the Pogroms in Germany', *News Chronicle*, 11 November 1938.
26 'Here is what Happened in Other Towns', *Daily Herald*, 11 November 1938.
27 'Jews Victim of Day of Vengeance', *Washington Post*, 11 November 1938.

The British Consul General in Frankfurt, Robert Smallbones, sent a report to London about the events in the city of Wiesbaden. The violence began at six in the morning, he wrote, 'with burning of all synagogues'. During the day 'organised groups of both political formations' – both the brownshirted SA and the blackshirted SS – 'visited every Jewish shop and office, destroying windows goods, equipment'. More than 2,000 Jews were arrested. Every synagogue in the district had been destroyed 'and all rabbis together with other religious leaders and teachers are under arrest'.[28]

In the province of Mecklenburg, the local Nazi newspaper reported how, in the town of Schwerin, all Jewish businesses were marked on November 9 for destruction the next day, and attacked on November 10, while at the same time the synagogue 'was made unfit for use'. In Rostock the synagogue was set on fire and Jewish businesses attacked. In Güstrow 'the synagogue, the temple in the Jewish cemetery and the shop of a Jewish watchmaker were set on fire, a number of shop windows broken and the contents of the shops destroyed and all Jewish residents taken into custody'. In Wismar, all Jews had been arrested.[29]

The destruction of synagogues was widely photographed. In the town square at Zeven, a bonfire was made of the interior furnishings of the synagogue, and the school director was ordered to bring his students to watch the blaze. They were photographed assembling for the spectacle.[30] At Ober-Ramstadt, as the synagogue burned, a photograph was taken of the firefighters saving

28 Robert Townsend Smallbones, telegram of 11 November 1938: Foreign Office papers, FO 371/21637.
29 *Niederdeutscher Beobachter*, 10 November 1938, reported by the British Consul General, Hamburg, 11 November 1938: Foreign Office papers, FO 371/21637.
30 'Synagogue Furnishings at Zeven', photograph: The United States Holocaust Memorial Museum photographic archive.

a nearby house.[31] The synagogue at Siegen was also photographed in flames.[32] So too was the synagogue at Eberswalde.[33]

In Regensburg the Jewish quarter was the oldest in Germany, dating back 918 years before Kristallnacht. That night the synagogue, consecrated in 1841, was destroyed. A Jewish community photographic record of the events included photographs of smashed shop windows, and of the Jewish men being marched away to Dachau, accompanied by laughing, uniformed stormtroopers. The Jews were forced to hold a large banner, 'Auszug der Juden': 'The removal of the Jews'.[34]

There are also photographs in the Yad Vashem Holocaust Archive in Jerusalem of the destruction of synagogues in four other towns: Wiesloch, Korbach, Eschwege and Thalfang.[35] The synagogue in Eschwege had been consecrated a hundred years earlier, in December 1838. That in Thalfang had been consecrated in 1822. In Adolf Diamant's study of synagogues burned, looted and destroyed on Kristallnacht there are photographs of more than ninety synagogues on fire or in ruins, and of post-war plaques set up on the sites of synagogues that were destroyed. The burned-out synagogues include those in the university towns of Heidelberg and Tübingen.[36]

* * *

31 'Synagogue Burns in Ober-Ramstadt', photograph: The United States Holocaust Memorial Museum photographic archive.

32 Reproduced in Yitzhak Arad (editor), *A Pictorial History of the Holocaust*, page 58.

33 'Synagogue set on Fire During Kristallnacht', United States Holocaust Memorial Museum, Photograph 55542.

34 'Der Fotoalbum der Jüdischen Gemeinde Regensburg, Kristallnacht 9–10 November 1938', Jüdische Gemeinde Regensburg, 16 June 2005.

35 Yad Vashem Photo Archives: 26891 (Wiesloch), 51741 (Eschwege), 63788 (Korbach), 5995/4 (Thalfang).

36 Adolf Diamant, *Zerstörte Synagogen vom November 1938*, pages 127–226.

In Bremen, three fire engines and seven fire ladders took up their positions at two in the morning of November 10 in the street where the synagogue and Jewish administrative building were located. They were still in position three hours later, at 5 a.m., when the synagogue was set on fire and – as reported by the British Consul T. B. Wildman – 'completely gutted'. While the synagogue was burning, the Jewish administrative building was sacked by SA men. At the same time, the house of prayer in the Jewish cemetery was burned. In the attacks on Jewish shops 'a lorry driver was ordered to drive into the windows of the various shops and, when he refused, an SA man jumped up beside him and forced him to do so'. The SA man then 'took away the goods, or a certain part of them, for the *Winterthilfe!*' – the annual German Winter Relief charitable appeal. Placards, prepared the previous day, were put in the shattered shop windows: 'Revenge for vom Rath', 'Death to International Judaism and Freemasonry', 'No dealings with races subservient to the Jews' and 'Away with Judaism'.

The Consul also reported that a Jewish dressmaker, Lore Katz, was forced into the street in her nightgown, and only allowed to get a coat after her shop 'had been despoiled of clothes'. Several Jews were said to have committed suicide. Others were forced to leave their homes at gunpoint during the night, 'and one man, named Rosenberg, a father of six children, who lived in the Neustadt, resisted, and was shot'.[37]

An estimated ninety-one Jews were killed in Germany on Kristallnacht. News of some of these deaths was reported by diplomats

---

37 T. B. Wildman, British Consul, Bremen, report dated 12 November 1938: Foreign Office papers, FO 371/21637.

and foreign correspondents. The Berlin correspondent of the *Daily Telegraph* wrote that the caretaker of the Prinzregentstrasse synagogue 'is reported to have been burned to death with his family'. The correspondent had also learned 'on good authority' that two Jews were lynched in Berlin's East End and two more in the West End. 'Numbers of further deaths were reported from other parts of the country.' There were also indignities. In Dortmund, a Romanian Jew 'was made to crawl a distance of two and a half miles this morning, beaten continuously by hooligans'.[38]

The Jewish community in Dortmund had already been forced to sell its Great Synagogue, built in 1900, to the Nazis: it was dismantled before Kristallnacht. The remaining synagogue was destroyed on Kristallnacht. In Heilbronn the high-domed synagogue, consecrated in 1877, was set ablaze.[39] Jews had first been recorded living in Heilbronn in the middle of the eleventh century, the date of a Hebrew inscription found inserted in the wall of the old synagogue, built in 1357. In Bad Homburg, a spa town that had been a popular meeting place for Russian Jewish intellectuals at the beginning of the century, the synagogue, consecrated on 9 November 1866, was likewise destroyed on Kristallnacht.[40]

In Bassum, where the synagogue was also destroyed, fifty-six-year-old Josephine Baehr saw her husband arrested and her home demolished. She committed suicide.[41] In Glogau, where both synagogues were set on fire, Leonhard Plachte was thrown out of a window and killed.[42] In Jastrow, where the synagogue was also

38 'Jews Shot Dead', *Daily Telegraph*, 11 November 1938.
39 Photographs of Heilbronn synagogue before and during destruction: Lionel Kochan, 'Kristallnacht', *Encyclopaedia Judaica*, Volume 10, column 1265.
40 Photograph of Bad Homburg synagogue before destruction: Bernhard Brilling, 'Homburg', *Encyclopaedia Judaica*, Volume 8, column 943.
41 Pages of testimony (Josephine Baehr), Yad Vashem Archive.
42 Pages of testimony (Leonhard Plachte), Yad Vashem Archive.

destroyed, Max Freundlich, a father of three, died while being arrested.[43] In Beckum, where the two synagogues and the Jewish school were completely destroyed, Alexander Falk was murdered. He was ninety-five years old.[44]

During November 10 the head of the German police, Heinrich Himmler, issued an order forbidding Jews to possess weapons. One London newspaper reported that evening that under Himmler's order, 'Any Jew found with arms will be imprisoned for twenty years.'[45]

Schoolboys were to be found at the forefront of many of the assaults on Jews, and smashing windows. Ulrich von Hassell, a German diplomat who was outraged by what was happening – and who was executed in 1944 for his part in the attempt on Hitler's life – noted in his diary five days after Kristallnacht that the organisers 'were shameless enough to mobilise school classes (in Feldafing, on the Starbergersee, they even armed the pupils with bricks)'.[46] A month after Kristallnacht, von Hassel lunched with a senior member of the German Foreign Office, who, Hassell noted in his diary, 'confirmed the story that teachers had armed school children with clubs so that they could destroy Jewish shops . . .'[47]

At five o'clock in the afternoon of November 10, Goebbels issued an order for a halt to the 'demonstrations'. It was broadcast over the radio in every city and town, whereupon police and Nazi Party officials began to send the sated and exhausted

43 Pages of testimony (Max Freundlich), Yad Vashem Archive.
44 Pages of testimony (Alexander Falk), Yad Vashem Archive.
45 'Anti-Jew Riots Raging', Evening News, 10 November 1938.
46 Diary entry, 25 November 1938: The von Hassell Diaries, page 14.
47 Diary entry, 11 December 1938: The von Hassell Diaries, page 19.

demonstrators home. Many synagogues were still burning. That night the American Consulate in Breslau had to be evacuated because a nearby synagogue was 'burning dangerously'.[48] Breslau's sixty-six-year-old New Synagogue was destroyed. The Sklowar synagogue, built in 1790, was only partially destroyed. It was later used by the Nazis as a wine cellar and warehouse. The Storch synagogue remained standing, but its Scrolls of the Law were taken by stormtroopers into the courtyard and set on fire. The Gestapo then arrested the rabbi, Dr Moshe Hoffman, as well as the cantor, who with six hundred Jewish men between the ages of sixteen and sixty were deported to Buchenwald.

Everywhere, Jews sought to avoid the Gestapo net. In Magdeburg, Ephraim Handler, a leader of the Jewish community, was saved from the round-up and deportation to Sachsenhausen by several non-Jewish friends, who helped him get the night train to Berlin. When the searchers came for him, he was already many miles away. Just before the outbreak of war he was able to travel to Palestine on a Palestine Certificate. His son Leo, who was in Palestine on Kristallnacht, with a return passage to Germany booked by sea via Trieste, received a coded message not to return. He went England instead.[49] Ephraim Handler had been saved by the goodwill of Germans brave enough to stand out against the prevailing hatred.

Evidence survives about three German villages where the parish priests and the mayors prevented a pogrom on Kristallnacht. These villages were Warmsried, Derching and Laimering.[50]

Almost no Jewish village community was spared from destruc-

---

48 ' "Eye for an Eye, Tooth for a Tooth" ', *News Chronicle*, 11 November 1938.

49 Arieh (Leo) Handler, conversation with the author, 28 June 2005.

50 Anthony Read and David Fisher, *Kristallnacht: The Nazi Night of Terror*, page 105.

tion. In the village of Hoengen, near the Dutch frontier, storm-troopers and villagers worked zealously side by side to smash the small synagogue with axes and sledgehammers. Eric Lucas witnessed the scene as his uncle Michael, the local butcher, who had built the synagogue, looked on in despair while the Scrolls of the Law were tossed from hand to hand, 'until they reached the street outside. Women tore away the blue and velvet and every-body tried to snatch some of the silver adorning the Scrolls. Naked and open the Scrolls lay in the muddy autumn lane, children stepped on them and others tore pieces from the fine parchment on which the Law was written – the same Law that the people who tore it apart had, in vain, tried to absorb for more than a thousand years.'[51]

Explaining why he did not order the police to stop the wreckers during Kristallnacht, Dr Goebbels told a meeting of foreign press correspondents in Berlin on the day after the destruction: 'I could not order our policemen to shoot at Germans, because inwardly I sympathised with them.'[52]

In a courageous response to the destruction and the brutality, the pastor of St Hedwig's Cathedral in Berlin, Bernhard Lichten-berg – who had been a military chaplain in the First World War – closed each evening's service after Kristallnacht with a prayer 'for the Jews, and the poor prisoners in the concentration camps'.[53]

In a leading article on Kristallnacht, published while syna-gogues throughout Germany were still smouldering, while the wreckage of several thousand shops was still strewn about the streets, and while thousands of German and Austrian Jews were

51 Eric Lucas, 'The Sovereigns'.
52 Quoted in the *Evening Standard*, 11 November 1938.
53 H. D. Leuner, *When Compassion was a Crime*, page 10.

either tending their wounds or being taken to concentration camps, *The Times* commented: 'No foreign propagandist bent upon blackening Germany before the world could outdo the tale of burnings and beatings, of blackguardly assaults on defenceless and innocent people, which disgraced that country yesterday.'[54]

54 'A Black Day for Germany', *The Times*, 11 November 1938.

2

Eye-Witnesses: Berlin

THE MOST WIDELY REPORTED VIOLENCE on Kristallnacht took place in Berlin, the German city in which the largest number of foreign correspondents were based. 'I have seen several anti-Jewish outbreaks in Germany during the last five years,' wrote Hugh Greene, the Berlin correspondent of the *Daily Telegraph*, 'but never anything as nauseating as this.' Beginning in the early hours of the morning, and continuing 'far into tonight', the pogrom – as the correspondent called it – 'puts the final seal to the outlawry of German Jewry'. German women who remonstrated with children who were running away with toys from a wrecked Jewish shop 'were spat upon and attacked by the mob'.[1]

Max Kopfstein was thirteen years old. 'My father's habit was to attend synagogue every morning,' he remembered, 'after which he would come home for breakfast, and then leave for the office. On the morning of 10 November 1938 Father came home much earlier, telling us that synagogues in Berlin were on fire. Our own synagogue, the Münchener Strasse, had not been torched, the reason being that it was situated in a courtyard and there was danger that the blaze could spread to the surrounding buildings.'

---

1 'German Mobs' Vengeance on Jews', *Daily Telegraph*, 11 November 1938.

Max Kopfstein's account continued: 'Not knowing what the day held in store, I was not allowed to go to school, but Father nevertheless went to work, not before a code – "There are guests" – had been arranged between us to warn him in case the Nazis came to look for him. Mother and I were alone, at home. Some time later, the doorbell rang. Mother opened the front door of our quite spacious apartment. There stood two Gestapo agents in civilian clothes, asking to see my father Walter Kopfstein. She answered that he was in his office, at the same time giving me a sign with her hand behind her back. I went downstairs via the back entrance to our flat, and ran to the public phone booth at the corner of the street, where I phoned my father in his office to say "There are guests." I then returned home.'

Meanwhile the Gestapo had asked Max Kopfstein's mother to phone his father 'and tell him to come home immediately, and not to say anything else, which she did. They then waited. After a short while they asked my mother: how old is your husband? Mother replied, whether intentionally or not I don't know, by giving the year of his birth "–85" instead of his age, then fifty-three. They misunderstood, thinking he was eighty-five years old, and exclaimed, "What, so old?" whereupon they left.'[2]

There were other narrow escapes in Berlin that day. Hannelore Heinemann was not yet three years old when two Gestapo agents appeared at her family's apartment door demanding her father and grandfather, both of whom had just left for a place of safety. Her mother Paula told the agents that neither man was there, and the agents left. The next evening the same Gestapo agents returned. This time the non-Jewish concierge of the apartment

2 'Kristallnacht' recollections, communicated by Max Kopfstein to the author, 6 June 2005.

building, Frau Müller, stopped them in the hallway. 'Herr Heine-mann and Herr Silberstein no longer live here,' she told them. 'Take my word for it. Only his wife and daughter remain. Why do you two want to disturb a young woman and a two-year-old child? Surely they are not a threat to the Reich.' The men turned away.

In later years Paula Heinemann would tell her daughter: 'People like Frau Müller were proof positive that not everybody in Germany was anti-Semitic, and some did care about human beings.' Heinrich Silberstein, who had fought in the German army in the First World War, had been unable to believe, when warned a few weeks earlier that he was on a Gestapo list for arrest, that 'such a betrayal of German Jews' was possible. 'But I am a law-abiding citizen,' he protested to his former fellow-soldier, a non-Jewish senior civil servant who had come to warn him. 'This is preposterous! There must be a mistake.'³

In the early hours of November 10, as the Gestapo prepared to set the Oranienburger Strasse synagogue on fire, the head of the local police precinct, Police Lieutenant Wilhelm Krützfeld, insisted that they stop. The synagogue, he told them, was a historic land-mark, a protected municipal building. This was indeed true; it had been so for many years due to its architectural importance. The Gestapo went away, and there was no fire – until 22 November 1943, during a British night bombing raid on Berlin. A photograph of the synagogue in flames that night in 1943 is often reproduced, in error, as a Kristallnacht photograph. For his successful act of defiance, Krützfeld was severely reprimanded.⁴

3 Hannelore Headley, *Blond China Doll: A Shanghai Interlude, 1939–1953*, pages 20–1.
4 Orianenburger Strasse Synagogue Museum, Berlin.

The rest of the destruction in Berlin proceeded without interruption. Late on the afternoon of November 10 a London evening newspaper described how during the day, 'with great precision', groups of stormtroopers and SS men, 'in civilian clothes, proceeding on motor-cycles, with sidecars filled with stones, went to stipulated points, where they threw the stones through the windows and then departed'. That was not the end. 'The street mobs quickly took up their cue. This afternoon scores of synagogues were in flames, thousands of Jewish shops were in ruins, and many thousands of Jews were in gaol.'

During the afternoon the Berlin correspondent of the Exchange News Agency saw a middle-aged Jew 'being chased through the streets, everyone who was near him striking him. A policeman stood by smiling.' Later that afternoon wrecking was still going on. Berlin's fashionable Kurfürstendamm was 'in ruins. Cartloads of broken glass and wrecked goods from the shops lay all over the road. Fires were still burning.' Eleven Berlin synagogues were in flames.[5]

'At the bottom of the street,' Serem Freier later recalled, 'a gang of Germans was busy in crashing the shop window of the bakery where we were wont to buy our Sabbath bread every Friday. In June of 1938, a law had been passed that all Jewish shops had to renew their nameplates according to a standard style, so as to make identification easy. The Germans, therefore, had no difficulty in finding suitable targets for their attacks. The gang came in the direction of our house. Our cook explained to us that her presence in our home was illegal. She had come to us at a time when the regulations stipulated that only Germans more than fifty years old were allowed to work in Jewish households. However,

5 'Streets in Ruins', *Evening Standard*, 10 November 1938.

meanwhile a new law had been promulgated. All Germans had been forbidden to work in Jewish households. She told us that if the Nazis were to enter our house she would have to flee. As the house had two staircases, she would run down whichever staircase was not occupied by the Nazis coming up. Fortunately, the Nazis did not come up either staircase. It was only later that we learnt that on this day, many Jewish homes were broken into by the Hitler Youth, furniture destroyed and the apartments ruined. In the streets, Jews were being pursued and assaulted by gangs of Nazis. We passed the day in fear.'

Towards evening, Serem Freier later wrote, 'news reached us that Goering had spoken on the radio and requested the Nazi gangs to stop causing further damage'. When Serem Freier woke up the next day his parents 'were nowhere to be seen'. Early that morning, when his father became aware that Jews were being deported, he had gone out into the street to tender help and support. During the day, however, a Gestapo officer told him that he was on the list of people to be arrested and advised him to go into hiding. He therefore disappeared. 'He hid with various friends of ours, until a few days later he obtained a tourist visa to Italy and immediately left for that country. From there, he proceeded to England where he remained for the next ten years.'[6]

'The great shopping centres looked as though they had suffered an air raid,' reported the *Daily Herald* from Berlin. 'Showcases were torn from walls, furniture broken, electric signs smashed to fragments.'[7] The *News Chronicle* reporter saw looters 'smashing with peculiar care the windows of jewellery shops and, sniggering,

6 Zerem Freier, letter to the author, 19 June 2005.
7 'Like Air Raid', *Daily Herald*, 11 November 1938.

stuffing into their pockets the trinkets and necklaces that fell on the pavements'. In Friedrichstrasse a grand piano 'was hauled out onto the pavement and demolished with hatchets amid whoops and cheers'.[8]

In the words of the *Daily Telegraph* correspondent in Berlin, 'Racial hatred and hysteria seemed to have taken complete control of otherwise decent people. I saw fashionably dressed women clapping their hands and screaming with glee, while respectable middle-class mothers held up their babies to see the "fun".'[9]

One young Jewish boy, Paul Oestereicher, later described how he was walking with his mother in one of the main shopping streets of Berlin, excitedly window-shopping, when in seconds the joy was over. 'What seemed like hundreds of men, swinging great truncheons, jumped from lorries and began to smash up the shops all around us.'[10]

Miriam Walk, who lived in a first-floor apartment opposite the Levetzowstrasse synagogue, recalled watching as 'the Nazis burned all the books in the street', and also the Torah scrolls. 'To this day I feel the stench of the burning and the fear – what next?'[11]

Helga Leib was a Berlin schoolgirl. On the morning of November 10 she left her house as usual at about twenty to eight 'to catch a tram to my school, which was in the Grosse Hamburger Strasse, about five minutes' walk from the Alexanderplatz. It was a cold, dull morning and the windows of the tram were misted over so I could not look out. On my five minutes' walk I also did

8 ' "Eye for an Eye, Tooth for a Tooth" ', *News Chronicle*, 11 November 1938.
9 'German Mobs' Vengeance on Jews', *Daily Telegraph*, 11 November 1938.
10 Paul Oestereicher, 'Terror, on Berlin's Night of Broken Glass', in *The Times*, 9 November 1978.
11 Miriam Spira (*née* Walk), letter to the author, 3 June 2005.

not see anything unusual. Arriving in my class I found everyone very subdued but could not find out why. When our teacher came in he explained the situation and told us that we all had to go back home again. We were not allowed to loiter in front of the school. We were let out of the school two by two at short intervals. On my way home we saw the broken shop windows and it was all very eerie and frightening.'[12]

Another schoolgirl in Berlin that day was Chava Rechnitz. Because her parents lived in the small town of Ratibor, on the River Elbe, she was staying in Berlin at the home of her friend Dörte. On reaching school by the S-Bahn suburban railway, she and her friend 'found it and the adjoining synagogue burning, also a Jewish Old Age Home located across the street. Many Hitler Youths were standing around, cheering and shouting "Raus mit den Juden" ("Away with the Jews"). We went back home and I put on my best dress and jacket, packed only a small suitcase and took a train back to Ratibor . . .'[13]

Fifteen-year-old Gerd Bochian remembered how, on the ground floor next to his family apartment, was a small house of prayer and religious seminary. The ultra-orthodox Jew who ran it, Rabbi Kupferstoch, had been a hero in Germany for having provided the German army in 1914 – while he was living in Russian Poland – with a crucial map before the Battle of Tannenberg. For this he and his seminary students had been welcomed to Berlin by the Kaiser. The German army honoured his patriotic contribution to that crucial battle – it was even said that he had a protective letter (*Schutzbrief*) signed by Hitler – and when SA thugs came to demolish his seminary, two German policemen

12 Helga Leib, letter to the author, 5 June 2005.
13 Chava Cohn (*née* Rechnitz), letter to the author, 3 June 2005.

armed with pistols were already standing guard and would not let them pass. 'This,' Gerd Bocian reflected, 'probably saved the building we were in.'[14]

Eleven-year-old Miriam Litke was also in Berlin on Kristallnacht. 'We lived in an apartment house which had our synagogue, Beth Zion, in the back courtyard,' she later wrote. 'Because there was a chemical factory behind the synagogue the Nazis were not allowed to burn it (it still stands). However, my mother, brother and I watched from our blacked-out window how they threw the contents of the synagogue into the courtyard. The benches, Torah scrolls, prayer books etc. were all piled up on the ground. We could hear the Nazis speaking to each other, yelling, shouting. We heard: "Da oben wohnen auch noch Juden" – "There are still Jews living up there." We were afraid that they would come up to our first-floor flat and hurt us. However, they left after doing their destruction.'

Later that morning, remembered Miriam Litke, 'when the Jewish shops were being broken into, the plate-glass display windows shattered, looting and destroying of goods continuing, my relatives who lived nearby called me. My uncle, Gershon Fachler, owned a large furniture store on the Kastonienallee, a beautiful boulevard lined with chestnut trees. He asked me to go there and watch what was happening to his store and to see that the "employees don't steal"! Thinking back one can see how ludicrous was the idea to send an eleven-year-old child to watch the Nazi destruction of his store. But my uncle with his beard certainly could not go there, neither could his grown sons, so they sent me, a fair-skinned, light-haired, blue-eyed girl with pigtails. I stood there with a crowd of people who were obviously enjoying

14 Jerry (Gerd) Bocian, conversation with the author, 14 September 2005.

the "show". What was I supposed to do? Keep anyone from looting? After a while I noticed some women were eyeing me and I overheard one say to the other: "This is a Jewish child." Hearing this I decided to go home.'[15]

Most visible in Berlin on November 10 were the burning syna-gogues. At least thirty had been set on fire by eight in the morning. That day a London evening newspaper reported that many of these fires 'were still blazing fiercely this afternoon'. So too were many shops and businesses. Any Jews who tried to enter their burning premises 'to rescue goods were prevented from doing so. They stood by and watched their possessions burn, while the crowds jeered.'

The synagogue burnings were accompanied by looting and vandalism. Before the mob broke into the Fasanenstrasse Syna-gogue in order to set fire to it, they first 'removed the altar cloths and ornaments, dumped them in the Wittenbergplatz, set them on fire, and danced round the bonfire'. Then, having set the synagogue on fire, they hired thirty taxis 'to take them on a tour of wrecking and incendiarism' in the Kurfürstendamm area. Huge crowds stood around the main synagogues as they were set on fire, 'watching the flames devour them, cheering wildly when the roof fell in'. Fireman directed their hoses only on adjoining non-Jewish properties, to save them from the blaze.

From the Kurfürstendamm area, the mob moved to the two other main areas of Jewish shops in Berlin, the Unter den Linden and the Alexanderplatz. There, one of Europe's largest retail estab-lishments, Israel's Department Store, a four-storey building, was 'raided and wrecked', watched by a 'crowd of thousands'. Some

15 Miriam Litke, letter to the author, 12 June 2005.

seven hundred of the 1,200 employees fled as the gang entered the building. After describing the raid, the announcer on Berlin Radio declared: 'All this is too mild. We need sharper measures. This is the signal.'

The signal was certainly understood – and heeded. As one London evening newspaper reported, even as Berlin's synagogues and Jewish shops were being reduced to ruin and ashes, 'mobs began to force their way into Jews' private houses and flats, beat up the occupants and smash their furniture. The police, when appealed to for assistance, shrugged their shoulders and declined to intervene.'[16]

That evening Eugen Lehmann wrote from Berlin to his son, who was already in Britain: 'It is now six-thirty and I can hardly think clearly. What happened to us Jews in Germany since four-thirty this morning is indescribable. In the whole of Germany there exists no synagogue that is not burned or still burning, there are no more store windows that are not broken.' At one Jewish-owned department store in Berlin 'all glass was broken by 2 p.m.', at another 'it was at twelve' and at a third 'at seven etc., etc. You can imagine what became of the displayed merchandise.'[17]

The Berlin correspondent of the *News Chronicle* reported 'two curious scenes' that he witnessed that day. One was the sight of passers-by hurling stones through a shop window, while on the balcony above the shop 'stood a grey-haired Jewess braving missiles and hurling imprecations at the crowd below, who were destroying her livelihood'. The other scene was outside a restaurant owned by a Hungarian Jew, where a crowd of young

16 'Streets in Ruins', *Evening Standard*, 10 November 1938.
17 Anne L. Fox, *Between the Lines: Letters from the Holocaust*, page 31.

men made an 'Aunt Sally' of the establishment, throwing stones through the broken window panes 'as they knocked vases, jugs, pewter plates and plaques off the walls', while inside the restaurant a small boy of school age 'collected the missiles, put them in a paper bag, and dropped them down to the crowd from the first storey so that they could start again'.

The correspondent noted that the 'average German looked on either apathetic or astonished'. He also reported that individual Jews had been 'chased through the streets by young Nazis, pummelled and knocked down'. One of the most 'deplorable features' of this spate of attacks 'was the number of young boys who gleefully took part'. He also quoted from the *Angriff*, Dr Goebbels' newspaper, which declared: 'The deed of murder falls on all Jewry. Every individual must account to us for every pain, every crime, every nasty action of this criminal race against the Germans; each individual Jew is responsible without mercy. World Jewry wants to fight us. It can do so on its own terms – an eye for an eye, a tooth for a tooth.'[18]

One courageous action was witnessed by this same correspondent, who reported 'the strange sight of two German army officers in uniform who intervened to prevent the destruction of a shop and who were threatened with bodily assault by a howling mob'. The officers were forced to retreat, their hands on their daggers. Meanwhile, the mob screamed at them: 'You owe us your very uniforms.' To the British journalist, these two officers 'seemed to be the only persons left in the Reich who dared to stand up for decency and restraint'.[19]

18 ' "Eye for an Eye, Tooth for a Tooth" ', *News Chronicle*, 11 November 1938.
19 'Powerless Officers', *News Chronicle*, 11 November 1938.

3

Eye-Witnesses: Vienna

NAZI RULE had reached Vienna in March 1938, with the German annexation of Austria. Eight months later the Jews of Vienna were caught up, like all the Jewish inhabitants of the German Reich, in the night and day of terror. 'To see our synagogues going up in flames,' recalled Bronia Schwebel, 'to see owners of Jewish stores walking in front of them with signs on their back "I am ashamed to be a Jew" while their stores were robbed, was frightening and heartbreaking. It was not only their stores being broken in, it was lives being broken . . .'[1]

Felix Seiler, a four-and-a-half-year-old boy at the time, described how all the family, except his father, were together in the cellar of their house. 'I remember my mother, grandfather and several others who I suppose must have been aunts and uncles. I thought the whole thing was a game and behaved accordingly. Usually, being an only child, I was the centre of attraction. Not so that night. As I now recall with hindsight everyone was very gaunt and tense.'[2] Later he learned that his father had been urged by his family to go to the house of a relative, to avoid arrest. The police, or Gestapo, came to the boy's house while his father was on his way

1 Bronia Sonnenschein (*née* Schwebel), letter to the author, 29 June 2005.
2 Felix Seiler, letter to the author, 6 June 2005.

to his relative. When they finally reached the relative's house, his father was on his way back home. In this way, he avoided arrest.

Helga Milberg's father was not so fortunate. She was eight years old during Kristallnacht. Her father's business in the Fleischmarkt had been broken into and damaged, the inventory stolen, the cash register, weighing scales and knives all taken. 'My father saw that the other storekeepers had helped themselves to everything,' she later wrote. 'When he complained to them, the SS beat him up. Made him clean up the mess that was left.' The business was then confiscated, but even then the government insisted that her father had to pay taxes on it. 'We had no income and no money. Father went out one night to sell his wedding band, and disappeared. We did not know what happened to him until many months later. He had been picked up and taken to Dachau. At Dachau he was frequently beaten and tortured . . .' The gold crowns on his teeth were knocked out.[3]

Professor Arthur Freud was fifty-six at the time of Kristallnacht. Born in a small Moravian town in what was Austria-Hungary until 1918, he held a Czech passport. After the First World War he became a journalist in Vienna and an active Zionist. 'On the gloomy autumn morning,' he later wrote, 'not very many Jews yet knew what actually was going on – but they were worried. Counting on my foreign passport, I walked in the direction of the Seitenstettengasse, in order to get more information at the office of the Jewish community . . . Usually I saw the house of the community besieged by poor Jews, who wanted to ask for food-stuff, help, the possibility of emigration, but this time there was only a detachment of armed people, whom I took for soldiers by their uniforms, but it was a detachment of one of the Nazi

3 Helga Milberg, recollections sent to the author, 10 July 2005.

organisations. They answered me with special politeness that entrance was free, so that I, stepping into the corridor, met with another such detachment. I was forced to pass in the middle, while these fellows wildly attacked me from both sides. Their commanding officer, a functionary in civilian clothes, had seized me by my coat collar at the entrance. As I told him my title and name I heard something like: "Now they had him." Apparently one or other of the fellows thought Sigmund Freud had been delivered to them.'

Although he was no relation to Sigmund Freud – who had been given refuge in Britain after the annexation of Austria eight months earlier – Professor Freud was ordered by the commanding officer of the detachment to take off his glasses. 'Nazi brutality under certain conditions,' Freud reflected, but after he loudly insisted that he was a foreigner, the officer allowed him to go. Freud was fortunate again early that evening, 'when two function- aries came to search my flat very rudely, pretending they were searching for arms; after one of them muddled up all my books, he discovered a row of back numbers of Kraus's *Fackel*' – a Viennese anti-Nazi magazine edited by Karl Kraus, who had died in 1936 – 'which he commanded me to burn immediately, he would himself check that I had done so tomorrow, and would arrest me if I had not done it, "because that one was the biggest Jewish filthy fellow". But my passport saved me from being taken away, after I had assured them that I was a "real" Czechoslovak and not perhaps one of the ceded Sudetenland. They simply took away my Vienna- born cousin. He returned after six weeks quite damaged and refused to relate what had happened to him; he persisted in his refusal to talk until his departure.'[4]

4 Professor Arthur Freud, 'Looking Back', manuscript.

Ruth Birnholz, then twelve years old, later recalled the scene in her family apartment in Vienna in the early hours of November 10, as 'people came storming in'. Her parents were in their bedroom. She heard the intruders 'smashing furniture and mirrors and yelling. And I was terrified. And people put pillows over my head, because if I had made a noise, they would have found . . . particularly, the young man, Hans' – her older sister's boyfriend – 'because that would have probably been the end for him.' The intruders took all her mother's jewellery and broke all the mirrors: 'it was a terrifying experience' for the young girl. 'It was being at the hands of anybody who could decide to hurt you in any possible way that was so frightening I think. For a child particularly.'[5]

Susanne Hatschek, who was only six months old during Kristallnacht, was later told by her mother how on November 10 they were both arrested by the Gestapo. 'There was a gun on the table pointing at us and my mother was ordered to hand over the keys to our flat. She refused, saying she needed the flat to take care of her baby. They went away, but the next day six armed Nazis came to the flat, searched it, threw our belongings into a sheet and dragged it down the stairs. They said they needed the flat for their own people, and the only reason they did not deport us was because we had a good name in the neighbourhood. The flat was sealed and we stood in the street homeless and penniless in the winter.'[6]

Lucie Draschler was a twelve-year-old schoolgirl. 'For me,' she wrote, 'the day started as usual by going to school, but there was a palpable tension in the air, we were sent home early and told not to dawdle on the way. When I arrived home, the whole family

---

5 Ruth Morley (*née* Birnholz), recollections: from the interview conducted by her daughter Melissa Hacker for her film *My Knees were Jumping: Remembering Kindertransports*, Bee's Knees Productions, New York, 1995.
6 Susan Ben Yosef (*née* Susanne Hatschek), letter to the author, 5 June 2005.

was there, everybody was anxiously waiting for me. I can still see us sitting there, talking, trying to keep calm, hiding from each other our fear.'

They did not have long to wait. 'Suddenly we heard loud noises in the building, shouting, the trampling of heavy boots and finally the dreaded knock on the door. Four armed stormtroopers burst in and fell upon my father, beating him and pushing him down the stairs. Two of them followed him, while the other two told my grandfather to come with them. Then the most amazing thing happened, my grandfather stood before them and refused to go, he told them that he was an old man, that he had served his Kaiser in the Great War, and that he would not leave his home.' It was a moment of danger. 'They could easily have taken him, he was quite frail, but strangely enough they turned on their heels and left without a word.'

After the men left with Lucie Draschler's father, 'we were all in shock. My grandfather collapsed, my grandmother was crying, and Evy' – her sister – 'and I sat huddled together, too frightened to move. My mother put Grandfather to bed, she tried to calm us down, but was not too successful.' Help was at hand. 'In the midst of all this one of our Gentile neighbours came in and took charge. She lived with her sister and brother on the same floor, but we hardly knew them. She insisted on taking me and Evy to their apartment, and we stayed there until the next day. They were all three elderly people, had never been married, and kept very much to themselves. When they witnessed what went on, they decided to take a stand and help. They fussed over us, talked to us, kept feeding us, and were so kind to us, that we slowly recovered.'[7]

*   *   *

7 Lucy Mandelstam (*née* Lucie Draschler), manuscript memoirs. Enclosed in letter to the author, 3 June 2005.

On the morning of November 10 many Viennese citizens on their way to work, having read in their morning newspapers that vom Rath was dead, turned on Jews waiting at the tram stops and beat them up. Nazi thugs moved through the streets encouraging such attacks, as well as battering down the doors and smashing the windows of Jewish-owned shops. A Jewish kindergarten was also attacked. From his bedroom window, twelve-year-old Fred Garfunkel saw the grocery shop below his family's apartment 'smashed to pieces', and trucks parked at every corner 'with soldiers picking up people off the streets'.[8]

At nine o'clock that morning, it was reported to London, fires broke out in the Hernalser and Hietzinger synagogues: 'The latter, a building in the Moorish style, and the largest and finest synagogue in Vienna, was completely gutted.' Two and a half hours later there were several explosions in the predominantly Jewish Second District, as 'a number of synagogues were blown up by bombs'.[9]

At noon on November 10 a mob broke into the Rabbis' School in the Grosse Schiffgasse, hauled the furniture into the street and made a bonfire of it. A few minutes later another mob set a synagogue in the Neudeggergasse on fire. The fire brigade arrived when flames were already breaking through the roof. A synagogue in the Hubergasse burned so quickly that it collapsed before the fire brigade could get there. It was noted that when the fire began in the Tempelgasse synagogue, explosions were heard: Brownshirts had deliberately placed cans of petrol inside.

From the roof of a synagogue in the Muttersteg, Nazi hooligans threw down the ornamental stone Tablets of the Law into the street. In the Jewish quarter of Leopoldgasse, the interior furnish-

8 Fred Garfunkel, conversation with the author, 21 August 2005.
9 'Vienna Synagogues Blown up', The Times, 11 November 1938.

ings, the Ark, and the Scrolls of the Law from four synagogues were piled up in the street and set on fire.[10] One report reaching the outside world that day told of how some Jews 'were given spades and taken to the destroyed synagogues where they were made to clear away the ruins'.[11] A day later the *New York Times* reported in one of its headlines: 'All Vienna's Synagogues Attacked; Fires and Bombs Wreck 18 of 21'.[12]

Throughout November 10, goods were taken away from Jewish shops throughout Vienna. A 'prominent' Nazi official told the correspondent of the British United Press: 'We began seizing goods from Jewish shops because sooner or later they would have been nationalised anyway.' The goods thus seized, the official added, 'will be used to compensate us for at least part of the damage which the Jews have been doing for years to the German people'.[13]

Fourteen-year-old Felix Rinde was in Vienna on Kristallnacht. 'Always living in fear since the Nazi takeover in March 1938,' he later wrote, 'we got up and cautiously peeked through curtains and blinds to the scene one storey below. We saw a large group of SA thugs herd a number of Jews towards the nearby Marienbrücke crossing the Donau Kanal. Among them was the bearded, elderly caretaker of an improvised synagogue and study hall located in the first floor of an apartment house around the corner in the Hammerpergtallgasse. He was carrying a heavy, sacred Torah scroll which, we found out later, he was forced to toss into the flowing waters of the Danube.'

'Being fourteen years old,' Felix Rinde noted, 'I crawled back

10 'Bombs Used to Set Synagogues on Fire', *Daily Herald*, 11 November 1938.
11 'Anti-Jew Riots Raging', *Evening News*, 10 November 1938.
12 'All Vienna's Synagogues Attacked . . .', *New York Times*, 11 November 1939.
13 'Goods Seized', *Daily Herald*, 11 November 1938.

into the warm bed. My parents and siblings, fearing the worst, soon followed. The next day I met a friend and together we went up to the synagogue. We found it trashed and devastated. Being Orthodox Jews, we picked up as many prayer books and torn shreds of pages as possible and after kissing them reverently, we returned them to the remaining tables and shelves. We were interrupted by two men, wearing the obligatory jackboots, swastika armband and Tyrolean hats who had come to relish the destruction. They yelled at us to get out and one aimed a kick at me, which being fit and agile I evaded with ease. We scurried down the stairs and sadly departed from the synagogue we had frequently attended with our parents.'

Felix Rinde's oldest sister had a prior appointment at the local register office to obtain a civil marriage certificate needed for a hoped-for emigration to the United States. 'Her fiancé had ordered a taxi and together they rode through deserted streets to the office. They were married without a hitch on 10 November 1938 and returned shaken but unharmed. Had the cab been stopped, her new husband would have wound up in Dachau, as did so many others. Months later they were married in a religious ceremony in a Baltic country on their way to the United States. My sister needed no reminder of her wedding date.'

Felix Rinde later reflected: 'Jewish life in Vienna came to a virtual end with the destruction of the many magnificent temples in the Leopoldstrasse, Tempelgasse, Grosse Schiffgasse and so many others. I'll always cherish the memory of Vienna prior to the Nazi Anschluss and the memory of my parents who saw the successful emigration of their six children. They were deported to the East in 1942. They did not survive.'[14]

14 Felix Rinde, letter to the author, 27 June 2005.

Hans Waizner was nine years old at the time of Kristallnacht. That day, his family were to move their belongings, under an earlier Nazi order, from their home on the Türkenstrasse to the Jewish area in the Second District, where his grandmother would take them in. He and his mother set off with the lorry carrying their furniture and possessions. 'As the lorry passed over the Danube into the Jewish District,' he recalled, 'I was amazed and frightened to see the violated shops, some burned, others with smashed glass fronts, "JUDE" was scrawled on the gutter. There were few people about.' Reaching his grandmother's street 'we came upon a crowd of people. They were throwing piles of books from a Jewish house of learning onto a fire and burning them. My *strongest*, my most physical memory of Kristallnacht was of our lorry bumping and rolling across that pile of smouldering religious books. I will never forget it.'

Towards nightfall, Hans Waizner remembered, 'I walked together with my mother back to the recently vacated apartment, for what purpose I don't know, perhaps to return the keys. At the top of the stairs two men were waiting. They wore civilian clothes and were very polite. They were from the Gestapo and asked my mother to accompany them to the police station. That was too much for me. The excitement and fear of the day, the sights that I saw, and now my mother being taken away made me break down. I cried and screamed and must have been hysterical. I threw myself to the banister and saw blurred through my tears the circling well of the staircase. How long I was there I don't know, but I felt my mother come to hold me and comfort me. The Gestapo had relented and had left.'[15]

Gary Himler was at home in Vienna when there was a knock

15 Hans Waizner, letter to the author, 5 June 2005.

on the door 'and several burly SA troopers in their brown shirts came into the apartment and arrested my father and me'. Gary Himler was six feet tall. 'Mother screamed at them that I was only thirteen years old. They took Dad away.' Despite his youth, Gary Himler was also taken away, to a public toilet. 'Then they gave me a pail of water and a rag and told me to clean the urinals. Although I had never heard of Tom Sawyer, I innocently told the SA man that I had never done this before, and did not know how to do it, and wondered if he could show me how it was done. He grabbed the rag from my hand and cleaned a urinal, to teach me how it was done. I then asked if he could please show me again how it was done, and so he cleaned a second urinal, and then I cleaned the other two. I was able to return to the apartment later in the evening.'[16] Several days later, Gary Himler learned that his father had been taken to Dachau.

Seven-year-old Kurt Füchsl was bewildered by the events of Kristallnacht, and by being forced to leave home with his family early on the morning of November 10. He later recalled: 'What happened, as recounted to me by Mother, was that an interior decorator had taken a picture of our beautiful living room and displayed this picture of our apartment in his shop window. A Frau Januba saw the picture and heard that we were Jewish. She came around to the apartment and asked if it was for sale. She was told it wasn't, but a few days later, on the morning of Kristallnacht, she came back with some officers and said, "This apartment is now mine." She showed a piece of paper with a swastika stamped on it and told us that we would have to leave by six that evening.' Kurt Füchsl's mother protested to the officers who were

16 Gary Himler, letter to the author, 4 July 2005.

accompanying Frau Januba that she had a sick child at home who was already asleep. 'All right,' they told her, 'but you have to get out by six in the morning.'

Next morning, as Kurt Füchsl remembered, 'when Frau Januba showed up, my father told her that she was stealing what he and my mother had worked for. She said, "Stop talking like that, or I'll have you sent to a concentration camp." I had seen this Frau Januba when she first came to look at the apartment, and when I saw what was happening now, I dashed in and yelled at her, "You lied to us when you were here last time. You're a bad woman!" She was terrified at this onslaught and said, "Get the child out of here!" And that is what happened. We packed up what we could, left the rest, and moved in with a neighbour.'[17]

Every day since the German annexation of Austria eight months earlier, there had been long lines of Jews outside the foreign consulates in the city, seeking exit visas. On November 10 those lines were noticeably shorter. Many men who had joined the lines that morning were taken away by the police, to prison cells and concentration camps. A London evening newspaper reported: 'A large crowd which gathered, terrified, outside the British Consulate in Vienna in the hope of getting a visa, was arrested en bloc and taken to prison.'[18] Jews who were standing in line outside the United States Consulate were, according to 'reliable reports', severely beaten and also arrested.[19]

That afternoon 'hardly a Jew' was to be seen in the streets of

---

17 Kurt Fuchel (Kurt Füchsl), recollections, in Mark Jonathan Harris and Deborah Oppenheimer, *Into the Arms of Strangers: Stories of Kindertransport*, page 67.
18 'Jews Flee into Vienna Woods', *Evening Standard*, 10 November 1938.
19 'Thousands of Jews Arrested', *The Times*, 11 November 1938.

Vienna. 'It was reported that they had fled to the Vienna woods.'[20] At five o'clock in the afternoon the order issued by Goebbels for a halt to the 'demonstrations' was broadcast over Vienna Radio. Police and Nazi Party officials immediately began to send the demonstrators home, whereupon, as one British newspaper correspondent reported, 'the situation became somewhat easier'.[21]

Shortly before Kristallnacht, an Austrian Jewish girl, Gertrude Reininger, her parents and her sister had been driven from their home in the provincial town of Neunkirchen. From there they made their way to Vienna. 'We sat in the dark, empty flat,' she later recalled, 'hoping anybody passing would think it was empty. My father hid in the inside, windowless bathroom, again without light. I know little of what went on outside as we did not dare go near a window. Fortunately nobody came to our flat . . .'[22]

The historian of the fate of the Jews of Austria, Gertrude Schneider, then a ten-year-old girl in Vienna, later recalled how 'four storm troopers' marched into her grandmother's Kosher restaurant – still open for business but, unknown to the intruders, already sold to a Nazi Party member – and proceeded 'in a rather methodical fashion, to break every chair, every table, the dishes, the glass vitrine where pastries were displayed, and, of course, the bevelled windows. They also ripped out the phone.'

Gertrude Schneider's grandmother, Bertha LeWinter, was cooking on the stove in the back room. Probably because she was listening to the radio, she did not hear the destruction in the restaurant. She was therefore surprised to see the four men 'come in and wreak havoc' in the kitchen.

First, Gertrude Schneider wrote, 'the thugs broke the modern

20 'Jews Flee into Vienna Woods', *Evening Standard*, 10 November 1938.
21 'Explosions, Fires, Panics', *News Chronicle*, 11 November 1938.
22 Gertrude Bibring (*née* Reininger), letter to the author, 17 June 2005.

refrigerator that had been installed only two years earlier. It extended over a whole wall; they ripped out its doors, its trays, broke off all the handles, and finally despoiled the food inside. They smashed the radio and then their leader, Alfred Slawik, whom all of us had known for years as a real bum, poured water over the range. As the fire went out, he asked grandmother with unconcealed glee whether she was satisfied. Although my usually unflappable grandmother was shaken to the core by this wanton destruction, she answered coolly: "The restaurant was sold, as is, to Party member Hans Maurer. He is the one who may not be satisfied!" [23]

Bertha LeWinter survived the war. After Kristallnacht she fled with her daughter to Belgium. When the Germans invaded Belgium they fled to France. There they were taken by the Vichy French militia to the Vichy-run concentration camp at Gurs, just north of the Pyrenees. From Gurs they escaped over the Pyrenees to Spain and Portugal, reaching New York by sea the day after Pearl Harbor.

Herbert Friedman was not quite fourteen years old on Kristallnacht. He remembered how 'The dreaded bang on the door and shouted command "Open up" about 9 p.m. on November 9 frightened us immensely. We froze when we heard that knock on the door.' Fearfully, his mother opened the door and two SA men in uniform entered. 'They asked for my brother, then sixteen years old. We said he was not home. They searched the apartment and not finding him decided to take me with them. My mother started crying, pleading, "He is only a little boy, he hasn't done anything, please, please, don't take him away." It was the comment of one

---

23 Gertrude Schneider, *Exile and Destruction: The Fate of Austrian Jews, 1938–1945*, page 31.

of the SA men that spared me, when he said, "It wasn't him." They said they would be back later for my brother and left. My mother then asked me to run down to the street (we lived on the fourth floor) to intercept my brother and tell him not to come home but to stay with a friend.'

Herbert Friedman's mother also asked him 'to warn my uncle, a Polish citizen, who had a candy store, not to go home but stay with his mother-in-law. The SA came there too looking for him. He slipped under the kitchen table, which had a long table-cloth. The Nazis searched the whole apartment but never looked under the table, they even pounded on the kitchen table as he lay under it and demanded that his mother-in-law report him if he showed up.'

The following morning Herbert Friedman decided to go to the Palestine Office to check on his application for emigration. 'As I came out to the street I saw a large crowd, laughing and jeering in front of Mr Springer's bedding supply store, next to our house. At first I did not realise what was going on, but then I saw a large truck and SA troopers looting the store of mattresses, blankets, sheets, etc. The police stood by but did nothing. The owner, Mr Springer, just stood by watching, scared and trembling.'

When the store had been emptied and the truck was about to leave, Springer approached the head SA man, asking for a receipt. 'The SA man turned to the crowd laughing and shouted, "The Jew wants a receipt." He then grabbed Mr Springer, turned him around and gave him a kick in the rear that sent him sprawling onto the pavement. Then, with the crowd cheering and laughing, he said, "There, Jew, this is your receipt." '

When the truck left, the crowd dispersed and Herbert Friedman continued on to the Palestine Office. 'Already, there was a large crowd of men and women waiting to talk to someone about their status. Suddenly SS men in their black uniforms appeared and ordered men to one side and women and children to the other. All the men were arrested and taken away. The rest of us were detained for about two hours then let go.'

When Herbert Friedman finally left the Palestine Office, more Jewish men were approaching it. 'I stood at the edge of the pavement and, turning my head not to speak directly, said, "Don't go in. Gestapo." Some asked me to repeat what I had said, and then walked away. I did not realise that an SS man was standing behind the door, several steps up, watching me. He yelled out for me to come back, then wanted to know what I was telling these men. I answered: "I was just telling them that I had been here three hours and just came out." He said, "That's a lie," and then struck me in the face and threw me down the steps. I picked myself up and ran home as fast as I could.'[24]

Thirteen-year-old Ilse Morgenstern was also a witness of the events of Kristallnacht in Vienna. It was, she wrote, 'the night I smelled smoke which came from a nearby synagogue being burned'. She added: 'It took only twenty-four hours for the local population to vandalise all Jewish businesses. I saw merchandise being tossed out of the windows of a nearby Jewish-owned department store which was carried home in big carts by the townspeople. In the summer of 1938, the German secret police had walked into my father's print shop and told him to get out immediately. They had confiscated his business and began using it for Party headquarters, where swastika flags were now flying.'

Ilse Morgenstern also recalled 'the frightening happening during which my older brother was sent out of our apartment by

24 Herbert Friedman, letter to the author, 8 August 2005.

my parents, in fear of being arrested ... He carefully walked the streets, hiding wherever possible when he saw SS men approaching. He was fortunate not to be caught that evening.' Others of her family were less fortunate. 'It sticks in my memory,' she wrote, 'that several of my cousins were arrested and brought to a public place. From there they were sent to Dachau. They never returned.' She also remembered 'the horrible moment when a Nazi who lived in our building came into my parents' apartment and told us to leave within five minutes and to move in with another Jewish family. Later, my father asked for permission to return and pick up more of our belongings. They granted his wish, and when we returned to our apartment there were now three men who had come to supervise what we were taking. Imagine, we were restricted in what we could carry from our own belongings!' The men had brought with them a woman 'to whom they had promised my new piano. Not realising the precariousness of the situation, I played once more a Viennese waltz which I had just learned. As they were beginning to move the piano, I let out a loud scream, to which the woman yelled back: "I no longer want that piano." My parents were able to give it to a non-Jewish family who had been sympathetic to us.'

'It was only two weeks after these events,' Ilse Morgenstern later wrote, 'that my parents were able to send me to a cousin in Holland who found a foster family who took me in.' After the German occupation of Holland in May 1940, 'I received an order from the German authorities to immediately go to a labour camp in Germany. Instead I was fortunate to find brave people who took me into hiding and saved my life. It was extremely dangerous and I was lucky not to have been betrayed. I stayed with these Christian rescuers by hiding for three years, until the end of the war in May 1945.' Her parents 'were unable to emigrate anywhere in the world and died in an extermination camp in Poland. Besides my brother, I am the only survivor of my family.'[25]

In all, 10,000 Jewish men were arrested in Vienna during November 10. Six thousand were released by nightfall, but the remaining 4,000 were taken under armed guard to Dachau.

Thirty Jews were reported to have committed suicide in Vienna on November 10. Twice as many were said to have tried to take their lives. 'By midnight,' reported the special correspondent of the British United Press, 'all the Jews of Vienna will have been examined either at a police station or in their homes, by police or stormtroopers.'[26]

The Jews of Vienna reached a traumatic turning point during Kristallnacht, from which there was no return.

25 Ilse Loeb (*née* Morgenstern), letter to the author, 11 July 2005.
26 'Bombs Used to Set Synagogues Afire', *Daily Herald*, 11 November 1938.

4

Eye-Witnesses
in Every Corner of the Reich

THE REPERCUSSIONS of vom Rath's murder were felt in a thousand German cities, towns and villages, in the early hours of November 10. A correspondent of *The Times* in Munich described how Jewish shops were attacked 'by crowds incited by Brownshirts, most of whom appeared to be members of the Putsch veterans who marched in Munich yesterday. The doors of shops were broken in, the windows smashed, and wares destroyed or looted. The fire brigade and police came on the scene after all the Jewish shops had been assaulted, and dispersed the rioters.'[1]

Large crowds, *The Times* reported, came onto the streets during the morning to look at the damage. 'The Kaufinger Strasse, one of the main streets, looked as if it had been raided by a bombing aeroplane. Half a dozen of the most fashionable shops in the street had been converted overnight into ruins, with their plate glass windows lying in splinters on the pavements, shelves overthrown, and wares lying broken or trampled on the floor.' As far as could be gathered, 'every Jewish shop in the town was partly or completely wrecked'.[2]

1 'Anti-Jewish Disorders in Munich', *The Times*, 10 November 1938.
2 'Havoc in Munich', *The Times*, 11 November 1938.

Inge Engelhard was eight years old on Kristallnacht. 'Our family lived at the back of our apartment block, near Munich's Deutsches Museum,' she later recalled, 'and therefore knew nothing of the events of the night until we almost reached our school. It was a bleak, cold morning, when a bigger boy, one of our usual tormentors, skipped passed us and said, "You'd better go home, poor old Joseph," and for once did not attack us. My brother and I were surprised, but as we neared the school, which was attached to one of the synagogues, we saw crowds watching the flames consuming the synagogue. Somehow we knew it wasn't going to be a normal schoolday, and made ourselves scarce. We went to our parents' shop. My parents ran the only Jewish laundry in Munich, which ironically did very well, because Jews could only patronise Jewish businesses, so we kept the whole of Munich's Jewish population clean.'

When they reached the laundry 'there were two huge Nazis telling my parents to close everything, but allowing them to deliver any laundry still there. One of the Nazis was more human than the second one, and probably more senior, because he told the other one to go to the next place on the list, whilst he told my father that when everything was delivered he should hand over the keys. Our business was not ransacked or the windows smashed – there really was nothing to loot, and the neighbouring shops had always been on good terms with our parents. So that was that: the end of my parents' business, their livelihood, and with a terribly uncertain future. We all went home, and relatives came to tell of the horrors they had been through.'[3]

Bertha Engelhard, Inge's older sister, remembered another sad aspect of that day: 'Father came home ashen-faced, because one

3 Inge M. Sadan (*née* Engelhard), letter to the author, 22 June 2005.

of the customers he had gone to deliver laundry to had committed suicide, both he and his wife.'[4]

Five hundred Jews were arrested in Munich on November 10. During the day it was announced that all the Jews in the city had forty-eight hours to leave Germany. Some tried to drive away from the city in their cars, but the petrol stations refused to serve them with petrol. It was a hundred miles to the Swiss border, but the Gestapo seized many passports, so that the foreign consulates in the city were unable to issue visas. When asked where they could go without passports, the Gestapo replied, as reported by a British journalist in the city: 'Well, they will have to shoot you all at the frontier.'[5] Many grocers and bakers put signs in their windows announcing that they would not sell food to Jews.

Among the Jews in Munich that day was Emil Kraemer, a partner in the largest remaining Jewish banking firm in Germany. As the bank windows were smashed, and the Nazis took control of the building, he committed suicide by jumping out of the window of his apartment. Or so the Nazi media reported. Within a few days, the Berlin correspondent of a British newspaper wrote that banking circles in Germany were wondering how Kraemer had managed to commit suicide by jumping out of a window, as 'the aged banker had been paralysed for two years and could scarcely walk with the aid of two sticks'.[6]

One good deed was reported from Munich that day, when the city's Catholic Archbishop, Cardinal Michael von Faulhaber, provided a truck for the community rabbi, Dr Leo Baerwald, to

4 Bertha Leverton (*née* Engelhard), recollections, in Mark Jonathan Harris and Deborah Oppenheimer, *Into the Arms of Strangers: Stories of the Kindertransport*, page 63.
5 'Munich Jews Told "Go in 48 Hours"', *News Chronicle*, 11 November 1938.
6 'Suicide Mystery', *News Chronicle*, 15 November 1938.

rescue religious objects from the Ohel Yaakov synagogue before it was pulled down.[7]

Renée Inow was a schoolgirl in Wuppertal. She remembered reaching school and the other children saying to her, 'Your synagogues are burning.'[8] Both synagogues in Wuppertal were burned that day, one dating from 1865 and the other from 1897.

Thirteen-year-old Gerhard Maschkowski lived in the East Prussian town of Elbing. His father, who had served in the German army in the First World War, had been blinded in action. His son took him into town on November 10. 'I had seen smoke coming from where the synagogue was,' Gerhard Maschkowski later wrote, 'and we walked towards there. The whole building was still smoking, and my prayer shawl and books and other religious items that were mine, all were burned. It was a shocking sight, and the Germans were cheering.'[9]

Marianne David was fifteen years old on Kristallnacht, at boarding school in Bad Kreuznach, more than three hundred miles from her home in Hamburg. Six decades later she described 'that awful night' in vivid terms. 'I was woken in the middle of the night by shouting and banging, then men in Nazi uniforms burst into my room screaming: "Raus, raus!" On the table was my new alto recorder, of which I was very proud, as I had so far only owned a soprano. One of the men picked it up and broke it by hitting it on the table's edge. I got dressed and went outside where everybody was gathering in a frightened group. Matron was there trying to keep everyone calm. The Nazis were bringing items,

---

7 A plaque at the site today records the location and fate of the synagogue, but makes no mention of the Cardinal's act.

8 Renie Inow, conversation with the author, 28 June 2005.

9 Gerhard Maschkowski, letter to the author, 12 July 2005.

books and other things, out of the building, piling them up to be set alight ... as I came out of my room into the long corridor, there was an SS man going along it with a club, systematically smashing the glass on each pretty nursery picture on the wall. Frightened as I was, it still struck me as such a pointless thing to do.'

Marianne David took the train back home to Hamburg, a seven-hour journey. 'How I got to the station or home from the station in Hamburg, is a mystery to me,' she later wrote. 'Of course, all this time I had no idea that what had happened to me that night had happened all over Germany. I thought it was just another isolated incident. But when I got to the house at last, pleased to have made it, a shock was waiting for me: my father had been taken away, as had nearly all other male Jews that were left in the town. Later it became known that they had been taken to Sachsenhausen concentration camp.'[10]

Four-year-old Edgar Gold was also in Hamburg that day. 'My father's business was targeted and all the windows were smashed,' he later recalled, 'but our house, which was next door, just had its windows smeared with horrid slogans and Stars of David. I remember noise and being frightened and my father being quite calm. Strangely, about a week later my father's business was confiscated, and to add insult to injury he had to reimburse the new "owner" for the broken windows!'

Josef Gold's business was a small but successful and well-known factory that made hand-made chocolates. It continued to operate under the Germans who seized it until July 1943, when it was destroyed in an Allied air raid.[11]

10 Marianne Geernaert (*née* David), recollections written in 2004, sent to the author 10 June 2005.
11 Edgar Gold, letter to the author, 9 September 2005.

The events in Hamburg were witnessed by the British Consul General, L. M. Robinson. In the early hours of the morning of November 10, he reported to the British Embassy in Berlin, attacks were made on large Jewish stores in the main shopping streets of the city. 'The plate glass windows of two drapery establishments, a fashionable ladies and gentlemen's outfitting shop, and a photo and optical shop were demolished, and the contents scattered on the pavements.' In the afternoon 'some sixty schoolchildren stoned the glass doors of a synagogue over the head of a policeman in the presence of some two hundred people'.[12] Ten of Hamburg's sixteen synagogues were burned out or destroyed on November 10, including the two-hundred-year-old synagogue in the suburb of Altona and the Oberstrasse synagogue, completed only six years before Kristallnacht.

Adina Koor was a schoolgirl in Hamburg on Kristallnacht. 'At the far end of the street where I lived stood the liberal synagogue, an impressive building,' she later wrote. 'In the morning on the way to school I saw thick clouds of smoke coming from the top of the building. Men dressed in the Nazi uniform patrolled the streets. I did not go to school but returned home instead. Across the street where I lived there were two stores both owned by Jews. It was early morning and the shutters were still on the windows. At eight o'clock the owners arrived, removed the shutters and opened the doors. No sooner were the stores open than a truck with men dressed in the Nazi uniform arrived. They jumped off the truck and began demolishing the windows and the stores. Most of the content was thrown into the street. The owners of both stores were marched away. On that day all Jewish men

---

12 Laurence Milner Robinson, letter of 10 November 1938: Foreign Office papers, FO 371/21637.

were taken to concentration camp. Those who were unfortunate enough to die during their stay in concentration camp, their ashes were sent to their families. I received a message that the Jewish school I attended was closed for the time being. Most teachers were taken to concentration camp.'[13]

As Brownshirts searched the streets of Hamburg for Jews to arrest, Carmen de Carvalho, the wife of the Brazilian Vice-Consul in the city, gave refuge to a Jewish doctor, Hugo Levy, hiding him in the Consulate. When the rampage subsided, she accompanied him to his home. Within two weeks she had obtained emigration papers to Brazil for the doctor and his wife Maria Margarethe, and on November 24 she drove them to the Hamburg docks to the ship that was to take them to Brazil. She protected them on the journey through the city by using her husband's consular car, and flying the Brazilian flag.[14]

Vera Dahl was seventeen years old on Kristallnacht. She was in Aachen that day, taken by her father for an appointment in the hospital: 'We went by tram – passed various Jewish shops on the way, partly very badly damaged, all windows broken or smashed, glass everywhere . . . Shops were being looted as we passed. I was petrified . . .' At the hospital 'no one said anything except when I was to come again'. Walking back, they passed a Jewish café where everything was 'smashed terribly badly and people stood outside eating stolen cream cakes etc.'.

Even before they could see the synagogue, Vera Dahl and her father could smell the burning. The synagogue was in ruins. It had been refurbished two years earlier when new stained-glass

13 Adina Koor, letter to the author, 24 June 2005.
14 Maria Margarethe Levy, notarised testimony, 25 November 1980. Yad Vashem, Righteous Among the Nations Archive, file 2305.

windows were installed. Non-Jewish singers from the local opera had been in the choir at the rededication ceremony. That night her father left town.[15]

An anonymous eye-witness of Kristallnacht in Bonn wrote to the leader of the British Labour Party, Clement Attlee: 'Under the guidance of the blackguards called the SS there came lorry loads of Nazi mobs, destroying everything according to lists which they carried with them.' After one shop had been destroyed 'they got into the same lorry and destroyed another in accordance with their checklist'. Two municipal rubbish carts, each a three-ton truck, were needed to remove the broken porcelain from the finest porcelain shop in the city.[16]

The Jews of Cologne suffered on Kristallnacht as Jews did in every German city. A report published the next day in London described how 'Windows of Jewish shops were broken and their contents scattered. A synagogue was entered. The seats torn up and the vestments thrown into the streets.'[17] 'We heard the fire department trucks go by in the direction of the Bonner synagogue, to protect the neighbourhood as they set it on fire,' recalled Hans Biglajzer, who was then ten years old. 'From our house we could see the smoke rising.' That was in the morning. 'The destroyers came at midday to break the display windows in the next building owned by the Levy family, a butcher shop.'[18]

November 10 was Rita Braumann's twelfth birthday. 'In the small hours,' she later wrote, 'the telephone rang. It was Mr

15 Vera Bier (*née* Dahl), recollections set down on 12 November 1988; sent to the author by her son David Bier, 1 September 2005.
16 Letter of 12 November 1938: Foreign Office papers, FO 371/21637.
17 'Here is what Happened in Other Towns', *Daily Herald*, 11 November 1938.
18 Hans Biglajzer, letter to the author, 6 June 2005.

Westhoven who said to my father, "Braumann, get out of town, go to Ruhrberg, you know where the keys to the house are hidden. The synagogue and the Jewish schools have been set on fire. Jewish homes are being wrecked and the men arrested." But we did not go. My usually pessimistic father was full of confidence, maintaining that nothing would happen to us because he had fought at the Front during the war and had even been decorated.'

Rita Braumann did not go to school that morning. 'My girl-friend Helga, who lived nearby, came to wish me a happy birthday and was still at our place when the doorbell rang at 10.30 a.m. My father, who had meanwhile pinned his wartime decorations to his lapel, opened the front door. There stood several storm-troopers, who asked politely: "Are you Braumann, is this house your property and is this your family?" When told that Helga was my friend they turned to this blonde and blue-eyed girl and said, "Du bist doch kein Judenkind?" (You couldn't be Jewish too?) When she nodded they yelled, "Mach dass du nach Hause kommst" (Get yourself home). She burst into tears and ran. To us they said politely: Go upstairs to your bedrooms and "Gruss aus Paris" (greetings from Paris).' Paris was the scene of the murder of vom Rath.

There were grim sounds from below. 'We then heard the sys-tematic destruction of all our furniture with tools they must have brought up from the cellar, because they were not carrying anything when they arrived. The noise was terrifying. We went out on the balcony, neighbours were on theirs and wanted to know what was happening, but we were too frightened to reply. Finally there was silence. The sight that awaited us downstairs was unbelievable. Absolutely everything had been demolished. Shattered glass made it dangerous to walk anywhere. Bottles of wine had been poured over Persian carpets, home-made jam had been emptied all over the place, making an impossibly sticky mess everywhere. Valuable paintings had been slashed with an axe or knives. Suddenly the telephone rang. When we eventually located the receiver it was the mother of one of my schoolfriends to enquire whether my scheduled birthday party was still taking place that afternoon!! In all this debris stood my new three-speed bike, only slightly damaged but never to be used by me.'[19]

Fourteen-year-old Esther Ascher lived in the Silesian city of Breslau. Her family were Polish-born Jews who had escaped the round-up on October 18 because of a tip-off from a girlfriend's father, who was the Jewish liaison person between the Jewish community and the Gestapo. 'The evening of 9 November 1938 was not different from any other evening,' she later wrote. 'My two older brothers were reading, my younger brother and I sat around and talked. We went to bed around 10.30. Suddenly we were awakened to the sound of shattering glass and loud shouts. All of us awoke, not knowing what this noise was about. We huddled close to the windows, and finally dared to part the curtains to look down. Below us we saw people ramming wood poles through the showcases of the Jewish store, we heard screaming, and saw people enter the showcases as looting began.'

The family's first instinct was to hide. 'We quickly retreated to the room, shaking our heads, attempting to guess the meaning of what we were witnessing. Our mother was not only afraid of what would happen to us, she was also a woman of action. She gave each one of us twenty marks, which was not a great deal of money, but I suppose that was all that she had. She gave instructions to

19 Rita Newell (*née* Braumann), recollections entitled '10 November, 1938' (written in 1980), enclosed with letter to the author, 28 June 2005.

hold onto this money in case we were separated. After a few hours, relative quiet returned to the street. We spoke quietly among ourselves as we waited for dawn. No amount of speculating as to the meaning of the breaking of the showcases led us to any conclusion.'

Esther Ascher remembered: 'I must admit, that I, a fourteen-year-old girl, even though I deep down knew that what happened could only mean disaster perpetrated against Jews, speculated about what I would be able to do with the sudden windfall of twenty marks. Would I be able to buy the sweater that I always wanted? There was not much time for daydreaming. The phone began to ring . . .'

It was members of Esther Ascher's family, and family friends. 'Everyone called frantically in the hope of getting an answer. The doorbell rang a number of times; my older brother's friends came to ask if they could stay with us, since it seemed that this action was aimed primarily against German Jews. We welcomed them, especially since we recalled that just a week earlier we had been seeking shelter with a German Jewish family, in addition to the Polish Consulate.'

Of all the family members, Esther Ascher was the only one 'who did not look Jewish, as a matter of fact I was always called "Shicksel" – a Yiddish word for a non-Jewish girl. Therefore the decision was made that I go out into the streets to explore what had happened to Jewish-owned stores, especially my uncle's, and attempt to find out as much as I possibly could. I was not especially fearful, since often, when I was with my youngest brother and children shouted at him "Dirty Jew, go to Palestine," and attempted to beat him, I ran after them. And so, conscious of not looking Jewish, I left the protection of our apartment building.'

It was quite an adventure. 'The streets were deserted except for

SS men, marching with a Jewish male between them. It became clear to me that these unfortunate people were on their way to a concentration camp. Nearby was a very large Jewish complex: a reform synagogue and a school. One could see doors open, books strewn about. The Storch synagogue that I frequented was too far and in a different direction. Only after a few days did I witness the destruction there. My parents attended a Stiebel' – a prayer house – 'which had been spared at that time, since it was located behind an apartment building.'

There was much to be shocked by. 'Many storefronts had been reduced to rubble, and it was clear that all those were Jewish stores. My uncle sold feathers for pillows and quilts. Next to his store was a Jewish liquor store. As I approached them, I saw feathers swirling in the air, feathers glued to the street where they had mixed with the wine flowing from the liquor store. Broken bottles were lying about; one could imagine that the best of the wines had been plundered, while some broke in the process of destroying the store. After that experience I had had enough, and turned to return home. The picture was the same: SS men leading Jews who followed them as innocent lambs. My mood changed from feeling adventurous to crestfallen. The harsh reality of what had happened, and what still might happen, began to sink in. By the time I reached our apartment, my family had heard the reason for the attack on Jews and their property. From that point on life changed for me. I had but one goal, to leave Germany . . .'[20]

Also in Breslau on Kristallnacht was Lutz Wachsner, a partner in a textile firm, and his family. The night itself, his nineteen-year-old son Frank remembered, 'we all survived without any problems'. But his father had already been warned by the local police

20 Esther Adler (*née* Ascher), letter to the author, 28 June 2005.

that something was going to happen and, determined that 'we should all leave as soon as possible', began to make plans for their emigration.[21]

In Siegburg, where the synagogue was destroyed and Jewish shops attacked, Fred Gottlieb, then aged nine, recalled that 'the Nazis went in convertible cars carrying long poles and breaking windows'. When a policeman entered his house, searching for all men aged between sixteen and sixty to be taken to concentration camps, he found a young neighbour. The questioning was brief. 'How old are you?' 'Sixteen.' The neighbour was taken away.[22]

After the synagogue was destroyed in Korbach, the rabbi, Moritz Goldwein, and his wife Rosa were able to send their son Manfred to the United States. They themselves were unable to leave, however, and later perished at Auschwitz.

Following the destruction of the hundred-year-old synagogue in Eschwege, a mob looted and vandalised Jewish property in the town. After being paraded through the main street, all Jewish men were taken off to concentration camp.

Five Jews were shot in Bremen that night, among them an elderly woman, Selma Zwienicki.[23]

In Mainz, Elsa Blatt was a month away from her nineteenth birthday on Kristallnacht. 'We woke to loud noises in the streets,' she later wrote, 'and became aware of people roaring and screaming outside.' Later that day the doorbell was rung by a member of a non-Jewish family whom her family knew well. 'He stood there, asking for the keys of our business. While we thought this an odd request, we had no idea what was going on.' The family 'had always been a decent family and had good relations with us.

21 Frank Wachsner, letter to the author, 11 September 2005.
22 Fred Gottlieb, letter to the author, 1 July 2005.
23 Pages of testimony, Yad Vashem Archives.

We gave him the key. Apparently he had printed large signs reading "Aryan Business" and had plastered this over the two entrance doors as well as the five shop windows.' The next time the doorbell rang it was the Gestapo, to take her father away. 'It was not until much later that we found he had been taken to Buchenwald.'[24]

Twenty-two-year-old Walter Loeb was in Karlsruhe during Kristallnacht. His father was the president of the synagogue. From an old tombstone in the cemetery his family had discovered that their name had existed in the town since 1696. 'We certainly were not newcomers,' he later commented. 'We had lived peacefully among our German neighbours with whom we had good relations. My father was a respected citizen, since he helped war widows with getting their pensions, and fellow Jews with emigration formalities.'

On the morning of November 10 Walter Loeb was on the main street, 'where a crowd had gathered, when I spotted a man with a beard whom I recognised as our gabbai, the rabbi's assistant. When I cast a friendly glance at him this was apparently intercepted by two Gestapo agents who ordered us to follow them. These two would-be agents were hardly older than myself, and I dared to ask them what I had done. One of them answered in a gruff voice, "You will find out!" When we got to the police courtyard there were other Jewish prisoners. Some showed marks of being beaten. A police spokesman then said we were there because of what had happened in Paris. Nothing would happen to us if we were to cooperate, and it was all for our own protection.'

It was protection of an unusual sort. 'We were taken into prison cells,' Walter Loeb recalled, 'and later in the afternoon they gave each of us a small loaf of bread. Late in the evening they marched

24 Elsa Kissel (*née* Blatt), letter to the author, 18 July 2005.

us to the train station, and a few onlookers jeered along the way. We boarded a special train with destination unknown. We stopped to pick up other prisoners on the way and travelled through most of the night, when our worst fears came true as we arrived at Dachau before dawn under blinding spotlights.'[25]

Charlotte Neumann was an eighteen-year-old pupil at a Jewish teachers' training seminary in Würzburg on Kristallnacht. She and the other girls were woken up at two in the morning by the caretaker, 'who was dressed in full "brownshirt" uniform'. He told the young women 'to dress quickly and run away, because "they" were burning, looting and destroying synagogues and Jewish homes and shops ... He said he himself was on duty, but had slipped away to warn us.' The girls fled to the nearby woods where they had often hiked 'in happier times', stumbling about in the darkness 'terrified and in despair. We could see a dull red glow from the town.'

Twenty-three years later, Charlotte Neumann (then Charlotte Lapian) returned to Würzburg with her eighteen-year-old daughter. 'I wanted to show her the seminary and there it was, exactly as I remembered it. We went up the stairs, and there was the same corridor, the same lockers – and the same caretaker, seemingly wielding the same wide broom, cleaning the same floors as of old. "Good morning, Herr Hüfner," I said, almost involuntarily. He turned, and did not look a day older. "Can I help you?" he said. I answered that I had been a pupil in the thirties, and wanted to show my daughter the place. He sighed, and said that it had been good, that it could and should have continued, and that it had been a dreadful time. What possessed me, I do not know; I burst out, "You Germans are all the same. Everything happened by

25 Walter Loeb, letter to the author, 11 July 2005.

itself and Hitler did it single-handedly." He looked at me without answering, and then he said, "If you were really here that night, you know what I did." At that I burst into tears and apologised. He said, "I understand how you feel," and we shook hands and left.'[26]

As soon as David Hess realised what was happening in Würzburg, he set off for the home of a Christian friend, an architect named Gourdon. 'When my father arrived at his friend's house,' David Hess's son Joel, who had left Germany for the United States two years earlier, later wrote, 'he told him what was going on in the city. Without any further words Mr Gourdon asked my father to come into the house, where my father remained for some time. Due to Mr Gourdon's act, taking his life in his hands, my father never, never saw the inside of a concentration camp and was able, together with my mother, to leave Germany in 1939.'[27] Both synagogues in Würzburg, one almost a hundred years old, were destroyed that night.

In Leipzig, Stefanie Bamberger was ten years old on Kristallnacht. 'At 4 a.m. there was a tremendous banging on the door. When we opened the door (my room was right by the front door so I was the first to get up) four unshaven, frightened-looking Gestapo barged in. At gunpoint my mother had to show them where she kept the jewellery and where the money was kept, but there was no money in the safe.' Stephanie's father, Ludwig Bamberger, whose leg was paralysed as a result of a wound received in action in the First World War, was ordered out of bed and told to hurry up and get dressed. He was then taken away to the local prison.

26 Charlotte Lapian (*née* Neumann), letter to the author, 17 August 2005.
27 Joel Hess, letter to the author, 6 June 2001.

As the Gestapo left, they called out: 'Go and look at your business and also at your beautiful synagogue.'

Stefanie and her mother made their way through Leipzig to their family business. What they saw was 'unbelievable – just a skeleton of a building, everything inside burnt – hundreds of rolls of material, coats, shirts, sweaters, and suits'. As for the building next door to theirs, owned by a non-Jew, 'not a centimetre was even charred, not one window broken'.

Going on to the synagogue, Stefanie Bamberger and her mother found it likewise burned and vandalised. They then went to the local Jewish hospital, where they were given white coats and went to work as nurses. 'Every morning at 4 a.m. the Gestapo came and took away any man who was able to stand up.' She and her mother were able to extract her father from the police station and take him to the hospital.[28]

The first news from Leipzig on November 10 was that two Jews had been arrested on a charge of setting fire to their own premises, 'in order to get the insurance'.[29] A Leipzig Jewish schoolgirl, Esther Reisz, was fourteen years old. 'The Nazis were given twenty-four hours' freedom to do what they wanted to with synagogues and Jewish homes,' she later recalled; but her family was lucky. 'In our apartment block there was a non-Jewish housekeeper,' she wrote, 'who would not let the Nazis come in to look for Jewish apartments. I remember us standing behind the curtain shivering with fright, and we heard the housekeeper shout to the Nazis, "Go away. No Jews live here."'[30]

Joseph Schwarzberg was a schoolboy in Leipzig on Kristall-nacht. He woke up on the morning of November 10 to see his

28 Stefanie Segerman (*née* Bamberger), letter to the author, 9 August 2005.
29 News item, *Evening Standard*, 10 November 1938.
30 Esther Reisz, letter to the author, 12 June 2005.

parents and their neighbours barricading themselves into their apartment. Through the slits of the closed shutters of his window he could see the apartment of one of his classmates, and the pavement in front of it. What he saw was his friend's brother, and his parents, being 'severely beaten on the street after they and some of their belongings and furniture were thrown out into the street. A group of mostly younger-looking men, some in brown uniforms, were screaming insults and beating with no mercy. The younger brother of my classmate was tied to a bicycle by his neck and had to run after the bicycle so as not to be choked. He was a big boy for his age of thirteen, but finally collapsed in complete exhaustion with many bruises.'[31]

The United States Consul in Leipzig, David H. Buffum, reported to his superiors in Washington that the three main synagogues, set on fire simultaneously, 'were irreparably gutted by flames'. He also noted that in the Jewish cemetery the Nazis practised 'tactics which approached the ghoulish', uprooting tombstones and violating graves.

In the city itself, Buffum reported, 'Having demolished dwellings and hurled most of the effects to the streets, the insatiably sadistic perpetrators threw many of the trembling inmates into a small stream that flows through the Zoological Park, commanding horrified spectators to spit at them, defile them with mud and jeer at their plight.'[32]

Among those who witnessed the outburst of destruction in Leipzig was a twenty-five-year-old Dutch Jew, Wim van Leer, who had arrived a few days earlier from England as an emissary of the

---

31 Joseph Schwarzberg, 'My Life Story', typescript, 1990. Sent by Joseph Schwarzberg to the author, 24 June 2005.
32 Letter dated Leipzig, 21 November 1938: submitted to the International Military Tribunal, Nuremberg, as Document L–202.

Quakers to take a group of young Jews to Britain. Walking in the city at about seven in the morning on November 10, he saw a truck draw up a few houses down the road from him, and 'some twenty louts jumped down'. One had a clipboard and directed the others to particular shops and houses. Van Leer watched as SA stormtroopers rang the doorbells, smashed the glass windows in the doors if there was no reply, and entered the Jewish houses.

'Suddenly,' van Leer later wrote, 'third-floor balcony doors were flung open and stormtroops appeared, shouting to their mates below. One yelled something about all blessings coming from above, and in expectation, that part of the pavement beneath the balcony was cleared. Next they wheeled an upright piano onto the balcony and, smashing the balustrade with one mighty heave – there must have been eight of them – they pushed the piano over the edge. It nose-dived onto the street below with a sickening crash as the wooden casing broke away, leaving what looked like a harp standing in the middle of the debris . . .'[33]

Fourteen-year-old Ruth Goldfein lived in Danzig. On Kristallnacht she was at the local Jewish youth club playing table tennis. The club was in a room above the synagogue. Warned that 'Nazi thugs' were waiting outside, she and her girlfriend Esther Goldman had the courage on the way out of the building to persuade a policeman standing there that an ambulance must be called for the beadle of the synagogue, who had had been taken ill. For this deed, she and her friend were summoned by the Gestapo. Her friend managed to leave Danzig for Poland a few days before the appointment; she later perished in a concentration camp.

33 Wim van Leer, *Time of My Life*, Jerusalem, 1984, pages 166–8.

At Gestapo headquarters, Ruth Goldfein was warned 'not to get involved ever again in such affairs'. On December 24 she left Danzig for Poland, and survived.[34]

Among the witnesses to Kristallnacht in Baden Baden was Dr Arthur Flehinger. Later he described how all Jewish men in the town were ordered to assemble on the morning of November 10. Towards noon they were marched through the streets to the synagogue. Many non-Jews resented the round-up. 'I saw people crying while watching from behind their curtains,' Dr Flehinger later wrote, and he added: 'One of the many decent citizens is reported to have said, "What I saw was not one Christ, but a whole column of Christ figures, who were marching along with heads high and unbowed by any feeling of guilt."'

While being marched up the steps to the synagogue, several Jews fell, only to be beaten until they could pick themselves up. Once inside the synagogue, the Jews were confronted by exuberant Nazi officers and SS men. Dr Flehinger himself was ordered to read out passages from *Mein Kampf* to his fellow Jews. 'I read the passage quietly, indeed so quietly that the SS man posted behind me repeatedly hit me in the neck. Those who had to read other passages after me were treated in the same manner. After these "readings" there was a pause. Those Jews who wanted to relieve themselves were forced to do so against the synagogue walls, not in the toilets, and they were physically abused while doing so.' Eventually the Jews were led away. Within an hour, the synagogue was in flames. 'If it had been my decision,' one of the SS men remarked, 'you would have perished in that fire.'[35]

---

34 Ruth Fluss (*née* Goldfein), typescript: letter to the author, 1 August 2005.
35 Dr Arthur Flehinger, 'Flames of Fury', *Jewish Chronicle*, 9 November 1979.

In the city of Bamberg, seeing the synagogue on fire and hurrying to it, Willy Lessing was 'beaten up by thugs', his granddaughter records. The following morning all Jewish men in Bamberg were seized and taken to Dachau, except Lessing, who was too badly beaten to be moved. He died in hospital two and a half months later. Unusually, the culprits of the beating were brought to trial after the war, and convicted. His widow Paula was able to get to England shortly before the outbreak of war, to join her son and sister who were already there.[36]

Ruth Herskovits was a schoolgirl in Hanover. On Kristallnacht she, her elder sister Grete and their parents went for safety to a Jewish family who were Czech nationals, and unlikely to be molested. After several days there, they returned to their apartment. 'As we walked up the three flights of stairs,' she recalled, 'we had carefully to pick our way on the stone steps to avoid stepping on glass and pieces of wood. And chaos confronted us when we opened our front door. In the spacious vestibule, three of the four doors to the two large yellowish oak linen closets were open. The closets had been emptied. Behind the still-closed fourth door, a few apparently forgotten older pieces of bed linen remained. Broken glass and broken dishes were strewn everywhere, and silver utensils and candlesticks were missing from their customary place in the dining room cabinet.' The furniture in the study, the room directly opposite the front door, 'had been methodically hacked to pieces. Hebrew books, their pages torn, were everywhere on the floor. Many of these were the Hebrew prayer books for the Sabbath and the different holidays, and father began to pick them up as he was stumbling over them: according to Jewish law and

36 Joan Lessing, letter to the author, 15 June 2005.

custom, Hebrew prayer books and texts, which usually include the name of God, are not supposed to lie on the floor. In the vestibule, the cabin trunk that had held linen bought for Grete's planned emigration lay empty. Dumbfounded, afraid to move, mother and the three of us just stood there.'

Samuel Herskovits tried to comfort his daughters. 'We should thank God that we are together and that we are unharmed,' he said. 'Luckily we decided to leave home and were not here when these people came.' But, his daughter Ruth remembered, 'while we continued to look at our ruined home, Father had other, much more terrible news: our synagogue had been totally destroyed'.[37]

Also in Hanover, a schoolgirl, Lore Pels, was walking to school with her brother Erwin when she passed a bedding store and was surprised to see policemen present. 'Windows were totally smashed, broken,' she recalled, 'feathers were all over. My first thought was that a burglary was in progress!! The next block was our school. We were NOT able to go into the building, instead we were greeted by police, or Nazis, who were standing in front of the building. They told all the children upon arrival to go back home. Erwin and I had NO idea what could have happened. Slowly word spread that our beautiful synagogue was burning . . . I remember being totally shocked, speechless, since we children spent so much time in the synagogue . . .'

Returning home, Lore Pels saw 'paper shreds' – the burned fragments of prayer books from the synagogue – 'flying in front of our windows'. Her father, Joseph Pels, switched on the radio, and turned the dial until he could hear a foreign radio station, something 'strictly forbidden for Jews'. That was how her family

---

37 Ruth Gutmann (*née* Herskovits), 'The Nazi Noose Tightens', typescript, sent to the author, 28 June 2005.

found out 'that there was no burglary at the store, and that the synagogue was burned, destroyed'. A few days later Lore Pels, her parents and her brother were forced to vacate their apartment, and to leave all their belongings behind. They were moved, with many other families, to a former Jewish school, with 'little more space than a bed' for each person.

As for all those who witnessed Kristallnacht, that night and day were a grim prelude. A cousin in the United States offered affidavits to Lore Pels's father for all four of the family to emigrate. Her father refused, 'stating over and over', as Lore Pels recalled, 'that he had served the Germans during World War One'. One of his brothers, Ivan Pels, had been killed in action in that war, fighting for Germany. When war came again, the family was still in the former Jewish school to which they had been uprooted before Kristallnacht, sharing one room. The building had been declared a 'Jewish House', and no ambulance was allowed to enter it. During the first heavy Allied bombing raid on Hanover, her father had a heart attack. Unable to be taken to hospital because of the ban, he died. A few months later his wife and two children were deported to Riga. His wife and daughter survived; his son Erwin died shortly before the end of the war, in Dachau, to which many of the surviving Riga deportees were taken as the Red Army drew near to the city.[38]

In Kippenheim, Ilse Wertheimer described how, as the Jewish men from the nearby villages of Altdorf and Schmieheim – both of whose synagogues had been destroyed – were marched into Kippenheim, 'the Hitler Youth threw dung and rocks at them and on their heads. Then the Hitler Youth from Lahr and from all

38 Lore Oppenheimer (*née* Pels), letter to the author, 6 July 2005.

over started to demolish the synagogue, put it on fire, and threw the books and Torahs – whatever they could find – in the brook, which went through the village. The windows in Jewish homes were broken. In front of our business we had all kinds of metal beams and machinery with which they broke all the windows, while we women watched behind the curtains in the living room, wondering how soon they would break the door down and kill us. They tried to break our front door when Dr Bernhard Weber in his SS uniform yelled, "That's enough now, stop!" I think that saved our lives.'[39]

In Worms, Herta Mansbacher, the assistant principal of the Jewish school, was among those who managed to put out the fire in the synagogue, but a gang of louts soon arrived to light it again. In a gesture of defiance, she barred the entrance. 'As much as they sought to put a Jewish house of worship to the torch,' the historian of Worms Jewry has written, 'she was equally willing to stop them, even at the risk of her life.'[40] Herta Mansbacher was eventually pushed aside, and the synagogue, set on fire, burned to the ground. A photograph survives of the burned-out ruin of a second, much older synagogue in Worms.[41] Founded in 1014, and enlarged in 1705, it was where the Jewish sage Rashi had studied 883 years earlier. Herta Mansbacher lived on in Worms for another three and a half years, until the deportation of the city's surviving Jews on 20 March 1942, eastward across German-occupied Poland to the death camp at Belzec.

In Bochum, before the synagogue was set on fire, the gold-

39 '10th Nov. 1938', report by Ilse Gutmann (*née* Wertheimer), sent to the author by her son, Benjamin Gutmann, 14 June 2005.
40 Henry R. Huttenbach, *The Destruction of the Jewish Community at Worms, 1933–45*, New York, 1981, pages 142–3.
41 Adolf Diamant, *Zerstörte Synagogen vom November 1938*, page 226.

plated Star of David that had been placed on top of the dome when the synagogue was remodelled in 1899 was, Ruben Moller recalled, 'torn off the dome and stolen', as were the gold-plated Stars of David on the small dome.[42] At Emmerich the Jews were forced to set the synagogue on fire themselves.[43]

In Nordhausen, seven-year-old Edith Welkemeyer remembered walking with her family's maid Anneliese on a morning shopping expedition. 'I adored our maid who always took time to explain everything I wanted to know. Suddenly there was the sound of breaking glass and Anneliese seized me urgently by the hand, pulling me away from the gathering crowds. "Why have they broken that shop window?" I wanted to know, but this time dear, gentle Anneliese wasted no time to explain. We reached home in record time and I was quite breathless.' And also 'quite bewildered'.[44]

The synagogue in Nordhausen, founded in 1845, survived until an Allied air raid in early 1945. By then Nordhausen was a centre of German military production; the Dora-Mittelbau slave labour camp was only three miles from the town.

In the East Prussian town of Schirwindt, the County Officer (Landrat) for the entire district, Wichard von Bredow, received orders from his Nazi Gauleiter to burn down the town's synagogue. In all, more than forty synagogues and houses of prayer in East Prussia were destroyed that night, but as the historian Stephen Nicholls has written: 'After receiving orders from his Gauleiter that all the synagogues in Germany were to be destroyed

42 Ruben Moller, 'A Brief History of the Moller Family', typescript sent to the author, 29 June 2005.
43 Adolf Diamant, *Zerstörte Synagogen vom November 1938*, page 26.
44 Recollections of Edith Forrester (*née* Welkemeyer), in Bertha Leverton and Shmuel Lowensohn, *I Came Alone: The Stories of the Kindertransports*, pages 94–5.

during the next few hours and that both the police and fire brigades were not to intervene, von Bredow donned his German Army uniform, said goodbye to his wife, the mother of their five children, and announced: "I'm going to the synagogue in Schirwindt where I want to prevent one of the greatest crimes in my district." He knew he was risking his life and that he could be sent to a concentration camp, but he added: "I have to do this." '

Nicholls added: 'By the time the SA, SS and Party members arrived with the incendiary materials, he was already waiting for them in front of the synagogue. He loaded his revolver in full view of this group, and realising they would only get into the building over his dead body, they left, not daring to attack the Landrat. The synagogue in Schirwindt was the only one in the district not destroyed.' Von Bredow was subsequently neither punished nor removed from office, but remained Landrat until the end of the war.[45]

Henry Stern was a fourteen-year-old schoolboy in Stuttgart on Kristallnacht. On the morning of November 10, he later recalled, 'I was on my way to school when I saw the flames and the smoke rising from the big synagogue (which was adjacent to the Jewish school). The fire engine stood by but did nothing. There was a huge crowd of people standing there and I remember clearly that there was a complete silence. (Not a jubilating crowd, as was generally reported in the German press.) I, of course, was in shock and ran home crying.' Later on, he heard Germans saying quietly: 'This won't end well, nothing good can come when you burn "Gotteshäuser" (the Houses of God).'

The main synagogue in Stuttgart was 'a very strong building',

45 Stephen Nicholls, manuscript, 'A Heroic Stand During the Night of 9th/ 10th November 1938'.

Henry Stern later wrote. It had been built in 1861. 'The fire "only" destroyed the interior and the cupola, which annoyed the Germans very much. So they ordered architect Ernst Guggenheimer to supervise the dismantling of the building stone by stone, and for that purpose brought Jewish prisoners from nearby camps to do the actual work. The big square stones were then sold to vineyard owners in the district and the cash went into the Gestapo coffers.'[46]

Edith Trzeciak was also in Stuttgart on Kristallnacht. Her stepfather told her to get dressed, 'and we took the streetcar to as close as we could to downtown. I remember a lot of fire and smoke and it scared me. All the big stores had broken windows and fire and smoke. I had never been near a fire before (but saw a lot of that in later years during air raids). There was a lot of noise. Shouting and screaming and some "bad" words I had never heard before. There were men in uniform, and Dad told me not to be scared. He was crying, and I vaguely remember seeing some other people cry too. But a lot were cheering and yelling "Heil Hitler." Dad started to tell me about the horror that was going on and I should never forget it, etc. And he told me that I should still be proud of my Jewishness (he was not Jewish).'

Edith Trzeciak had one fear, 'that some kids I knew would see me and laugh at me, because my Dad was carrying me like a baby and hugging me close to him. And I do recall seeing some kids whom I knew in Hitler Youth and Bundesmaedel uniforms. Not being one of them was the great tragedy of my life at that age, and now they would see me like a baby. Little did I know how lucky I was.' It was one of her earliest memories 'of anything to

46 Henry Stern, letter to the author, 4 June 2005.

do with the Nazis and my being different'.[47] Within five years, Edith Trzeciak's mother and little brother were murdered at Auschwitz.[48]

Batya Emanuel was a thirteen-year-old schoolgirl in Frankfurt-on-Main on Kristallnacht. 'This November 10 had started out no different from any other day,' she later recalled. 'When I woke up a subdued light shimmered through the curtains. I let myself luxuriate in semi-drowsiness.' As she lay in bed, she could just make out the deep red plush cloth on the oak table in the middle of the room, a tablecloth 'that did splendid service as King Ahasuerus's royal mantle on the Jewish festival of Purim, which celebrates our people's deliverance in ancient Persia from Haman, the king's wicked vizier'.

On that November 10 'these pleasant thoughts were rudely interrupted by the door opening. Surely, it wasn't time yet to get up? It was Mother who woke us up in the morning, but here was Papa striding into the room, with the telephone, which was kept in our parents' bedroom at night, tucked under his arm, and he was in braces, without a waistcoat and jacket. I don't think I had ever seen him not fully dressed before. He nodded curtly in my direction, plugged in the phone and dialled: "Is that the police? I wish to inform you that the synagogue at the back of Rutschbahn 11 has been broken into and is being vandalised at this very moment – you are sending your men? Thank you."

'Gitta and I were out of bed in a flash, and barefoot we rushed to our parents' bedroom at the back of the flat where we stood glued to the window. A weird spectacle met our eyes.' Behind

47 Edith Rogers (*née* Trzeciak), letter to the author, 28 June 2005.
48 Edith Rogers, *No Childhood*, page iii.

their back garden stood a small synagogue. 'Through its windows we saw the chandelier swing like a pendulum, moved by invisible hands, swaying backward and forward in ever-widening revolutions – crash – darkness. A window was pushed open, a chair flew out, tumbled to the ground and broke into splinters. It was followed by another chair and yet another, and then there was silence. What were they up to now? We had not long to wait: a white snake jumped down from the windowsill and slithered down, down to the ground below, it seemed unending.

'"Scrolls of the Law, Torah scrolls," we gasped, not wanting to believe our eyes. Papa ran back to our room, which overlooked the street. He returned a moment later: "Yes, they're there, several policemen on the other side of the street – waiting for those godless vandals to complete their work of destruction." And so it turned out to be. Non-Jewish neighbours from upstairs had gone to the police station and had personally brought the policemen back in their car.'[49]

Of the forty-three synagogues and houses of prayer in Frankfurt-on-Main, at least twenty-one were destroyed or burned out that morning. The fate of fifteen is unknown.[50]

Benjamin Marx was also living in Frankfurt at that fateful time, as was his sister Claire. Both went to a Jewish school. 'When Claire and I arrived at our school,' he later wrote, 'we realised something was amiss. The usual noise and chatter of students greeting each other as they made their way to the classrooms was missing. The students stood in the hallway; none had yet gone to their rooms. Most stood quietly, a few talked only in whispers. Claire and I joined our friends and classmates. One boy whispered

49 Batya Rabin (*née* Emanuel), 'Friendly Aliens, or Uprooted but not Rootless', typescript.
50 Adolf Diamant, *Zerstörte Synagogen vom November 1938*, pages 29–31.

to me that the nearby synagogue was burning. A few teachers, all women, stood nearby, also talking in subdued voices. Finally the head of the school arrived, somewhat out of breath. She demanded quiet, though everyone had stopped talking.' 'The school will be closed for the day,' the head teacher announced. 'Go home at once, do not loiter on the way, and make as little noise as possible. Your parents will be told when classes resume.'

With that the children were dismissed. 'That the school was closed because of the fire at the synagogue made not much sense to me,' Benjamin Marx remembered. 'We did as we were told. Claire and I made our way home without any incidents. Our parents were anxiously waiting for us. The first reports of trouble came from Radio Strasbourg. During the late night of November 9, the station reported, spontaneous attacks on Jews had occurred in a number of German cities. The station gave no indication of the scope of the violence.'

Throughout the morning Marx's father 'sat by the radio turning the dial. Perhaps he could get more details from other stations; but he had little success. Finally and somewhat reluctantly, he turned to Radio Madrid. In November 1938 Spain's capital, Madrid, was still in the hands of the anti-Fascist forces. Radio Madrid's newscasts consisted mostly of anti-Fascist propaganda, hence when the station reported on the scope and violence of the pogrom my parents took the reports with scepticism. As the day wore on and other non-German stations gave more detailed reports, Madrid's reports appeared to have been confirmed.'[51]

'Every synagogue in the district has been destroyed,' the British Consul General, Robert Smallbones, reported from Frankfurt on

---

51 Hans Benjamin Marx, 'Tales from the Other Side; Growing up Jewish in Nazi Germany', manuscript.

November 12, 'and all rabbis together with other religious leaders and teachers are under arrest.'[52]

Six-year-old Joseph Wohlfarth later wrote about the events in Frankfurt on the morning of November 10: 'There must have been a rumour or warning that Hitler Youth were breaking into Jewish homes, because my mother took me and my brother upstairs into my uncle's flat, where we hid in the bathroom. Eventually they broke in and there was a lot of noise, the sound of broken glass and furniture being thrown about. They came up into the apartment where we were hiding and found us, but because there were no men there they left us alone. After they left we went back down to our flat and found the place ransacked. I remember the first thing I saw was a wardrobe lying across the floor in the hall with my train set scattered over it and the engine without any wheels. I think this upset me more than anything else. I suppose the natural reaction of a child of my age.'[53]

Sixteen-year-old Reiner Auman was also a witness to the events of the day in Frankfurt. Early on the morning of November 10, he recalled, 'I packed my satchel, I packed my lunch box, grabbed my prayer shawl and phylacteries because it was a Thursday, and Mondays and Thursdays I would go to synagogue to listen to the praying. I took my bicycle and I rode toward the synagogue.' When he was within two minutes of the synagogue he saw his grandfather coming in the opposite direction. 'When he saw me he waved to me and said, "Reiner, come over here, don't go to the synagogue, the synagogue is burning." But I was a very impetuous young fellow. I took my bike. I went to the synagogue and there I saw the fire engines,

---

52 R. T. Smallbones, report of 12 November 1938: Foreign Office papers, FO 371/21637.
53 Joseph Wohlfarth, 'A Snapshot of the Events as I Remember Them', speech notes.

policemen standing around not really doing anything, because the fire hadn't really started yet to burn big. I saw people carrying in buckets of kerosene, bales filled with paper and old clothing soaked in kerosene. They were trying to really get the fire started.'

In the meantime, Reiner Auman remembered, 'the rampage went on throughout the whole day as hordes of people were milling around in the streets, running through the streets and making a noise that was deafening. As they came closer and closer to our house I kept on going out to see which way they were headed, and told my parents, "Look, they are coming closer to our house, what are we going to do?" My father, who had been through World War One for four years in the German army crawling on his belly as an infantry soldier, was not easily scared. He said, "Let's sit tight, let's see what is going to happen." And by that time afternoon had arrived and evening was coming fast, since it was November and getting dark early, when by some miracle we were spared.'

Reiner Auman understood later what the miracle had been. The house in which they lived 'was owned by a non-Jew, and he let the SA know beforehand "that they better not come into his house because they would be responsible for any damage that they might do to his property". Here we were, watching from behind drawn blinds, as the hordes were marching past our house to other Jewish homes. They went from one Jewish home to another doing their work. I saw pianos, I saw merchandise, I saw all kinds of dishes, I saw clothing being thrown out of the third- and fourth-storey windows hitting the ground and being smashed. That went on until well into the evening,' when it got dark, 'at which time the crowd gradually dispersed.'[54]

*   *   *

54 Reiner J. Auman, 'Kristallnacht', a speech delivered on 9 November 1988.

In Hanover, according to a British newspaper report, 'the furniture and household property of the Jews was taken to a square and burned in the presence of a cheering crowd'. In Kassel 'nearly all the homes of the Jews have been destroyed. There the arrested Jews were paraded in the open, the fire brigade was called out, and the hosepipes were turned on them, so that they were all completely drenched before being sent to the concentration camp at Buchenwald.' At Göttingen the fire brigade 'observed that a charwoman was inside a burning synagogue. The firemen rescued her, although the crowd tried to prevent them from doing so.' At Zwickau 'all homes of German and stateless Jews were demolished by hooligans armed with hatchets while the police looked on'. The three synagogues in Bremen had been burned down 'and all adult male Jews have been arrested', as they had also been in Erfurt.

The newspaper also reported that throughout Germany 'Jewish homes and institutes for the poor and aged and ailing have been destroyed'. The Jewish children's home at Caputh, near Berlin, one of the finest such institutions in Europe, 'had to be evacuated at short notice before being demolished inside by an organised gang'. At Nuremberg all the inmates of the Jewish hospital, 'including the sick, had to parade in the courtyard while the inside of the building was demolished'.

At Ems 'the Jewish home for aged people had to be evacuated during the night, and the personal property of the inmates was destroyed with the furniture and fittings. One of the inmates, who had stayed in bed because he could not move, was injured by splinters of furniture that was being smashed with hatchet blows. He was found the next day, bleeding from several wounds, by a second gang, which had arrived to complete the work of destruction'.

At Bad Soden the patients in the home for consumptives 'were driven out during the night and the home was demolished'. At Isenburg the home for Jewish infants was destroyed, as were homes and institutes for children at Lehnitz and Ellguth.'[55]

Fifty miles from Frankfurt, in the medieval market town of Marktbreit-on-Main, a schoolboy, Lassar Brueckheimer, was still in bed on the morning of November 10 when his mother 'rushed into my bedroom and told me to get up immediately: there were sounds of crashes coming from the synagogue'. His account continued: 'As we came down the stairs from our flat and passed the synagogue entrance, we saw the destruction. The huge oaken door was smashed, its panels splintered, the inner door was missing altogether, and broken benches lay higgledy-piggledy all over the place. As we rushed past, there was insufficient time to note the smashed windows, the far-flung Torah scrolls, the broken silver.' Many weeks later 'we discovered that the benches from the ladies' gallery had been heaved over the railings and thrown on top of the seating below. Just at that moment all we wanted to do was to rush unhindered out of the building.'

The synagogue had been built 224 years earlier, in 1714. Lassar Brueckheimer's account continued: 'When we arrived at grand-father's house we heard that the local police had arrested him.' His mother and grandmother 'were in a state of apprehension and worry, and it was not long after that that two plainclothes Gestapo men arrived and asked for my mother to unlock our flat so that they could search the schoolroom.' While his two brothers, Nathan, aged five, and Maxim, aged three, remained behind, 'I insisted on accompanying my mother and never left her side. The

55 'Extent of German Pogrom', *Manchester Guardian*, 18 November 1938.

search in the schoolroom was perfunctory, until they came to a cupboard in which some of the archival documents from one of the "liquidated" communities – communities dissolved between 1933 and 1938 – were stored. I said, "These papers are my father's," and received a slap round my head that rocked me back and sent my cap off my head onto the floor. One Gestapo man ordered me to pick up my cap, but I just stared back at him. When they locked and sealed the room without taking anything away with them, my cap was still lying on the schoolroom floor. When we got back to Grandfather's house, he had returned from his arrest.'

At about eight o'clock that evening, Lassar Brueckheimer recollected, 'we heard noises in the street both from the Tachauer house opposite and from the Oppenheimer house a little further up the street on our side. We heard the sound of splintering wood and crashes and rushed downstairs, when the stout wooden door to the street just caved inwards. About five or six louts armed with long-handled axes rushed towards us as we hugged the wall to one side of the hall. But they did not harm us. Instead they smashed every panel in all the wardrobes, cupboards and doors throughout the house. Within five minutes the entire contents of the house were destroyed; then they rushed out without saying a word. When we were finally able to move our limbs we inspected the damage and found that the luggage we had packed was also smashed, even the storage cupboard in the cellar in which the home-made jam was kept had been destroyed and its contents were dripping onto the stone floor.'

As Lassar Brueckheimer, his mother and two brothers walked disconsolately about the ruined house, 'with the front door gaping open, there was a hiss from the door leading to the backyard. A neighbour, Frau Niess, had gone along the narrow passage between the houses to call us to follow her back to her flat. We put string around our damaged suitcases and went along the passage to relative safety. However, it was only fair to make our rescuer aware of the risk she was running by giving us shelter, and after some time we decided to seek help from the police . . . We could not have given a description of the vandals since they were all strangers to us, probably not even citizens of our town, and any argument that this pogrom had been spontaneous was negated by this fact. How could strangers coming to Marktbreit have known which were the Jewish houses? It must have been organised months in advance, only the excuse for the pogrom had to be found.'

It was late at night when Mrs Brueckheimer, with her three children at her side, went to seek help from the police and to report the attack. 'They told us to go away, the matter had nothing to do with them. This, too, proves that the police had their instructions well beforehand. Probably we were one of the few families who were still innocent enough to believe that the police would be even-handed. We wandered through the streets with nowhere to go. We could not return to Frau Niess, since this would draw attention to the fact that she was giving us shelter; Grandfather's house was wide open and unoccupiable, and mother would not return to our own flat because she was on her own with three children and she would have had to pass the smashed synagogue door. So one woman and three small children (the youngest just three years old) walked through the silent and deserted streets of Marktbreit at about eleven o'clock at night, carrying slashed suitcases tied with string.'[56]

As the mother and her three children crossed the marketplace,

---

56 Lassar Brueckheimer, unpublished memoirs, enclosed with letter to the author, 5 June 2005.

'we were called by someone at the third-floor window of the house in the top right corner and went towards the voice, which was barely above a whisper. The mother of Heinz Kraemer had been looking out of her window to see whether the noise of the destruction had finally ceased, and had seen us cross the marketplace. She told us to come up to her flat, and when we had climbed the stairs she explained that we would be quite safe there, because the man living below, a non-Jew, had stated that he would not allow anyone to pass through his flat. He had stopped and questioned us, since the stairs to the third floor passed for some unknown reason through the lower flat rather than at the side of it. How we spent the night there I cannot remember, but stay we did.'[57]

Inge Neuberger, then an eight-year-old girl in Mannheim, later recalled how, during the evening of November 9, 'my family, which consisted of my father, mother, my maternal grandmother, my older brother, and I were eating dinner when there was a knock at our front door. I can still picture my father's somewhat ruddy complexion turning white, and the quizzical look that passed between my parents. My mother said she would answer the door, and I went with her. There stood a German woman who worked in our home as part-time housekeeper. When my mother asked her what she was doing there, she answered that my father had to leave the house the next day. I recall her saying that something was going to happen, although she did not know what. And she left as quickly and quietly as she had come.'

The next morning when Inge Neuberger got up to get ready

57 Lassar Brueckheimer, unpublished memoirs, enclosed with letter to the author, 5 June 2005.

for school she had 'more or less forgotten about that incident. My father was not at home, but he always left very early because his factory was out in the country a distance from Mannheim. I met my cousin and we walked to school together. I remember that it was a relatively long walk, and as Jews we could not ride the trolley car. We walked along a broad, pedestrian street and came upon an "army" of men marching four or more abreast. They wore no uniforms but were dressed as working men would have been. Each had a household tool over his shoulder. I remember seeing rakes, shovels, pickaxes, etc., but no guns. My cousin and I were puzzled by this parade, and watched for some minutes. Then we continued on to school.'

When they came near to the school, which was next to the synagogue, 'we saw a bonfire in the courtyard in front of the building. Many spectators were watching as prayer books and, I believe, Torah scrolls were burned. The windows had been shattered and furniture had been smashed and added to the pyre. We were absolutely terrified. I am fairly certain that the fire department was in attendance, but no attempt was made to extinguish the flames. We ran back to my home to tell my mother what we had seen. She told us that we would leave the apartment and spend the day in Luisenpark, a very large park in town. We spent the entire day in the park, moving from one area to another.'

Because of the warning from the cleaning lady, on November 10 Inge Neuberger's father, who had returned home late the previous night, 'had picked up my uncle and a friend of his and had driven to Heidelberg. There he drove up the hill as far as he could and hid the car under some trees or bushes. There was no road above him, so he could not be seen, but as they looked out on the road below they saw a troop of SS marching.' Returning to Mannheim, her father 'spent the next six weeks in the attic of our building. I was given strict orders that if anyone asked about my father's whereabouts I was to say that I didn't know where he was. I remember how strongly this was impressed on me.'[58] The main synagogue in Mannheim was burned out. The 230-year-old smaller synagogue was demolished. Rolf Dörmann, a young Catholic teenager, later remembered witnessing the destruction of the main synagogue, 'when furniture was thrown out of the upper windows and Jews were beaten and forced into the street'. Recalling the events thirty-five years later, he 'could still hear the crash of furniture and still felt shame'.[59]

Margot Wertheim and her younger brother Kurt – she was eleven and he nine and a half – lived in the small town of Fulda. Together, they later remembered how 'the windows in our ground-floor flat were smashed with rocks taken out of the front garden while we were cowering under the furniture inside. That night we slept in an office some way from home, as our parents were afraid to let us sleep at home. Our synagogue was burned to the ground. The next day our father, Abraham Wertheim, went to friends to discuss the situation. While he was there, two policemen – not Gestapo – came to arrest the head of the family in the general round-up of Jewish males over sixteen. Our father knew them from childhood, friends until now. They said to him: "Abba, disappear, we haven't seen you." Foolishly, he went to another family, and the same two policemen came there too. They said: "You are making life difficult for us, we will be in serious trouble if we are found out, disappear entirely, leave town." So we all, parents and three children, went off to Frankfurt where we were not known, to stay

58 Janet Ettelman (*née* Inge Neuberger), letter to the author, 15 June 2005.
59 Report of a conversation with Rolf Dörmann (in 1973) recalled by Dr Stephen Nicholls, letter to the author, 7 July 2005.

with distant relations in their flat already packed with other fleeing relations.'

When Margot and Kurt's mother returned to Fulda from Frankfurt after Kristallnacht, she was confronted by the local chief of police, who knew her husband, and who, her children recalled, 'said to her, "Why didn't you come to me to avoid the round-up?" Mother said, "What could you have done?" The police chief: "Put him in prison and look after him." Jews in prison were not taken to concentration camps.'[60]

Also in Fulda lived Manfred van Son. On Kristallnacht, he later wrote, 'my mother and I were alone in the flat when we heard the sound of heavy army boots on the stairs. The footsteps stopped outside our door, and I waited in the dark on the other side, knowing and fearing what was about to happen. To my amazement, however, the expected knock on the door never came. On the other side I heard the two SS men consulting one another, then deciding that people with the aristocratic name of von Son ("v. Son", as it appeared on our nameplate) couldn't possibly be Jews. The heavy feet descended the stairs. My mother and I had gained a brief reprieve.'

On the following day, Manfred van Son remembered, 'I took my bike and went down to our synagogue which was burning, surrounded by a crowed of onlookers. As I stood there, somebody sidled up to me and said "Hau ab" (Buzz off) and I cycled into town, where I still remember the sound of broken glass being swept up. I went home but left my bike behind somewhere. I told my mother what I had seen, and phone calls came from various members of the family enquiring as to whether I had managed

60 Margot Wohlmann and Naftali (Kurt) Wertheim, letter to the author, 9 June 2005.

to avoid being rounded up and to tell who had been arrested or had fled.'[61]

Martin Lowenberg was ten years old on Kristallnacht: 'After being forced to move in spring of 1938 from our small village, Schenklengsfeld, to Fulda, renting a small flat not able to accommodate six persons in the centre of town next to the Judengasse directly behind the synagogue, we had to make the very best of it,' he later wrote. 'Since everything seemed very convenient, being near the school as well as going to prayer services etc., it seemed rather perfect, except on November 9, when stones came through the windows. At once classes were dismissed. We rushed home. The next day we could not recognise the school which was attached to the synagogue, and that was in flames behind our apartment.'[62]

Oskar Prager was nine and a half years old on Kristallnacht, living in Furth. 'In the night, at about 2 a.m.,' he later recalled, 'I was rudely awakened by a man in brown uniform whom I recognised as an SA man. He shouted at me to get up and get dressed quickly. I was stunned at his tone, and whilst dressing I saw him throw my wristwatch, which I had got for my ninth birthday, on the floor – and with his heel he ground it into the floor. Then I saw him take my books, tear them up and throw them around the room. They were not Hebrew books but standard German reading books which children had at that time.'

Oskar Prager continued: 'My parents were rushing around the apartment getting my three other sisters up, two of whom were twins of about one and a half years old, and the older sister was

---

61 Salomon van Son, *The van Son Family*, Jerusalem, 1991, privately printed, page 105.
62 Martin Lowenberg, letter to the author, 24 September 2005.

just about four years old. There were a number of SA men around the apartment, and in relatively short time we were ushered by all the Brownshirts down the stairs into the foyer of the building. On leaving the apartment I saw that the glass front door was smashed and broken glass was all over the floor and corridor. None of us were allowed to use the toilet prior to leaving.'

Outside in the street it was 'very cold and foggy. The air smelled of burning and I could see that the sky was reddish. Because of the fog I couldn't see clearly if something was burning because it was some distance away. So we were marched by four SA men, two at the side of us and two behind us, my mother was pushing the pram where the twins were who were crying or screaming. My father was holding my sister's and my hand. And so we arrived at a large area, which in fact was a tram terminal in the middle of town. My constant questions to my father were answered with a sharp "Don't talk," so we remained silent.'

During the walk to the tram terminal, Oskar Prager added, 'I remember stepping on broken glass which was on the pavement, and I also noticed that many other people were walking or being walked to the same area. Having got there, we were told by the SA men to stay put and not to move, and to keep totally quiet. Thus we stood maybe for two hours or so in the cold, foggy, smelly air. Suddenly I saw movement and realised we were being marched to another place, and when we got there I realised it was the local high school. We were pushed inside and made either to stand or squat on the floor. This time however I saw all men being removed, including my father. I had no idea where they all went.'

It was about six in the morning when Oskar Prager's mother 'took my sister's and my hand, and with the pram in which the twin girls were, we trooped off home but without our father, who was nowhere to be seen. At the exit to the school we were told by the SA man not to talk to anyone about our experience. The walk home did not take long; it was still dark and foggy but the air smelled much more of burning. The streets were a patchwork of broken glass. At the entrance to our building I saw someone had painted the words "Juden Raus" (Jews Out) on the walls.[63]

After the synagogue had been destroyed in the German border town of Kehl, across the Rhine from the French city of Strasbourg, the Jews were ordered out of their homes and marched in double file through the streets, 'escorted', a British newspaper reported, 'by Nazi guards who struck and insulted them', while the towns-people 'massed on the pavement and spat upon the Jews'. As they marched, the Jews were forced to sing without cease: 'We have betrayed the German Fatherland. We are responsible for the Paris assassination.'[64]

Forced to join this march were Jews brought into Kehl from the surrounding villages. They too were insulted by the towns-folk, who had been summoned to watch the 'entertainment', and spat upon them to cries of 'Down with the Jews' and 'Dirty dogs.'[65]

It was a six-hour train journey from Berlin to Ratibor. There Chava Rechnitz, whose recollections of Berlin earlier in the day had been so vivid, made her way home. 'I found our flat deserted and five of the rooms totally destroyed,' she wrote, 'broken windows, broken furniture, even my mother's beloved grand piano, a Bechstein, was in pieces. However the guest bedroom,

63 Oskar Prager, letter to the author, 6 June 2005.
64 'Here is what Happened in Other Towns', *Daily Herald*, 11 November 1938.
65 'Jews Marched in Streets', *News Chronicle*, 11 November 1938.

the nursery and my small bedroom and the kitchen and the two servants' bedrooms were untouched.'

It was a non-Jew who had come to the rescue as the destruction of her home in Ratibor was taking place. 'I learned later,' Chava Rechnitz wrote, 'that our long-time chief maid, Paula, had stood in the middle of the long hallway and told the Hitler Youth that behind her were only the servants' rooms, that the furniture belonged to her as my mother had given it to her, as she was getting married shortly. They believed her and so we had at least a place to sleep.'[66]

In Bayreuth, home of Wagner's operatic genius – and performances that Hitler himself often attended – sixty Jewish men and women were arrested and kept all day in a cowshed. Some of them, the Exchange News Agency reported, 'were kicked downstairs by secret police agents and suffered concussion'.[67] Bayreuth's 188-year-old synagogue was demolished.

In the small town of Ladenburg, the inside of whose synagogue was totally demolished on Kristallnacht, six-year-old Lea Weems recalled 'a loud knocking on the door. My father opened it and I saw three Nazis standing there. They looked big to my childish eyes and they were carrying axes, hammers and saws. They pushed us aside and began to destroy everything in our house. Of course I did not understand what was happening, and my parents tried to protect my sister and me. When everything was broken, they pushed my father and my grandfather down the stairs. I was screaming and pulling on my father's sleeve trying to keep him from leaving. I saw a row of men standing in the street – they had been arrested – and my father and grandfather were taken

---

66 Chava Cohn (*née* Rechnitz), letter to the author, 3 June 2005.
67 'Here is what Happened in Other Towns', *Daily Herald*, 11 November 1938.

away with the others. My mother, sister and I were unable to live at home any more, and some neighbours took us in and we slept on the floor of their house. This is what I remember, vividly, of Kristallnacht. I learned later that the men were taken to Dachau.'[68]

Glatz, a Silesian town fifty miles from Breslau, had a small Jewish community. Ten-year-old Ruth Prager later described the morning of November 10: 'I walked to school as usual, passing some destroyed shops and seeing the burning synagogue in the background, but I did not think about these events. On my arrival at the school, my class teacher called me aside and recommended that I should go home and that she would talk with my mother later. I left crying, because I thought I was expelled for something I had done wrong. Apparently my homecoming was the first realisation my parents had of the happenings of the day. In the afternoon, I was playing with my best non-Jewish friend when my father entered my room accompanied by two men, kissed me and said goodbye, but I was so absorbed in my game that I hardly looked up from it. Fortunately my mother managed to free my father from detention after a couple of days, but the tension was too much for him and he suffered a stroke two weeks later and died in February 1939.'[69]

Seventeen-year-old Margot Schwarz lived in the small town of Horb. November 9 was her father's birthday. That evening she stayed at home with her grandfather, while her parents spent the evening with friends. 'My parents returned home earlier than usual, father white-faced: vom Rath had died, no good will come out of it.' She went to bed. Whether her parents managed to sleep

---

68 Lea Weems, letter to the author, 9 August 2005.
69 Ruth Lewin (*née* Prager), letter to the author, 19 June 2005.

that night she did not know. 'I awoke from the shattering of glass. Stones were flying through every window of the house, causing all kinds of damage in the rooms. Father's hobby was cactuses, which stood at the windows. Each one of them was a target.' Opposite Margot Schwarz's house was her father's shop. 'It was broken into. Bales of cloth lay scattered in the street.'

Margot Schwarz's account continued: 'Very early in the morning they came to arrest my father. Grandfather they left at home. He was over eighty. Horb was a little town, everybody knew everybody. The man who arrested my father grew up with him. They even served together in the First World War. One of them even excused himself: "I am sorry, but this is an order." That's what they always said. Later we saw a group of men of the Jewish Community Council being led to the police station.'[70] The two-hundred-year-old synagogue in Horb was not destroyed: after the war it was dismantled and taken to Israel.

An eye-witness of the events in the Silesian town of Sprottau, Fraenze Hirsch, set down her recollections six months later, when she was safely in Britain. 'As we were approaching our house in Sprottau,' she wrote, 'we saw crowds of people everywhere, so that we knew that something was going on, but we thought that a meeting of some kind must have ended, and went straight to bed. Early next morning we heard a tremendously loud knocking; the Schindlers' shop window was broken and all the shelves and shutters were destroyed and the goods thrown down onto the floor, so that eiderdown feathers were everywhere, all mixed up with slivers of glass from the cupboards. It was simply awful.'

The knocking sounded 'so terribly loud to us', Fraenze Hirsch

70 Margot Wilde (*neé* Schwarz), recollections written in November 1980, sent to the author 5 June 2005.

explained, 'because we were sleeping at the front of the house, our parents in the front room and I in the little room, right next to the Schindlers' wall. Also, as bad luck would have it, the window was open. So at about six a.m. someone shouted: "Jews live there, too. Close the window, dogs!!!" Mama closed it straight away.'

The next morning Fraenze Hirsch's father 'went as usual to get milk and the post', and saw a friend being taken away by two policemen. After breakfast 'he went over to the synagogue and saw that there was nothing inside, just bare walls. Those beasts had dragged everything out into the square and burned it. Papa managed still to see the pile of ashes. Nearby stood a fire extinguisher, in case anything happened! It had all been done by a handful of SS men.'[71]

In the city of Dresden the Chief of Police had expelled 724 Polish-born Jews – all German citizens – to the Polish border east of Beuthen during the mass expulsions on the night of October 27–28. On Kristallnacht there were 1,800 Jews still in the city as mobs rampaged through the Jewish-owned businesses on the main shopping street, Pragerstrasse. They were on their way to the magnificent synagogue designed by Gottfried Semper, who had also designed the Dresden opera house.

Opened in 1840, two years after the Jews of Saxony had been granted full rights of citizenship, the Semper synagogue was a mixture of the Byzantine and Moorish styles. By the time the mobs appeared, the SA had already set it alight. When firemen arrived to put out the flames they were prevented from

71 Fraenze Vanson (*née* Hirsch), letter of 15 March 1939. Archive of Dorothea Shefer-Vanson (Fraenze Vanson's daughter).

entering by a cordon of SS and SA men. Later that day the High Burgomaster of Dresden, Dr Kluge, was able to announce that 'the symbol of the hereditary racial enemy has finally been extinguished'.

From the burning synagogue, the mobs moved on to break up and loot Jewish shops in Seestrasse and Schlosstrasse. A local painter, Otto Griebel, later described how uniformed SA men 'hauled a group of totally distraught looking and deathly pale Jewish teachers from the nearby Jewish community house. They forced crumpled top hats onto their heads and exhibited them to the baying crowd, to whom the unfortunate victims were forced, on command, to bow deeply and take off their hats.' While the crude charade was being enacted, Otto Griebel noted that 'a well-dressed, grey-haired passer-by, who looked like an actor, found this too much, and he called out, full of outrage, "Incredible, this is like the worst times of the Middle Ages!" But no sooner had he uttered these words than he was seized by Gestapo officials present among the crowd and taken away.'

A few days later the blackened shell of the Semper synagogue was dynamited, the scene being filmed by a camera crew as an 'instructional' documentary. While the synagogue was still burning, a local character, Franz Hackel, turned to Otto Griebel and muttered: 'This fire will return! It will make a long curve and then come back to us.'[72] That fire was to come to Dresden six years and three months later.

Crowning the Semper synagogue was one of the fine sights of Dresden, a golden Star of David. A German firefighter, Alfred Neugebauer, saved it from the blaze and hid it in a box filled with sand for more than sixty years. At the dedication of the new,

72 Frederick Taylor, *Dresden: Tuesday 13 February 1945*, pages 69–75.

modern synagogue in 2001 he was given the honour of fixing the star above the main entrance.[73]

Kristallnacht was at an end. The words of the Psalmist had found a terrible, literal echo: 'They have cast fire into thy sanctuary, they have defiled *by casting down* the dwelling place of thy name to the ground. They said in their hearts, Let us destroy them together: they have burned up all the synagogues of God in the land.'[74]

The toll on Kristallnacht has never been fully determined. On November 11 a report was presented to Heydrich that set out the 'provisional' results. Seventy-six synagogues had been destroyed and a further 191 set on fire. Twenty-nine Jewish-owned department stores had been demolished and 815 other shops destroyed, as well as 117 private houses. Thirty-six Jews had been murdered – this figure was later raised by the Nazi Party Supreme Court to ninety-one.[75] The number of shops destroyed and homes looted was in fact many thousands. The total number of synagogues destroyed was more than a thousand – within less than twenty-four hours.

73 'Through Fire and Water', *Ha'aretz* (English edition), 17 June 2005 (reporting on the Dresden floods).
74 Psalm 74, verses seven and eight.
75 Günther Deschner, *Heydrich: The Pursuit of Total Power*. London: Orbis, 1981, page 157.

5

Bitter Prelude

KRISTALLNACHT WAS THE CULMINATION of more than five years and nine months of systematic discrimination and persecution. From the first days of Hitler's regime in Germany, anti-Jewish measures followed with disturbing frequency. The half million Jews of Germany, who constituted a mere 0.76 per cent of the country's population, were singled out by the Nazi propaganda machine as the enemy within, the cause of Germany's defeat in 1918 and of her subsequent economic difficulties. As a scapegoat, the Jews were vulnerable. Their prominence in many aspects of German scientific and professional life made them, despite their small numbers, the objects of a jealousy that the Nazis skilfully and explosively inflamed. Despite the intense patriotism of the German Jews during the First World War – when 12,000 were killed in action – they were presented in the Nazi ideology as disloyal shirkers, and parasites on the German body politic.

Jewish communities in Germany dated back a thousand years. For the fifty years before Hitler came to power German Jews had integrated fully into German life and culture. They were proud Germans, bewildered to be singled out as an evil influence, and trusting that the excesses of Nazism must, in the normal evolution of things, moderate and decline.

Anti-Jewish persecution began from the first days of Nazi rule. So, too, did the courage of German non-Jews willing to take a stand against anti-Semitism. The initial testing time came in Berlin on 1 April 1933, two months after Hitler came to power, during a one-day boycott of all Jewish shops. Tens of thousands of passers-by witnessed the first public humiliation of Germany's Jews as the entrances to their shops were barred by SA men. When Julie Bonhoeffer, the ninety-year-old grandmother of Pastor Dietrich Bonhoeffer – who was himself to be executed by the Nazis shortly before the end of the war – saw the cordon of uniformed stormtroopers and Hitler Youth barring the way into a Jewish-owned shop in Berlin, she pushed past them, entered the shop and made her purchases. She was determined to show her solidarity with a persecuted people, and her contempt for a spiteful punishment. 'The cordon fell back to let her pass,' writes Bonhoeffer's biographer Mary Bosanquet. 'Only her expressive and distinguished face spoke her unmistakable thoughts.'[1]

In Aachen, with a Jewish population of more than a thousand, where many of the citizens opposed Nazi policy, a 'rare demonstration' against the persecution of the Jews was held a week after the boycott.[2]

During 1933 the German government enacted forty-two laws restricting the right of German Jews to earn a living, to enjoy full citizenship, and to educate themselves. The most draconian of these, promulgated on April 7, six days after the Berlin boycott, was a law 'for the reconstruction of the civil service'. It forbade Jews from continuing to work in any branch of the civil service,

1 Mary Bosanquet, *The Life and Death of Dietrich Bonhoeffer*, page 119.
2 Shmuel Spector (editor in chief), *The Encyclopedia of Jewish Life Before and During the Holocaust*, Volume 1, page 18.

which they had to leave immediately. The civil service included schools and universities. In reaction to the dismissal of all Jewish professors, an Academic Assistance Council was set up in Britain, which launched an emergency fund to find university positions and financial help for the dismissed scholars. In the words of its secretary, Tess Simpson, the aim of the Council was 'to salvage the displaced academics'.[3]

In its first three years, the emergency fund helped 1,300 displaced German Jewish academics to find permanent professional employment. The Quakers (the Society of Friends) were active in helping German Jewish schoolteachers – also dismissed under the law of 7 April 1933 – find work in Britain. In 1934 Ludwig Rosenberg, from Berlin, was among those invited by the Quakers to teach in Britain: he came with his wife and their two-and-a-half-year-old daughter.[4] In the United States, an Emergency Committee for Aid to Displaced German Scholars also enabled Jewish refugee scholars to work, helped by the Rockefeller Foundation.[5]

The Turkish government also welcomed German Jewish scholars from the first year of Nazi power. At the end of 1933 the Hungarian-born Philip Schwarz, who had been dismissed from his professorship of pathology at the University of Frankfurt-on-Main because he was Jewish, was invited to set up a medical school at the University of Istanbul. He did so, serving for twenty years as head of the Institute of Pathology.[6]

3 R. M. Cooper (editor), *Refugee Scholars: Conversations with Tess Simpson*, page 31.
4 Ludwig Rosenberg's daughter, conversation with the author, 24 March 2002.
5 Jean Medawar and David Pyke, *Hitler's Gift: Scientists Who Fled Nazi Germany*, pages 55, 61.
6 Jean Medawar and David Pyke, *Hitler's Gift: Scientists Who Fled Nazi Germany*, page 66.

In Britain, many schools made an effort to take in German Jewish youngsters. At King's School, Taunton, the headmaster, Dr R. D. Reid, found a place for Kurt Abrahamsohn, from the Baltic port of Stettin. Abrahamsohn (later Kenneth Ambrose), remembered how Dr Reid 'saw it as his duty to look after me in loco parentis'.[7] Headmasters, headmistresses and teachers throughout Britain did likewise. A school specially set up for German Jewish refugee children was opened at Stoatley Rough, south of London. The Chairman of the Governors was a leading Quaker, Bertha Bracey. The headmistress, Dr Hilda Lion, herself a Jewish refugee, made several journeys back to Germany in 1933 and 1934 to find girls to bring back with her.[8]

The pressure against the Jews of Germany was continuous. During 1934 the German government enacted a further nineteen discriminatory laws. In protest, several Jewish and non-Jewish groups outside Germany instituted an economic boycott on German goods. That May, Goebbels accused the Jews of Germany of responsibility for the boycott. During 1935 the German government enacted a further twenty-nine discriminatory laws. The most draconian were the Nuremberg Laws 'for the protection of German blood and honour'. Signed personally by Hitler, these laws prohibited marriage, and also extra-marital sexual intercourse, between Jews and non-Jews.

Another law introduced shortly after the Nuremberg Laws created a new definition of German citizenship: no Jew, and no person with 'Jewish ancestry', could be a German citizen. Shortly

7 Kenneth Ambrose, 'The Suitcase in the Garage: Letters and Photographs of a German Jewish Family, 1800–1950', manuscript.
8 Katherine Whitaker and Michael Johnson, *Stoatley Rough School, 1934–1960*.

afterwards, Jews were excluded from the financial benefits of the German Winter Relief charitable fund, to which, hitherto, they had been both contributors and beneficiaries.

For some travellers to Germany after 1933, showing contempt for Nazi persecution of the Jews was a natural reaction to the abomination of racism. Lord Drogheda, who in 1935 went for his honeymoon to Bavaria, actually pretended to be Jewish 'in order to be turned out of a restaurant which displayed prominently a sign "Juden hier Unerwünscht" (Jews not wanted here)'.[9]

Another of those who witnessed the persecution of the Jews in those early years was Prince Philip of Greece, the only son of Prince Andrew of Greece, and a great-great-grandson of Queen Victoria. He later recalled how, at the age of twelve, he had 'first-hand experience of the anti-Semitic frenzy that was gripping the members of the National Socialist Party in Germany in those days. I had just moved from a private school in England to attend the boarding school at Salem in the south of Germany belonging to one of my brothers-in-law. The founder of the school, Kurt Hahn, had already been driven out of Germany by Nazi persecution and this was well known throughout the school. It was the custom of the school to appoint a senior boy to look after the new arrivals. I was unaware of it at the time, but it so happened that our "Helper", as he was called, was of Jewish origin. One night he was overpowered in his bed and had all his hair cut off. You can imagine what an effect this had on us junior boys. Nothing could have given us a clearer indication of the meaning of persecution. It so happened that I had played cricket for my school in England and I still had my cricket cap

9 Lord Drogheda, *Double Harness: Memoirs by Lord Drogheda*, page 59.

with me. I offered it to our Helper. I was pleased to see that he wore it.'[10]

In Berlin, Pastor Heinrich Grüber, Dean of the Protestant Church in the capital, set up a rescue operation in 1935, organising escape routes for Jews to cross into Holland. It became known as the 'Grüber Office' by those Jews using it to leave Germany. 'The valiant churchman preached by day against Hitler's Jewish policies and operated escape routes for the Jews by night,' wrote Henry Walter Brann on the twenty-fifth anniversary of the outbreak of the Second World War, when Grüber was made an honorary citizen of Berlin.[11]

Also living in Berlin was Countess Maria von Maltzan, one of whose brothers was in the SS. As Hitler imposed increasingly repressive measures against the Jews – there were a further twenty-four laws aimed solely against them in 1936, and another twenty-two in 1937 – the Countess made contact with members of the Swedish Protestant Church in Berlin, who were systematically smuggling Jews out of Germany. She forged visas, ration books and other official documents, and drove vegetable lorries full of refugees out of Berlin. Her relaxed, aristocratic manner helped her to hoodwink officials and to outwit the Gestapo who frequently called her in for questioning.[12]

German policy between Hitler's coming to power in January 1933 and the outbreak of war in September 1939 was to encourage

10 Prince Philip, Duke of Edinburgh, speaking at Yad Vashem, Jerusalem, 21 October 1994, at a ceremony honouring his mother, Princess Alice of Greece. Yad Vashem Righteous Among the Nations Archive, file 6080.
11 Henry Walter Brann, 'Pastor who Rescued Jews is Honoured', *Jewish Week*, Washington DC, 20 August 1970.
12 Henry Walter Brann, 'Pastor who Rescued Jews is Honoured', *Jewish Week*, Washington DC, 20 August 1970.

Jewish emigration. Both the United States and Britain had quotas, within which they were able to give refuge to a large number of German Jews. The United States took in by far the largest number during this period: almost 200,000, as a result of its long-established quota of 25,000 German immigrants a year. Britain took in the second largest number, more than 65,000 in the same six-year period. Between them, Britain and the United States gave refuge to more than half of all German Jews living in Germany in January 1933.

The British Mandate in Palestine had been similarly receptive. Between January 1933 and March 1938 more than 35,000 German Jews were granted immigration certificates to Palestine. Following the outbreak of the Arab revolt in 1936, however, restrictions were imposed to placate Arab sentiment. Only 8,000 Jewish immigrants were allowed into Palestine in the eight months from August 1937 to March 1938. From April to September 1938 only 3,000 were admitted.

Diplomats stationed in Germany were at the centre of many rescue efforts. In 1937 the British Consul General in Munich, John Carvell, issued certificates for the British Mandate in Palestine that led to the release of three hundred Jewish men being held in Dachau concentration camp. The men had been accused of 'race defilement'.[13]

Even as the emigration of German Jews accelerated, the number of Jews within the confines of Germany increased dramatically. On 12 March 1938, German troops entered Vienna, and on the following day Austria was annexed to Germany. A further 183,000 Jews came under Nazi rule. Added to those Jews still in

13 Benno Cohn, 'Address on the Occasion of the Planting of a Forest Near Harel in Remembrance and in the Name of Major Foley, 10 July 1959', Yad Vashem Righteous Among the Nations Archive, file 8378.

Germany, this made almost half a million people in search of a haven.

Within hours of the German annexation, anti-Semitic assaults became commonplace throughout Austria. Leo Spitzer, the son of Viennese Jews who later emigrated to Bolivia, often heard their recollections and that of their friends about the mood in Vienna following the annexation: 'Visas! We began to live visas day and night. When we were awake, we were obsessed by visas. We talked about them all the time. Exit visas. Transit visas. Entrance visas. Where could we go? During the day, we tried to get the proper documents, approvals, stamps. At night, in bed, we tossed about and dreamed about long lines, officials, visas. Visas.'[14]

In Germany, on the day of the annexation of Austria, in one of the thirty-eight discriminatory laws against Jews promulgated that year – laws that henceforth also applied to Austrian Jews – all Jewish associations, religious and secular, were deprived of their legal status.

On March 13, the day of the German annexation of Austria, President Roosevelt asked for an increase in the German quota. As a result of this request, on March 24 Congressman Emanuel Cellar (Democrat, New York) and Congressman Adolph Sabath (Democrat, Illinois) introduced a Bill 'to assure certain aliens legal admission for permanent residence in the United States'. The Bill was referred to the House Committee on Immigration and Naturalization, but no action was taken on it: in Congressional parlance, it 'died in committee'.[15]

Following the German annexation of Austria, all foreign

14 Leo Spitzer, *Hotel Bolivia: The Culture of Memory and a Refuge from Nazism*, page 35.
15 Bill HR 10013: Library of Congress.

ambassadorial duties in Vienna were transferred to Berlin, leaving only consulates in the former capital. The number two at the Chinese Legation in Vienna, Dr Feng Shan Ho, was made Consul General of a much-reduced staff. He knew the dangers facing Jews in Vienna. On one occasion he had been held at gunpoint in a café while uniformed Nazi Brownshirts sought out Jews to seize and beat up.

For the German authorities to allow Jews to leave Germany or Austria, proof of emigration was required: either a ship ticket or a visa. Dr Ho provided visas. With them, Jews could leave for China. Many Jews, having reached a German or Italian port as a result of Ho's efforts, went on to Britain or the United States. At least four hundred went to Palestine. Most went to the Chinese city of Shanghai, part of which was then under Japanese occupation, and part under international administration (predominantly British, French and Italian).

One beneficiary of Ho's visas was Ady Bluds. She and four other members of her family left Austria by train for Britain, and then sailed from Southampton to Shanghai. In this they were helped both by Ho and by a Swiss national, William Seiler, Director of the American Express office in Vienna. It was Seiler who acquired the five ship tickets for them. Ady Bluds noted: 'Had it not been for Feng Shan Ho and William Seiler, we would not have escaped the Holocaust that followed, just as, to my bitter regret, my parents and many relatives did not.'[16]

Dr Ho continued issuing visas despite growing pressure from his superior, the Chinese Ambassador in Berlin, that he should not do so. The Ambassador, eager to win favour from the German

16 Testimony of Ady Bluds, New York, 18 November 1998: Yad Vashem, Righteous Among the Nations Archive, file 8688.

government, sent an emissary to Vienna to report on Dr Ho's breach of instructions, and then caused a 'demerit' to be put on his diplomatic record.

Ho's son Monto, then aged eleven, was with his father in Vienna. He later told his sister, who was born after the war, of 'a man waiting in line outside the Chinese embassy who saw that he had no chance of getting in before the office closed. Seeing a consulate car drive up, he threw his application in the open window.' Dr Ho was in the car. The applicant received a note the following week: 'Your visa is ready, please come pick it up.'[17]

Another diplomat who was active in expediting the escape of Jews from Germany was Captain Frank Foley, the British Passport Control Officer in Berlin, and an undercover British agent. Reporting in June 1938 to the Foreign Office in London on the plight of Germany's Jews, Foley wrote: 'In Berlin as well as in other parts of Germany there were systematic house to house searches for, and arrests of Jews; cafés were raided and even cinema halls were emptied of Jews so that they could be arrested in concentration camps. In Berlin the methods of persecution were particularly severe.' Foley added: 'It is no exaggeration to say that Jews have been hunted like rats in their homes, and for fear of arrest many of them sleep at a different address overnight.'[18] Foley helped several thousand German Jews leave for Palestine between 1936 and the outbreak of war. His biographer has estimated the number at 10,000.[19]

Jews wanting to leave often had to use convoluted methods to

17 Etgar Lefkovits, 'Chinese Consul General Honoured for Saving Austrian Jews', *Jerusalem Post*, 23 January 2001.
18 Berlin Consular Report (Foley), 16 July 1938: Foreign Office papers, FO 371/21635.
19 Michael Smith, *Foley: The Spy Who Saved 10,000 Jews*.

escape. Foley participated in and even initiated such methods. Sabina Comberti wrote of how, when it became clear that her father, Wolfgang Meyer-Michael, an aspiring potter, could not raise the £1,000 needed for a 'Capitalist' certificate – the most common requirement for emigration to Palestine – Foley suggested finding the money through someone who would vouchsafe it. 'Just get a promise – you don't have to use it,' was Foley's comment. 'My father then looked up a cousin in Holland, who understood the dilemma. They drew up two documents. In one, the cousin promised to lend my father £1,000 when/if he needed it. In a second my father declared the first one invalid and promised not to make use of it. Mr Foley knew of course that this was a ploy but issued the visa immediately.'[20]

The British Counsellor of Embassy in Berlin, Sir George Ogilvie Forbes, also helped expedite the emigration of German Jews. John Schnellenberg later wrote, from New Zealand: 'My father, Rudolf Schnellenberg, was service manager for a Ford car dealership in Berlin. One of his customers was Sir George Ogilvie Forbes, counsellor at the British Embassy. One day in 1938, Forbes came to my father and advised him that it would be well to take his family out of Germany as soon as possible. Further, Forbes undertook to provide papers for any country in the British Empire that my parents chose. So it came about that they chose New Zealand, papers were duly provided, and the three of us arrived safely in Wellington on 28 March 1939. None of my three surviving grandparents were able to escape, nor my mother's sister, and all perished.'[21]

20 Sabina Comberti, letter to Mordecai Paldiel, 14 January 1999: Yad Vashem Righteous of the Nations Archive, file 8378.
21 John Schnellenberg, letter of 14 March 2001: Yad Vashem Righteous of the Nations Archive, file 8378.

In Vienna, a Jewish student at the Diplomatic Academy, George Weidenfeld, and his mother obtained an interview with Captain Kendrick, the British Passport Control Officer. 'Just as he was about to end the interview with a lugubrious mien and a shrug of his shoulders,' Weidenfeld later wrote, 'my mother broke down and sobbed. Captain Kendrick relented and gave me the flimsiest of all visas – the right to enter England for a period of three months in transit for a final destination.' It was enough. A month later Weidenfeld took the train to Switzerland, on his way to England, where he was to have a distinguished career as a publisher. 'After the bellowing, self-important Nazi guards, the phlegmatism of the Swiss border police came as a relief' as he crossed the German–Swiss border. 'In Zurich I spent the first full day of freedom at a lakeside café listening to Swiss military music. It sounded heavenly after the harsh, syncopated tones of the SS anthems or the Prussian military marches played by Austrian bands with exaggerated zeal.'[22]

In Britain, many families offered a helping hand to refugees. In Grantham, Muriel Roberts had an Austrian Jewish penfriend, Edith. Muriel's sister Margaret (later Margaret Thatcher) recalled how, after the German occupation of Austria, 'Edith's father, a banker, wrote to mine asking whether we could take his daughter, since he very clearly foresaw the way events were leading. We had neither the time – having to run the shops – nor the money to accept such a responsibility alone; but my father won the support of the Grantham Rotarians for the idea, and Edith came to stay with each of our families in turn until she went to live with relatives in South America. She was seventeen, tall, beautiful, well dressed, evidently from a well-to-do family, and spoke good

22 George Weidenfeld, *Remembering My Good Friends*, pages 76–8.

English. She told us what it was like to live as a Jew under an anti-Semitic regime. One thing Edith reported particularly stuck in my mind: the Jews, she said, were being made to scrub the streets.'[23]

Another future British Prime Minister, Harold Macmillan, gave shelter to a number of Jewish refugees, as his Principal Private Secretary later confirmed: 'He lent them a house on his estate'[24]

On 6 July 1938 an international conference opened at Evian, on the shores of Lake Geneva, to discuss the future reception of refugees. By that time more than 250,000 Jews had already left Germany and Austria. The largest group, 155,000 by then, had been admitted to the United States. The British government had already admitted 40,000 and a further 8,000 into Palestine. France had taken in 15,000, whose fate would again hang in the balance within a few years, when France was defeated by Germany. Many were then to be saved a second time, in hiding, as a result of the courage of French men and women. Switzerland had taken in more than 14,000, who were to survive the war thanks to Swiss neutrality.[25]

More than 300,000 German and Austrian Jews were still seeking safe havens. As the number of Jews attempting to leave grew, the restrictions against them also grew: Britain and the United States both tightened their rules for admission. Four South American countries, Argentina, Chile, Uruguay and Mexico, adopted laws severely restricting the number of Jews who could enter; in the

---

23 Margaret Thatcher, *The Path to Power*, pages 26–7.
24 John Wyndham, letter to the author, 17 August 1963.
25 Statistics in J. Hope Simpson, *The Refugee Problem: Report of a Survey*, pages 323 (France), 340 (Britain), 397 (Switzerland), and 473 note 1 (United States).

case of Mexico that limit was a hundred a year. The Republic of Ireland declined to take in any refugees. The representative of Australia, Colonel Thomas White – a Cabinet Minister – declared that 'as we have no real racial problems, we are not desirous of importing one by encouraging any schemes of large-scale foreign migration'.[26] That year, Australia took 1,556 Jewish refugees, a thousand more than in the previous year.

In Berlin, Captain Foley redoubled his efforts to expedite Jewish emigration to Palestine. A German Jew, Simon Wertheimer, later recalled how his father, Eliezer Leopold Wertheimer, had been imprisoned in 1937 'on a flimsy charge to deprive him of his livelihood as a textile merchant'. He was sentenced to a year in prison, to be served in Nuremberg. 'As by 1937/38 the Nazis were in the habit of transferring released Jewish prisoners to concentration camps, my mother was strongly advised to obtain visas to Palestine. All her efforts through Jewish aid organisations and the directly concerned British Consulate were of no avail.' Then a Jewish aid organisation referred her to Captain Foley, who issued her a Palestine Certificate 'for the sake of the child', as Foley told Simon Wertheimer's mother.[27]

That summer the Mossad, the Intelligence arm of the Haganah – the defence force of Palestine Jewry – decided to accelerate 'illegal' Jewish emigration from both Austria and Germany, ignoring the British Palestine restrictions and conditions. A Mossad agent, Pino Ginsberg, travelled to Berlin, where he obtained Gestapo

26 Paul R. Bartrop, 'The Dominions and the Evian Conference of 1938', in Paul R. Bartrop (editor), *False Havens: The British Empire and the Holocaust*, pages 64–5.
27 Letter of 17 January 1999 to the Department for the Righteous. Yad Vashem Righteous Among the Nations Archive, file 8378.

permission both to reside there and to organise groups of young Jews for emigration to Palestine, despite their not holding Palestine certificates. A second Mossad agent, Moshe Bar-Gilad, went to Vienna, where he negotiated with Adolf Eichmann, the SS Captain who had been put in charge of the Central Bureau for Jewish Emigration.

Eichmann offered to set up training farms and facilities for young Austrian Jews, who would then be taken by the Mossad to Palestine, 'illegally', without the necessary British permits. By the time of Kristallnacht, a thousand Jewish youngsters were in these farms, awaiting their clandestine journey.[28]

The pre-Kristallnacht fate of the main synagogue in Munich was later described by Benno Cohn of the Berlin Zionist Organisation, who travelled to Munich in June 1938 for a meeting of Bavarian Zionists. 'When I came to the Jewish community hall I looked through the window towards the spot where there had stood the large and stately synagogue – and I no longer saw the synagogue – it was gone. And I asked my friends what had happened. There was a parking lot there instead. I was told the Führer had been there some time ago and had asked what that building was, and had said: "When I come to Munich next time, I don't want to see this building again!" So they pulled down the synagogue. That was not published in the press. There was a severe ban on publishing it. But I saw it with my own eyes.'[29]

The Great Synagogue was located next to the German Art House. For this reason Hitler had ordered it, and the adjoining

---

28 Jon and David Kimche, *The Secret Roads: The 'Illegal' Migration of a People, 1938–1948*, pages 16–19.

29 Testimony of Benno Cohn, Eichmann trial, 25 April 1961, *The Trial of Adolf Eichmann*, Volume 1, page 222.

Jewish community building, to be torn down, and to be gone before German Art Day, July 8. The demolition order was given on June 8 and carried out the following day. As compensation, the Munich municipality paid the Jewish community one-seventh of the real value of the two buildings.[30]

That July, the leading German anti-Semitic magazine, *Der Stürmer* ('The Stormer'), published an issue headed 'Synagogues are Robbers' Dens. The Shame of Nuremberg'. Following this article, the leaders of the Jewish community in Nuremberg were summoned by the police and the city administration and told that their main synagogue, which had served them for so many years, would have to be demolished, as it was 'spoiling the look of the city'. They were allowed to hold one final Friday-night service. The synagogue and the adjacent Jewish community building were demolished on August 10. The 'Jewish stone', a remnant of the earlier medieval synagogue that had served as the base of the Holy Ark in the new one, was saved by a non-Jewish architect.[31]

On 17 August 1938 a new law was promulgated in Germany and Austria. Its official title was: 'Second Decree to Implement the Law Regarding the Changing of Surnames and First Names'. The law stated that from 1 January 1939, all Jews who were German subjects must add a second name: Israel for men and Sarah for women. Jews would thereby be identified as Jews on all official documents, including passports.

On August 18, a day after this order, the Swiss authorities closed

---

30 Henry Wasserman, 'Munich', *Encyclopedia of the Holocaust*, Volume 3, pages 998–1001.
31 Henry Wasserman, 'Nuremberg', *Encyclopedia of the Holocaust*, Volume 3, pages 1073–6.

their frontier with Austria to anyone who did not have a Swiss entry visa. Hundreds of Jewish refugees from Germany and Austria were trapped on the German side of the border. Those who did manage to cross were held in a refugee camp at Diepoldsau and then sent back to Germany. But the Police Chief for the region, Captain Paul Grüninger, did everything possible to allow the refugees to stay. In the three months following the new Swiss regulation, more than 2,000 men, women and children were admitted as a result of his initiative and sense of decency.

Grüninger went so far as to issue fake documents to prevent the expulsion of Jews from Switzerland. He sent writs of summons to Jews inside Austria, instructing them to appear for a 'hearing' in his office in the Swiss town of St Gallen. He also sent Jewish prisoners in Dachau letters of invitation to Switzerland.[32]

At the border, the Germans confiscated all valuables and jewellery from the refugees. In order to circumvent this, Grüninger arranged for a secret depot at an inn in the western part of Austria. From the Swiss Consulate in the Austrian town of Bregenz, a Swiss diplomat, Ernest Prodolliet, regularly sent a diplomatic courier to the innkeeper, collecting the valuables and jewellery in order to bring them to Switzerland.[33] By the end of 1938, Prodolliet had enabled three hundred Austrian Jews to cross the border into Switzerland. After the German annexation of Austria he had been rebuked by his superiors for letting Jews continue to cross the border, and disciplinary measures were taken against him.[34]

On 19 August 1938, the day after Switzerland closed its borders to Jews trying to flee from Austria, the London weekly magazine

32 'The Righteous Among the Nations of Swiss Nationality' website, www.switzerland.taskforce.ch/
33 Meir Wagner, *The Righteous of Switzerland*, pages 36–7.
34 Yad Vashem Righteous Among the Nations Archive, file 2393.

the *Spectator* published an article, signed 'An Aryan Englishman', telling of the plight of the Jews of Vienna. This Englishman wrote critically of the attitude of many of the foreign consuls in the city. After describing the 'pitiful' scenes at Vienna station, 'where whole families were splitting up', he continued: 'And no less pitiful are the queues in the sun-baked streets outside the consulates, queues which form up, as for a theatre premiere, in the early hours of the morning. But the prima donna in the consulate is far more inaccessible than any film star, and I have met Jews who have waited every morning from 5 a.m., sometimes waiting only for information and sometimes for the visa or permit they have been told to collect.'[35]

Reflecting on this criticism, Norman Angell, who in 1924 had won the Nobel Prize for Peace, and Dorothy Buxton, a leading Quaker, jointly wrote a short book intended to alert the public to the refugee problem. Many refugees, they wrote, 'now knock at the doors of the greatest Empire in the world, asking sanctuary', and they went on to ask: 'Shall those doors be closed against them?'[36]

On September 6, as the refugees clamoured for places of safety both in Europe and beyond it, Pope Pius XI told a group of Belgian Catholic pilgrims at the Vatican, after a reading about Abraham, 'our Father, our Ancestor': 'Anti-Semitism is not compatible with the sublime thought and reality which are expressed in this text. It is not possible for Christians to participate in anti-Semitism. Spiritually, we are Semites.'[37]

---

35 *The Spectator*, 19 August 1938.
36 Norman Angell and Dorothy Frances Buxton, *You and the Refugee: The Morals and Economics of the Problem*, page 44.
37 Quoted in Michael Phayer, *The Catholic Church and the Holocaust, 1930– 1956*, page 3.

Emigration continued. Bernard Wulkan left for the United States from Hanover on 'the night of Munich'.[38] That was the night of September 30, when Britain and France, urged to do so by Hitler, put pressure on Czechoslovakia to cede the Sudetenland to Germany. Wulkan and his parents were three of more than 25,000 German and Austrian Jews who were admitted to the United States in 1938.

Rachel Man, a Viennese teenager, later described how, 'on a chilly October afternoon', equipped with her Student's Certificate for Palestine, she boarded a train in Vienna for the Italian port of Trieste, and proceeded by ship to Palestine.[39] She was one of more than 7,000 German and Austrian Jews who were able to enter Palestine legally in 1938.

On October 15, the German authorities announced that the passports of all German Jews were cancelled. Future would-be emigrants would have to apply for passports anew, a long and fraught process. Two weeks later there was an attack in Antwerp on a party of German tourists by a group of Belgian Jews protesting against German anti-Jewish legislation. The German government responded at once. 'In accordance with the official policy of avenging the misdeeds of Jews outside Germany upon their co-religionists within the Reich', one British newspaper explained, a ban had been placed inside Germany on all meetings of Jews, and on 'all Jewish work for adult education'. Adult education was regarded by most German Jews as 'an essential preliminary to emigration'.[40]

38 Dov Bar-Ner (formerly Bernard Wulkan), letter to the author, 7 June 2005.
39 Rachel Man, letter to the author, 16 July 2005.
40 'The Jews in Germany', *The Times*, 10 November 1938.

Among outsiders, the instinct to help remained strong. In the first week of November 1938 the Bible College of Wales, in Swansea, applied to the Home Office in London to take in twenty Jewish refugees who had written to the college from Germany, Austria and Italy. There were four doctors among them. In the hope of being able to bring over as many as a hundred more Jewish refugees, the college asked the Swansea Corporation to give it the tenancy of a large house in the city that had earlier been used to house Spanish Republican refugee children. The director of the college, the Reverend Rees Howell, was also planning to go to Palestine to negotiate for the purchase of a college and a hospital, and also to buy land for Jewish refugees there.[41]

This encouraging item was published on November 7. That day there was disturbing news from Vienna. In eight days' time all Jewish shops and businesses would have to display 'the name of the firm in Hebrew characters as large as the German name over the shop in order to distinguish them from Aryan firms'.[42]

That same day, November 7, Herschel Grynszpan carried out his fatal attack on Ernst vom Rath in Paris.

---

41 'Bible College and Jews', *Manchester Guardian*, 7 November 1938.
42 'Marking Jewish Shops in Austria', *Manchester Guardian*, 8 November 1938.

6

Harsh Aftermath

ON 10 AND 11 NOVEMBER 1938, throughout Germany, Jewish men between the ages of sixteen and sixty were seized in their homes or on the streets, and sent to three concentration camps: Dachau, Sachsenhausen and Buchenwald. These arrests continued for several days, until more than 30,000 had been incarcerated. Conditions in the three camps were terrifying. When Henny Prilutzky's father came back from Dachau he told her and her mother: 'Never, never ask me what I've seen.' Fifty years later his daughter asked him, 'Can you tell me now?' to which he replied, 'No.'[1]

One Viennese family was fortunate on the night of November 10. Following the German annexation of Austria, the thirty-three-year-old composer Erich Zeisl had been stripped of his position at the Vienna Conservatory of Music, all performances of his works had been cancelled, and his name added to the list of composers whose music was considered 'degenerate' ('*Entartete Musik*'). On November 10 his wife Trude hid him and his brother in the laundry room in her mother's attic, as the Gestapo went from house to house in search of Jews to be sent to Dachau.

1 Henny Handler (*née* Prilutzky), conversation with the author, 28 June 2005.

That evening the Zeisls managed to get a sleeping compartment on the night sleeper to Cologne. Jews were systematically pulled off the ordinary carriages of the train at each stop, but the Gestapo avoided the sleeping cars, not wanting to create a bad impression on the foreign tourists who mostly used the sleepers.

The Zeisls had with them their passports, undated visas, and an American affidavit from a plumber in New York with the same surname. He was the only one of the Zeisls in the New York telephone book who had responded that summer to their desperate appeal.[2] From Cologne, where the Zeisls were warned not to go to the American Consulate because their incomplete papers might be confiscated, they flew to Paris. There, Erich Zeisl completed the 'November Pieces' that he had begun composing immediately after Kristallnacht. It is the bittersweet work of an artist who, 'about to flee his land and traditions, confronts and finally accepts his Jewish identity'.[3]

November 11 was Armistice Day, commemorating the end of the First World War twenty years earlier. That morning, at a meeting of the Zionist General Council in London, the head of the Jewish Agency for Palestine, Chaim Weizmann, told his fellow delegates: 'While millions of people of all nations celebrated the Armistice today, there was no peace for the Jews. We open this session in the light of synagogue burning throughout Germany, and to the

2 Bret Werb, programme notes, 'November Pieces', solo piano premiere, United States Holocaust Memorial Museum, Washington, 21 May 2003. On the eve of war the family were able to take the Holland-America liner *Vollendam* to New York.
3 Margaret Shannon, programme notes for the first Washington performance of Eric Zeisl's 'Requiem Ebraico', Washington National Cathedral, 13 November 2005, based on Malcolm S. Cole and Barbara Barclay, *Armseelchen: The Life and Music of Eric Zeisl*, page 39.

groans of the murdered and the cries of thousands of Jews in the concentration camps.'[4]

That day the senior British diplomat in Berlin, Sir George Ogilvie Forbes, telegraphed to the Foreign Office in London that all Jewish schools, newspapers and cultural organisations 'have been suspended or closed until further notice'.[5] Other measures were being promulgated. Jews would only be allowed to live and to do business in certain prescribed districts. Jewish-owned shops and apartments would be expropriated, and exchanged for shops and apartments in the 'segregated quarters'.[6]

That night an elderly Jew was trampled to death in Berlin near the Kurfürstendamm. The names of five other Jews who had been killed in Berlin, and one in Innsbruck, were known in London within three days. Also known was the fate of the inmates of a Jewish home in Düsseldorf for the poor and aged. On November 11 they were ordered to leave the home within forty-eight hours. The following morning they were told 'to clear out at once'. Men and women in their sixties and seventies, 'and without any means of subsistence were turned out on the streets'.[7]

Greed and theft permeated every aspect of Kristallnacht and its aftermath. In Königsberg – all six of whose synagogues were destroyed on Kristallnacht – Arthur Propp, a prosperous Jewish businessman, forty-eight years old, was imprisoned on November 10 and held in prison until he agreed to give his captors what they wanted: his three properties.

4 'We Open our Session to the Light of Synagogue Fires', *Palestine Post*, 13 November 1938.
5 Telegram timed at 9.16 p.m., 11 November 1938: Foreign Office papers, FO 371/21637.
6 'Nazis Planning the Revival of the Ghetto', *Evening Standard*, 11 November 1938.
7 'Britain and the Pogrom', *Manchester Guardian*, 15 November 1938.

Propp's story mirrored many thousands of others. First he had to transfer one of his properties to his former secretary, who saw her chance of loot and came to the prison to ensure it. Then he had to transfer his villa to the wife of the local Gauleiter, Herr Dzubba: she too came to the prison to obtain her loot. Finally, the Party District Economic Adviser, Herr Schultze-Roever, who had been interested in the third property for some time, came to the prison to confirm that Propp had long been wanting to 'dispose' of it. 'This was a nice turn of events for him,' Propp later wrote, 'to get it for free.' No longer addressed as 'Jew' Propp but as 'Herr' Propp, Arthur Propp was released from prison and left Germany. He went to Britain, and then to Bolivia.[8]

In an article released for publication on the evening of November 11, Goebbels ascribed the events of Kristallnacht to the 'healthy instincts' of the German people. He went on to explain: 'The German people is anti-Semitic. It has no desire to have its rights restricted or to be provoked in future by parasites of the Jewish race.'[9] In Washington, anti-Nazi demonstrators converged on the German Embassy. In Holland and Switzerland, both of which had borders with Germany, newspaper criticism of Kristallnacht was much stronger than the German Propaganda Ministry had expected.

From the Sudeten region of Czechoslovakia, which had been annexed by Germany less than six weeks earlier, Jews were fleeing across the new Czech border. On November 11 several hundred crossed over the border to the Czech town of Louny. Many had been badly injured by Sudeten German Nazis as they were taken

8 Arthur Propp, 'November, 1938 in Königsberg', *Midstream*, February 1987.
9 *Daily Telegraph*, 12 November 1938.

from their homes and driven to the border. A British newspaper correspondent reported from Prague: 'They had been robbed of all their property, brought in German army lorries to the new Czechoslovak frontier, and forced to creep into Czechoslovakia on hands and knees, being warned never to return to Germany.'[10]

On the night of November 11 there was a small item of good news. A hundred German and Austrian Jews – men, women and children – who had left Germany before Kristallnacht and reached Britain, sailed from Liverpool on board the *Duchess of Bedford* for Montreal, on their way to Australia and New Zealand. All the men were skilled workers, wanted in the Antipodes. Some of the women, however, 'had to leave their husbands in Germany because they had not enough money for their fares'.[11]

During November 11 the Vatican joined British and French leaders in protesting against the excesses of Kristallnacht. That evening the Nazis organised mass demonstrations in Munich against both Jews and Catholics. The Nazi Gauleiter of Bavaria, Adolf Wagner, warned an audience of 5,000 at the Munich Circus: 'Every utterance the Pope makes in Rome is an incitement of the Jews throughout the world to agitate against Germany.'[12]

In was in Munich that the Catholic Archbishop, Cardinal Michael von Faulhaber, had provided a truck for the community rabbi to rescue religious objects from the Ohel Yaakov synagogue before it was pulled down on Kristallnacht. Following the Gauleiter's tirade, a mob attacked the Cardinal's Palace, smashing all the windows on the first and second floors. 'Next morning,'

10 'Refugees Crawl Over Frontier', *Daily Telegraph*, 12 November 1938.
11 'Sailing for Dominions', *The Times*, 12 November 1938. It was on the *Duchess of Bedford* that the author, then aged three and three-quarters, sailed with several hundred other evacuee children from Liverpool to Canada in the summer of 1940.
12 'Nazi Attack on the Pope', *Daily Telegraph*, 12 November 1938.

the acting British Consul General, Wolstan Weld-Forester, noted, 'a small and almost dumb crowd of people collected to stare at the damage. Scarcely any expressions of approval or condemnation were to be heard, but some people gave way to silent manifestations of grief. Those who did so were quickly moved on by plainclothes police.'[13]

At eleven on the morning of November 12 a meeting was held in the Air Ministry in Berlin, under Field Marshal Goering's chairmanship, at which the German Ministers of the Interior, Propaganda, Finance and Economics were present, to discuss the 'Jewish question'. Goering began the proceedings by announcing: 'Gentlemen! Today's meeting is of decisive importance.' He had received a letter 'on the Führer's orders' from Martin Bormann, the Chief of Staff of Hitler's Deputy, Rudolf Hess, 'with instructions that the Jewish Question is to be summed up and co-ordinated once and for all and solved one way or another. A phone call from the Führer to me yesterday again gave me instructions that decisive coordinated steps must now be outlined.'

Goering pointed out that at an earlier meeting of Ministers before Kristallnacht, when it had been decided 'to Aryanise the German economy, to get the Jews out of the economy, to make them debtors on a pension, we unfortunately only made very fine plans, but then dragged our feet in following them up'. Goering then made a proposal that was to have disastrous consequences for the Jews of Germany. He told his colleagues: 'The German Jews as a whole, as a punishment for their abominable crimes, etc., etc., will have to pay a contribution of one billion. That will do

13 W. Weld-Forester, Munich, report of 13 November 1938: Foreign Office papers, FO 371/21637.

it. The swine won't hurry to commit another murder.' Goering added: 'In general I must say once again: I should not like to be a Jew in Germany.'

Of a suggestion to close down or 'Aryanise' 12,000 or 14,000 of the 17,000 Jewish businesses in Vienna, Goering commented: 'I must say that this proposal is marvellous. Then the whole business would really be cleared out by Christmas or the end of the year in Vienna – one of the chief Jewish cities, so to say.'

The Minister of Economics, Walter Funk, declared that this could also be done in Germany. He had 'prepared a regulation for this matter that states that from 1 January 1939, Jews are forbidden to operate retail stores and commission agencies, or to operate independent artisans' businesses. They are also forbidden to hire employees for this purpose, to offer such services, to advertise them or to accept orders. Where any Jewish trade is carried out it will be closed by the police. From 1 January 1939, a Jew can no longer be the manager of a business . . . Where a Jew is in a leading position in an economic enterprise without being the official manager his employment can be terminated by the manager with six weeks' notice. At the end of the period of notice all claims of the employee deriving from the terminated contract will be void, including pension rights where these existed.'[14]

Action was immediate. Later that day it was announced from Berlin that all the damage done to Jewish property would have to be paid for by the Jews themselves. In addition, the Jews would have to pay a massive fine, in the words of the official announcement, 'as punishment for the brutal murder in Paris'.[15] The fine was equivalent to almost £90 million: more than £3 billion ($5.3

14 International Military Tribunal, Nuremberg, Document PS–1816.
15 'Plight of German Jewry', *Observer*, 13 November 1938.

billion) in the money values of 2006. The announcement stunned German Jewry, already, as one British journalist in Berlin described it, 'broken and cast down by the burning of its places of worship, the wrecking of its shops and businesses, and wholesale arrest of its menfolk'.[16]

Also on November 12, Josef Goebbels announced that from 1 January 1939 no Jew could be a retailer, an exporter, or a manager of a business. No Jew could be a foreman or chief clerk in any store or factory. No Jew could engage in handicrafts. All Jewish shops 'will gradually be taken over into Aryan hands'. Any business that had not been sold to Aryans by the start of the New Year would be taken by the state.[17]

These measures, promulgated within forty-eight hours of Kristallnacht, impoverished a whole people, feeding the avarice of their adversaries and breaking their ability to acquire anything but the most basic necessities of daily life. That night, November 13, a British journalist reported from Munich how, through the cobbled sidestreets, 'cowering from every lighted corner, creep the Jews. They are searching for food. Every shop in this fourth biggest city in Germany today bears the inscription "NO JEW ADMITTED". Food stores, cafés and restaurants, pharmacists, fruiterers and banks – in all of them hangs the same sign. And the Jews may buy their bread, their milk, only after nightfall, at back doors – if they happen to know a friendly shopkeeper.'[18]

That evening the United States Ambassador to Germany, Hugh Wilson, was told by a number of American journalists in Berlin that, 'realising the gravity of the measures they had reported to

16 'German Cabinet Decisions: Jewish Businesses Wiped Out', *Observer*, 13 November 1938.
17 'Dr Goebbels Explains', *Observer*, 13 November 1938.
18 'Munich Jews Barred from Buying Food', *Daily Herald*, 14 November 1938.

their papers, only events which had been seen by them personally or by members of their staffs'. Most of the correspondents, Wilson reported to Washington, 'anticipate trouble with Goebbels, but are in frame of mind almost to welcome it as they are more than ordinarily sure of their facts and seething with indignation'.[19]

There was also a complete ban on the entry of Jews into theatres, concerts, cinemas, music halls, dance floors and other places of entertainment. Any such places that allowed Jews to attend would be punished, Goebbels warned, 'but the Jews who are attending them will be punished even more severely'.[20]

In defending the exclusion of Jews from all places of entertainment, Goebbels told a Berlin audience on November 13: 'It is equivalent to degradation of German art to expect a German to sit next to a Jew in a theatre or cinema. If the parasites had not been treated much too well in the past, it would not have been necessary to make such short work of them now.' The very fact that such legislation was possible, he added, 'proved to the world that the Jews had been having much too good a time in Germany'.[21] That night Sir George Ogilvie Forbes telegraphed to the Foreign Office in London that many Berlin Jews 'are wandering about in the streets and parks afraid to return to their homes'. He added: 'I can find no words strong enough in condemnation of the disgusting treatment of so many innocent people, and the civilised world is faced with the appalling sight of 500,000 people about to rot away in starvation.'[22]

19 Telegram of 13 November 1938: National Archives and Records Administration, Washington DC.
20 'Hitler's New Blow', *Evening News*, 12 November 1938.
21 Dr Goebbels, speech, reported by Sir George Ogilvie Forbes to London, Berlin, 14 November 1938: Foreign Office papers, FO 371/21637.
22 Telegram sent at 9.20 p.m., 13 November 1938: Foreign Office papers, FO 371/21637.

'Most tragic of all,' wrote the Berlin correspondent of the *Sunday Express* on November 13, 'are the ex-servicemen, many of whom lost limbs fighting for Germany during the war. I saw one today wearing an ex-serviceman's badge in the lapel of his coat, helping to nail up planks in front of his windows.' The former soldier told the journalist: 'I don't know what to do.'[23]

For the Jews of Germany the imperative was to leave, to find a country willing to receive them, and the necessary visas to enter it. The world was not entirely a welcoming place. Also on November 13 the *Sunday Express* published a critical note in its editorial column. 'For the Jews of Britain,' it stated, 'this is a word of warning. Do not seek to admit too many foreigners into our country. Some, yes. But do not go beyond the limits caution dictates.' Already, the editorial continued, there were stories that the immigrant Jewish population in Britain 'is getting outside the capacity of British Jews to provide sustenance for them. Such a situation will bring its punishment upon all.'[24]

Emigration had become the urgent need of the hour. A Munich schoolboy, Pesach Schindler, later recalled the 'enormous lines outside the travel agencies as people attempted to get out. Every week my class diminished in size.'[25]

From the Princely States in India – nominally independent but under British supervision – came offers of help. 'Can we afford to sit idle and look on the monstrous phenomenon helplessly?' asked D.V. Tahmankar, joint editor of the London-based *India*

---

23 'The Pogrom Goes on', *Sunday Express*, 13 November 1938.
24 *Sunday Express*, 13 November 1938.
25 Pesach Schindler, letter to the author, 15 June 2005, and Pesach Schindler, manuscript, 'A Jewish Child Growing up in Nazi Germany', Jerusalem, 2004.

Bulletin, in reporting that the state of Cochin 'has invited Jews there to establish themselves in peaceful avocations'. Although the Jews would need to be 'fully equipped with means to settle down there', the Maharaja had shown 'his readiness to give some financial aid to the very needy Jews'.

Four other Indian states, Travancore, Hyderabad, Baroda and Kashmir, were also 'contemplating throwing open their doors to the oppressed Jews'. Several Congress Party provincial administrations – established as self-governing by the British three years earlier – were considering employing Jewish doctors. In Bihar Province, the Congress Minister for Education and Development, Dr Syed Mahmud, agreed to employ Jews in industrial schemes.[26] Several hundred German Jews were able to avail themselves of these distant but sincere offers.

The pattern of increased discrimination was relentless. On November 14 the German Minister of Education, Bernhard Rust, issued a decree forbidding any Jew to enrol at any German or Austrian university, or to attend lectures. The decree was telegraphed from Berlin to all campuses. On the following day, in the culmination of more than five years of being pilloried and discriminated against in the classroom, German Jewish children were barred from German schools. All such children 'are to be dismissed at once'. Telegrams had been sent to all high school authorities 'to dismiss their remaining Jewish scholars'.[27]

On November 15, at a press conference in Washington, President Roosevelt announced that he could 'scarcely believe' that

26 D. V. Tahmankar, 'India's Example to the Dominions', letter to the editor, *Manchester Guardian*, 15 November 1938.
27 German Ministry of Education announcement: reported to London by Sir George Ogilvie Forbes, 15 November 1938: Foreign Office papers, FO 371/21637.

Germany's anti-Jewish campaign 'could occur in the twentieth century of civilisation'.[28] Departing from his usual practice at press conferences, the President allowed himself to be quoted directly. That same day it was announced that the United States Ambassador in Berlin, Hugh Wilson, was being recalled to Washington, and that, according to what the Exchange Telegraph press agency correspondent was told by 'a very reliable authority', he would not return to Berlin 'until Herr Hitler handles the Jewish problem with greater restraint'.[29]

The following day in New York, as a gesture of his anger at what had happened in Germany, Mayor Fiorello la Guardia – whose mother was Jewish, and who had once caused a diplomatic incident by referring to Hitler as a 'brown-shirted fanatic' – appointed three Jewish police chiefs to be in charge of guarding the German Consulate in the city. 'Under this Jewish command,' reported the New York Times, 'a detail of sturdy Jewish patrolmen is to take over from the Alien Squad the task of protecting the German Consul General and his staff, as well as any other visiting German notables, and German property,' particularly the piers of the North German Lloyd shipping company, 'which already have been the scene of demonstrations'.[30] On the previous day, more than 4,500 protesters had given a 'noisy' send-off to the North German Lloyd ocean liner Bremen.[31]

On November 15 the American Consul General in Stuttgart reported that 'In a figurative sense, my home has been bombarded

28 'Roosevelt on Persecution of German Jews', Manchester Guardian, 16 November 1938.
29 'Ambassador to Report', Manchester Guardian, 15 November 1938.
30 'Police Detail Made up Solely of Jews . . .', New York Times, 17 November 1938.
31 'Bremen Picketed by 4,500 at Sailing', New York Times, 16 November 1938.

by visitors and telephone calls giving evidence of the distressing circumstances in which many people are finding themselves.' Hundreds were appealing 'for help and encouragement, and with husbands in concentration camps many are without funds'.

The previous day the Consulate had received almost one hundred telegrams, 'and almost as many today'. Many of these were from the United States, 'and have expressed the utmost interest in their relatives in Germany'. In the majority of cases the male members of the families concerned were ascertained to be in concentration camps. 'Even up to this minute arrests have been made in Stuttgart and telegrams are constantly being received, although it is late at night.'

For more than five days, the Consul noted, his office had been 'inundated with people'. Each day 'a larger and larger crowd has besieged the Consulate, filling all the rooms and overflowing into the corridor of a building six storeys high. Today there were several thousand. Each person has been handled with the greatest possible consideration and each person must have felt that he or she had been as courteously and sympathetically handled as the enormous crowd would permit . . .'[32]

The situation was dire, however, for those tens of thousands of Jews desperate to emigrate. 'Rumours that certain countries have relaxed their restrictions result in hundreds of Jews hurrying to their consulates only to find out that the rumours are false,' a British newspaper correspondent in Berlin wrote on November 15. 'This occurred at the Argentine and at the Paraguayan Consulates today. Out of three hundred Jews who went to the Argentine Consulate yesterday only two qualified to make applications for

---

32 Telegram of 15 November 1938: National Archives and Records Administration, Washington DC.

entry into the country, which only admits those who have had five years' experience of farming.'[33]

Also on November 15, another British correspondent in Berlin wrote of how 'crowds of harried and frightened Jews' continued to throng the British and United States Consulates there, 'begging for visas to enable them to leave the country. To very few of them, however, are the visas being granted.' Despite the events of the previous week, the correspondent added, 'I understand that neither Great Britain nor the United States are making any concessions, and that for the great majority of those applying there is little hope of getting what for them would be the only possible way of returning to a normal life.'

Normality inside Germany was impossible, the correspondent wrote, because 'those Jews who have not been arrested are in constant fear that they may be taken at any moment. It is this fear that prevents many of them sleeping in their own homes, or even in the same place, two nights running. It is this fear that keeps the crowds at the British and American Consulates small enough to be accommodated in the waiting-rooms or near the door.' Those who could not get inside the Consulate buildings found some other place to shelter inside, 'for they dare not be seen standing outside'.

These were grim days for the Jews of Berlin, as for those elsewhere in Germany. 'Their look of despair and hopelessness is dreadful, and the expressions worn by the young men and women, yes, even by the terrified Jewish children, hurrying home from their schools past the closed and wrecked shops which belonged to people of their race are, indeed, piteous.' One rarely saw a Jew

33 'Throwing Responsibilities on Other Countries', *Manchester Guardian*, 16 November 1938.

on the streets. 'None of them leaves his hiding-place, unless on urgent business.'

Sometimes, the correspondent reported, a slim shaft of light pierced the darkness. 'I am told of cases where kindly Aryan neighbours have taken food and other necessities to Jews in hiding. This human kindness does great credit, not only to the charity of the Germans concerned, but also to their courage. More than one good Aryan has had a beating-up for attempting to assist even aged Jews in distress.'[34]

Reflecting on the reports that had reached him from Germany, Michael Cresswell, the head of the German Department of the British Foreign Office, noted: 'This far exceeds any other barbarities which the Nazis have been guilty of in the last five years. It is of quite a different order.' With winter beginning in Berlin, he added, 'the outlook for these miserable people is absolutely hopeless, and one cannot be surprised if large numbers of people prefer suicide to death by starvation and exposure. At the same time, tens of thousands are being sent to concentration camps.'[35]

On November 15, the day of Cresswell's dire assessment, the *Schwarze Korps*, the official newspaper of the SS, with a circulation of half a million, declared that in the event of any reprisals by Jews outside Germany for the ill-treatment of their fellow Jews in Germany, 'We shall use our Jewish hostages in a systematic way, no matter how shocking some people find it. We shall use the principle proclaimed by the Jews – "an eye for an eye and a tooth for a tooth". But we shall take a thousand eyes for one eye, a thousand teeth for one tooth.'[36] The *Schwarze Korps* added: 'Woe

34 'Victims Seek Permits to Leave', *Daily Herald*, 16 November 1938.
35 Minute of 15 November 1938: Foreign Office papers, FO 371/21637.
36 Text in the *News Chronicle*, 18 November 1938.

to the Jews if another of them, or a helper employed or incited by them, should raise his hand against a German.'[37]

That day, in Washington, the National Negro Congress asked Roosevelt 'to provide in America a free haven for the oppressed Jewish people'. The National Secretary of the Congress, John P. Davis, explained in his telegram to the President: 'Negro people in America, representing a minority in our democracy, are deeply concerned over the inhuman barbarism being practised upon the Jewish minority in Nazi Germany.'[38]

A debate had begun between Britain and the United States about the upsurge of German Jews who were in daily search of visas to leave. The British position, accurately reported in the British newspapers, was that the government would be 'willing and able to provide temporary refuge' for any number of Jewish emigrants whom the United States would be willing to take in 'within a reasonable time'. To this the Americans stated that they were 'willing enough' to let Britain be a conduit for the refugees, but that under the existing quota law they could only take some 30,000 German and Austrian immigrants a year, 'and that to alter the quota would mean legislation changing the whole basis of the immigration laws'. The United States, noted a British Foreign Office official, 'do not appear to be willing to make any further substantial contribution' to the refugee problem.[39]

For its part, the United States government wanted to know why the refugees could not be given a home somewhere within the

---

37 'Reprisals Mean "1,000 Jews Will Die for One"', *News Chronicle*, 16 November 1938.
38 'Negroes Urge Haven for Jews', *New York Times*, 16 November 1938.
39 Note of 19 November 1938: Foreign Office papers, FO 371/21637.

British Empire. To this, one newspaper explained, 'the British reply that the Dominions are their own masters, and that so far as the Colonial Empire is concerned, it is very hard to think of any territories suitable and available for large-scale Jewish settlement'. There were also problems for Jews escaping from Germany to other countries in Europe. When five hundred Jews managed to cross from Germany to France by digging a tunnel at night under the border wire, four hundred were sent back by the French border police.[40]

The United States had already given refuge to more than 120,000 German Jews between 1933 and Kristallnacht, by far the largest number of any country. One possibility being discussed, wrote W. N. Ewer, a British diplomatic correspondent, 'is that United States government might ask Congress to pass an Act temporarily increasing the German and Austrian immigration quota. But in such a matter both decision and initiative must necessarily come from Mr Roosevelt himself. Nor is it likely that Congress would agree in the present economic situation to any big-scale Jewish immigration.'

A second idea being 'canvassed' was that the United States, if not by government grant, then by private subscription, should provide money for Jewish settlement elsewhere than the United States, 'if some other Power can provide suitable territory'. But the problem of finding a suitable territory was 'a thoroughly perplexing one'. The interior of a British South American colony, British Guiana, was being spoken of for large-scale settlement of German Jews. It had already been thoroughly examined four years earlier, when the League of Nations was looking for somewhere to settle Assyrian Christian refugees fleeing from persecution in

40 'Tunnels Dug by Escaping Jews', *News Chronicle*, 16 November 1938.

Iraq. In mid-November, Britain offered the vast territory for up to 10,000 German and Austrian Jews, but only if it were found suitable.

The British Guiana project was abandoned when the remote, harsh jungle expanses were surveyed. Ewer commented: 'Land unsuitable for Iraqi Assyrians is hardly suitable for German Jews.' Brazil, the uplands of Madagascar, Uganda and Tanganyika, were also under consideration. 'But so far one can only say that the quest goes on without much result.'[41] On November 16, in the Dominion of Newfoundland, the editor of the *Evening Telegram* urged a toughening of his country's immigration policy – it had taken in a few dozen refugees since 1933 – to prevent Newfoundland 'being overrun by peoples who could not possibly be absorbed in the population'. The following day a letter to the editor declared that when Newfoundland needed a larger population 'we should first look to British stock'.[42]

No foreign observer then in Germany doubted the severity of the implications of Kristallnacht. Sir George Ogilvie Forbes wrote to London from Berlin on November 16 that Kristallnacht had 'let loose forces of medieval barbarism'. The position of the German Jews was, he commented, 'indeed tragic', and he added: 'They dwell in the grip and at the mercy of a brutal oligarchy, which fiercely resents all humanitarian foreign intervention. Misery and despair are already there, and when their resources are either denied to them or exhausted, their end will be starvation.' The

41 William Norman Ewer, 'World Talk of Home for Jews', *Daily Herald*, 17 November 1938.
42 Quoted by Gerhard P. Bassler, 'We Should First Look to British Stock', in Paul R. Bartrop (editor), *False Havens: The British Empire and the Holocaust*.

Jews of Germany, he feared, were 'not a national but a world problem which if neglected contains the seeds of a terrible vengeance'.[43]

The cruelties of Kristallnacht were about to spread beyond the already enlarged borders of the Third Reich. The senior Nazi representative in the Free City of Danzig, Gauleiter Forster, announced on November 15 that the Nuremberg Laws would be introduced into Danzig in eight days' time. Henceforth no Jew living there could hold public office, vote, or marry an 'Aryan' German. Steps would also be taken to eliminate the remaining Jewish retail businesses in the city. The League of Nations High Commissioner in Danzig, the nominally responsible authority for the Free City, had no power to act against this. On November 17 the British Consul General there, Gerald Shepherd, telegraphed to London that the position of the Jews of Danzig 'is now similar to that of those in Germany, synagogues burned, houses and shops wrecked, furniture destroyed, a few personal injuries and arrests without explanation'.[44]

Also on November 17, in Vienna, it was reported that a commission of 'Nazi connoisseurs and the Gestapo' had begun travelling from Jewish apartment to apartment, seizing old masters, carpets, antique furniture, which were crated up on the spot and taken in vans to the city's National Museum.[45]

German Jewish children were being sent out of Germany in whatever way their parents could devise. On November 17, 'a very cold and dark, foggy morning', Rita Braumann, who had been in Cologne on Kristallnacht, was driven by car with several of her

43 Sir George Ogilvie Forbes, Despatch No. 1224 of 16 November 1938: Foreign Office papers, FO 371/21637.
44 Telegram of 17 November 1938: Foreign Office papers, FO 371/21637.
45 'Nazis Seize Jews' Valuables', *News Chronicle*, 18 November 1938.

young cousins across the border to Holland. 'I did not have time to be afraid,' she recalled. 'It was all a total surprise.'[46]

On November 17, the Spanish Republican government, struggling on the battlefield to hold back the steady advance of the Nationalists under General Franco, published an official Note offering shelter to all those 'persecuted for their origin, politics, or religion. Catholics, Israelites or Protestants who wish to work peacefully . . .' The Note went on to attack Nazi Germany's 'Jew-baiters'.[47] But this was the offer of a government under siege, which had less than a year to survive. Also on November 17, a week after Kristallnacht, Frances Perkins, the United Sates Secretary for Labor, stated that the German/Austrian quota was already filled 'for at least fourteen months': that is, until after January 1940. This meant that 32,000 Germans and Austrians, the majority of them Jews, had permits to land.[48]

Inside Germany, a week after Kristallnacht, Pastor J. von Jan preached to his Lutheran congregation in Memmingen, whose synagogue had been burned down on Kristallnacht: 'Houses of worship, sacred to others, have been burned down with impunity – men who have loyally served our nation and conscientiously done their duty, have been thrown into concentration camps simply because they belong to a different race. Our nation's infamy is bound to bring about Divine punishment.' Dragged out of his Bible class by a Nazi mob, Pastor von Jan was brutally beaten, then thrown onto the roof of a shed. The mob then smashed his vicarage, just as, a week earlier, so many Jewish houses had been

46 Rita Newell (*née* Braumann), recollections entitled '10 November 1938'. Sent to the author, 28 June 2005.
47 'Spain Asks Refugees', *Daily Herald*, 17 November 1938.
48 *New York Times*, 18 November 1938.

smashed. As a punishment for his courageous stand, Pastor von Jan was imprisoned.[49]

The distress of German Jewry continued. A report from Berlin on November 18 related: 'One case is known where a well-to-do couple already granted their clearance papers appeared at their police station on Monday to claim the passports that were then ready for them. The police superintendent then suggested that the husband should contribute a substantial sum before leaving for the benefit of the Jewish community left behind. The man agreed, wrote out a substantial cheque, and was told to come again next day to receive his passport. When he came on the following day he was informed that his clearance papers were no longer valid.'[50]

In a report from Munich on November 18, Reuters news agency described how Jews owning houses were summoned before the Nazi Party Labour Front in Nuremberg 'and persuaded to sign a document turning their property over to the Labour Front'. This transaction was reported to have been carried out 'at the taxation value of the houses concerned of which the Labour Front kept 90 per cent while the Jewish owners received 10 per cent. The Jewish house owners were kept at the Labour Front office, it is stated, from about 10 p.m. until five the next morning, and most of them signed the document.'

The Reuters report continued with a modicum of good news: 'Jews can buy food again in Munich'. The district Nazi Party administration 'has allowed the Jewish Cultural Society to establish selling depots where Jews can buy all necessities, including foodstuffs'. But the rest of the report was without redeeming

49 H. D. Leuner, *When Compassion was a Crime: Germany's Silent Heroes*, pages 113–14.
50 'Nazis Make New Difficulties', *Manchester Guardian*, 19 November 1938.

features: 'In the window-smashing incidents all Jewish shops were more or less destroyed, and since then all Aryan shops have displayed notices, "Jews are not desired here." Jews have therefore had no means of buying anything.'

A number of suicides had been reported from Frankfurt-on-Main. Among them were those of Dr Löwe of the Jewish Hospital, 'who was in charge of the X-ray station and former chief doctor of the hospital, another doctor of the Jewish Hospital named Rosenthal, and a Jewish lawyer named Hochschild. A Jewish business man named Blum has committed suicide after his stores had been ransacked.'[51]

On November 19 the burning of synagogues broke out in the Free City of Memel, on the Baltic. This autonomous region of Lithuania had been part of Germany until 1918. Following the attack on the synagogues, almost all Memel's 2,500 Jews fled into neighbouring Lithuania. That day, in Germany, the authorities imposed a draconian barrier to the ongoing Jewish emigration. No Jews would be allowed to leave until the thousand-million-mark fine on the Jewish community had been paid in full, or until the family seeking to emigrate had no financial assets or obligations left – including the collective fine. All passports had to be handed in. They would be returned only when the passport holder produced an official certificate showing that all his or her financial assets had been handed over to the government. In a move that further depressed the would-be emigrants, the Finance Ministry had begun, a few days earlier, to refuse to issue any further certificates.

51 'Jews Forced to Sign Away Their Property', Reuters News Agency: *Manchester Guardian*, 19 November 1938.

A week after Kristallnacht, the head of the Intergovernmental Refugee Committee, George Rublee, had sought to negotiate with the German government to allow German Jews to leave Germany with at least part of their possessions, to enable them to make what the *New York Times* called 'a new start in a new land'. But on November 19 the *Essener National Zeitung*, known as Goering's 'mouthpiece', declared that henceforth Germany, 'like the Pharaohs, will not permit any part of the Jewish possessions to leave the country'.[52] While insisting that its Jewish policy was to allow and accelerate emigration, by this decision the German government made it much harder for Jewish would-be refugees to find a country willing to take them in. The penniless were, for most countries, the least acceptable category of refugees,

In Berlin and Vienna the lines of those Jews with passports and Finance Ministry certificates had started to grow again at the foreign consulates. In Vienna they were particularly long at the Chinese Consulate General, where Dr Feng Shan Ho continued to issue the visas that would enable the holders to leave Germany for Shanghai. Dr Ho had discovered that these visas could be used to secure the release of Jews who had been taken to the concentration camps after Kristallnacht. He acted with alacrity, helping to expedite cases that had previously not been seen as urgent.

A young Viennese Jew, Eric Goldstaub, later recalled how, before Kristallnacht, he had obtained visas for his whole family 'in a Consulate representing a country that to me at that time was like the end of the world – China'. On the strength of those visas the Goldstaub family had been able to book a passage on an Italian liner from Genoa to Shanghai, 'for departure on

52 'Reich Insists Jews Depart Penniless', *New York Times*, 20 November 1938.

20 December 1938'. On Kristallnacht, six weeks before the ship was to sail, the family shop in Vienna had been destroyed and everything in it plundered. 'Both my father and myself were arrested and most of our co-sufferers then sent to concentration camps. The fact that we had a visa for China as well as ship tickets for the end of December enabled us to be released within a few days and we were on our way by train to liberty in China.'[53]

At the height of his activities Dr Ho was issuing between four and five hundred visas a month. He was later to say: 'I thought it only natural to feel compassion and to want to help. From the standpoint of humanity, that is the way it should be.'[54] 'He was a Christian,' his daughter Manli Ho later reflected, 'and basically thought it was a natural thing to do.'[55]

In all, 18,000 German and Austrian Jewish refugees reached Shanghai while it was still possible to leave Europe.

The plight of those who had witnessed Kristallnacht was varied and often cruel. On 30 December 1939 the river boat *Uranus*, with 1,310 Jews on board – an 'illegal' transport bound for Palestine, organised in Vienna by a Mossad agent, Ehud Uberall – was forced by the freezing-over of the Danube to shelter in the Yugoslav port of Kladova. When the ice melted, the British government pressed Yugoslavia not to allow the ship to continue. The refugees were interned in the Yugoslav town of Sabac. There, in mid-1940, 207

53 Testimony of Eric Goldstaub, Ontario, Canada, 22 December 1997: Yad Vashem, Righteous Among the Nations Archive, file 8688.
54 Roberta Kremer (editor), *Diplomatic Rescuers and the Story of Feng Shan Ho*. Vancouver Holocaust Education Centre, Vancouver, 1999. This brochure was produced in conjunction with Eric Saul's exhibition 'Visas for Life: The Righteous Diplomats', and Dr Ho's daughter, Manli Ho.
55 Quoted in Douglas Davis, 'Ho Fengshan: The Chinese Oskar Schindler', *Jerusalem Post*, 20 February 2000.

teenagers under sixteen received their Palestine Certificates and went on to Palestine by train through Istanbul. The remaining 1,003 refugees were still in Sabac in October 1941, when, six months after the German conquest of Yugoslavia, they were mass-acred. Among those killed was Gertrude Reininger's younger sister Martha. Gertrude herself had gone safely to England on a dom-estic servant permit in February 1939, to work in a vicarage in Leeds.

In November 1940, off Palestine, the British seized more than 3,500 'illegals' who had reached the coast on three ships. Taken to Haifa, they were put on board a fourth ship, the *Patria*, to be sent to the Indian Ocean island of Mauritius and held there in detention camps. Determined to remain in Palestine, some of the would-be deportees set an explosive charge to disable the ship. The charge was more powerful then they realised, and 250 of the refugees were drowned: they had come from Berlin, Munich, Frankfurt-on-Main, Vienna and a dozen other German and Austrian cities; only to perish in the waters of Haifa Bay.

7

Between Good and Evil

SIX WEEKS BEFORE KRISTALLNACHT, the British Prime Minister Neville Chamberlain had returned from the Munich Conference proclaiming 'peace in our time'. Kristallnacht was a blow to that hope. On 18 November 1938 the Chancellor of the Exchequer, Sir John Simon, spoke of how the prospect of peace 'has been thrown within the last few days in the forefront of a development which has deeply stirred and shocked the world'. The fate of Germany's Jews, Simon added, 'inevitably raises strong sentiments both of horror and of sympathy'.[1]

The effect of Kristallnacht on British parliamentary opinion was also considerable. 'This is due entirely to the Nazi attack on the Jews,' reported the *Observer* on November 20, 'and has had an inevitable influence on the immediate outlook. Ministerialists have no illusions. To their lasting regret they recognise that all that has happened in Germany in the past ten days spells a definite setback to the prospect of appeasement in Europe.'[2] In New York, President Roosevelt declared on November 19: 'It is fitting that we offer prayers for the unfortunate people in other lands who are in dire distress at this, our thanksgiving season.'[3] Within a

1 Speech of 18 November 1938: *Manchester Guardian*, 19 November 1938.
2 'Parliament and Refugees', *Observer*, 20 November 1938.
3 'America Warns Germany', *Observer*, 20 November 1938.

week of Kristallnacht the American Federation of Labor called for a 'moral ring' around Germany.[4] In Philadelphia, 3,000 men, women and children 'howled their hatred as a Hitler effigy was burned in the street'.[5]

Inside Germany, the persecutions and humiliations continued unabated. On November 20, a Sunday, the Evangelical Church authorities ordered all churches with Jewish Biblical names carved above their doors to remove them. This was because anti-Jewish mobs in Saxony had tried to burn down churches with the name 'Jehovah' carved above their doors.[6]

That day, in Britain, the Chief Rabbi's office organised a Service of Prayer and Intercession for the Jews of Germany. One prayer that was recited that day was addressed to Germany: 'Man is brought low; human brotherhood is become a mockery; and there is neither truth, pity nor freedom in the land. And they have set their face utterly to defame and destroy the House of Israel.'[7]

On November 20, President Roosevelt announced that he would ask Congress to allow between 12,000 and 15,000 German refugees already in the United States on visitors' visas to remain there 'indefinitely'. It would be 'cruel and inhuman', he said, 'to compel the refugees, most of whom were Jews, to return to Germany to face possible maltreatment, concentration camps or other persecution'.[8]

Roosevelt said nothing, however, about asking Congress to accelerate or increase the annual immigration quota, or to establish a special refugee category. The combined German and

---

4 'America Warns Germany', *Observer*, 20 November 1938.
5 'Crowd Burns Hitler Guy . . .', *Sunday Pictorial*, 20 November 1938.
6 'Churches Attacked', *Daily Herald*, 21 November 1938.
7 *A Service of Prayer and Intercession for the Jews of Germany*, 20 November 1938: Jewish Museum, London, Archive.
8 'Shelter in US for 15,000 Refugees', *Daily Herald*, 21 November 1938.

Austrian annual quota of 27,000 was already filled until January 1940. The American Jewish organisations had asked for the quotas for the following three years to be combined, allowing 81,000 Jews to enter immediately. This proposal was rejected by the United States administration.

The British government was also under pressure to do more for refugees. On November 21 in the House of Commons, Alderman Logan, a Labour Member of Parliament, called on Britain to take the initiative. 'I speak,' he said, 'as an orthodox Catholic, feeling to the depth of my heart the cause of the Jew. I hear mention made of the question of money. If we cannot have civilisation contented, if we cannot bring sunshine into the lives of people, without being concerned with the question of money, civilisation is doomed. Today an opportunity is offered to the British nation to take its proper stand among the nations of the world.'[9]

In the spring of 1937 the British government had taken in 4,000 Basque children, refugees from the civil war in Spain. More than half of these had later returned to their homes.[10] On November 21 in the House of Lords a leading British Jew, Viscount Samuel, the former head of the Liberal Party, reminded the government that in 1915 many thousands of Belgian children – refugees from the German advance through Belgium that had precipitated Britain's declaration of war on Germany – had been found refuge in British homes.[11] When the debate was over, the government announced that 'very large numbers' of German Jewish children would be allowed into Britain.

*   *   *

9 *Hansard*, Parliamentary Debates, 21 November 1938.
10 'Spanish Refugees Add to Burdens of Europe', *New York Times*, 5 February 1939.
11 *Hansard*, Parliamentary Debates, 21 November 1938.

The fate of the Jews who had been seized during the Kristallnacht and sent to concentration camps was becoming widely known and publicised. On November 23 the *News Chronicle*, a London newspaper, reported the arrival of sixty-two Jews, including two rabbis, at Sachsenhausen, north of Berlin. The arrested men had reached the camp gates under police escort from Berlin. At the gates, the police were made to hand them over to an SS unit. The sixty-two Jews were then forced to run a gauntlet of spades, clubs and whips.

According to an eye-witness, the police, 'unable to bear their cries, turned their backs'. As the Jews were beaten, they fell. As they fell they were beaten further. This 'orgy' of beating lasted half an hour. When it was over, 'twelve of the sixty-two were dead, their skulls smashed. The others were all unconscious. The eyes of some had been knocked out, their faces flattened and shapeless.'[12]

Thirty-one-year-old Ernst Gerstenfeld, from Vienna, was registered in Dachau on November 12. 'The three months my Grandpa was in Dachau were quite brutal,' one of his grandsons later recalled, 'but he hid most of the stories from us. He would learn to stand in a formation of men in the middle or sides, but never in front; those in front were beaten with rifles or fists of guards. He took blankets from dead men and made himself a cap. He also bought a set of gloves from the camp store and used them in slave labour.'[13] Among the Munich Jews sent to Dachau was the community rabbi, Dr Leo Baerwald, who was severely ill-treated there.

On November 21 it was announced in Berlin by the Nazi authorities that 3,767 Jewish retail businesses in the city had either been transferred to 'Aryan' control or closed down. Further

12 *News Chronicle*, 23 November 1938.
13 Ted Shealy, letter to the author, 28 June 2005.

restrictions on Jews were announced that day. To enforce the rule that Jewish doctors could not treat non-Jews, each Jewish doctor had henceforth to display a blue nameplate with a yellow star – the Star of David – with the sign: 'Authorised to give medical treatment only to Jews.' German apartment managers were told to give notice to their Jewish tenants. Bookmakers were forbidden to accept bets from Jews, denying them even of the lottery of possible monetary gain.

In Washington, the Secretary of the Interior, Harold Ickes, put forward to the Alaskan Territory's Chambers of Commerce a plan to settle large numbers of German and Austrian Jewish refugees in the vast emptiness of Alaska. The Mayor of Seward, Don Carlos Brownwell, telegraphed to Ickes that the fertile but virtually un-inhabited 120-mile-long Kenai Peninsula could support a quarter of a million additional inhabitants, 'regardless their creed or condition their personal finances'.

Brownwell was supported by two other mayors, those of Skagway and Petersburg. But it was not enough: four Alaskan Chambers of Commerce – those of Anchorage, Fairbanks, Juneau and Valdez – passed resolutions opposing the settlement plan. The Juneau Chamber, citing a recent experience with a Federal agricultural colony, predicted that a heavy tax burden would fall on the territory to support the required roads and schools. The Anchorage Chamber of Commerce feared that a colony made up entirely of immigrants would 'stifle assimilation and will prevent them from becoming Americanized'. Despite Ickes's desire to do something for the refugees, the settlement plan was dead.[14]

14 Tom Kizzia, 'Sanctuary: Alaska, the Nazis, and the Jews: The Forgotten Story of Alaska's Own Confrontation with the Holocaust', *Anchorage Daily News*, 16, 17, 18 and 19 May 1999.

Felix Cohen, one of the Interior Department lawyers, later told a new member of the department, Ruth Gruber, how Ickes 'was determined to help refugees', but that 'a whole group of Alaskans came all the way down here just to fight us'. These Alaskans 'said there was no anti-Semitism in the Territory now because there were only a few Jewish families in each town. Bringing five thousand Jews a year would start race riots.'[15]

In the Caribbean, the Legislative Assembly of the Virgin Islands – an island group the United States had acquired from Denmark twenty-one years earlier – passed a resolution on November 18 offering a place 'for Refugee peoples of the world' on the islands, where they could find 'surcease from misfortune'. The islands' population having declined from 43,000 to 22,000 in the previous hundred years, there was certainly room. But a month later, on December 15, the United States Secretary of State, Cordell Hull, sent a letter to all the authorities concerned in the matter, calling the islanders' resolution 'incompatible with existing law'.

It was to take more than a year before the Department of Labor, which had been consulted on the plan, concluded that the invitation to take in refugees was 'consistent with existing law and unobjectionable from the standpoint of policy'. Even then the Attorney General, Frank Murphy, asked in October 1939 by the Secretary of the Interior, Harold Ickes, to give a legal opinion, with a view to reviving the rescue plan, refused – in his reply in March 1940 – even to study the issue, 'for the reason that the Secretary of State had not invited such an opinion'. With that, the proposal died.[16]

15 Ruth Gruber, *Inside of Time: My Journey from Alaska to Israel*, pages 13–14.
16 'Chronological Account of Inter-Departmental Negotiations on Admission of Alien Visitors into Virgin Islands', United States National Archives, Record Group 126.

On November 20 the Jewish National Council for Palestine, in a telegram from Jerusalem, offered to take 10,000 German Jewish children into Palestine, to be dispersed among the existing 250 Jewish agricultural settlements and urban centres there. Homes would be found for 5,000 of the children 'at once', and for the second group of 5,000 'within four weeks'. The full cost of bringing the children from Germany and maintaining them in their new homes, as well as their education and vocational training, would be borne by the Palestine Jewish community and by 'Zionists throughout the world'.[17]

The Jewish National Council's offer was discussed in the British Cabinet three weeks later, together with a subsequent offer by the Council to take in 10,000 adults in addition to the children. The Colonial Secretary, Malcolm MacDonald, told his Cabinet colleagues: 'There could be no question of allowing the adults to enter Palestine, but the question of the children, on which he had been strongly pressed, was more difficult. There were homes available for all the 10,000 children and there was no doubt that they could be received in Palestine without causing injury to anyone's interest. There were, however, other points which must be considered.'

MacDonald then referred to the forthcoming conference, to be held in London, between the British government and representatives of Palestinian Arabs, Palestinian Jews, and the Arab States. Both the British High Commissioner in Jerusalem and the British diplomats in the neighbouring Arab countries, MacDonald reported, 'had all said that, if these 10,000 children were allowed to enter Palestine, we should run a considerable risk that the

17 '10,000 Child Refugees, Palestine Plan', *Manchester Guardian*, 21 November 1938.

Palestinian Arabs would not attend the Conference, and that, if they did attend, their confidence would be shaken and the atmosphere damaged'.

Lord Zetland, the Secretary of State for India, whose responsibilities included the loyalty of the sixty million Muslims in British India, also opposed the plan, warning the Cabinet that he was 'satisfied that the admission of these 10,000 children to Palestine at the present time would have a very adverse effect on Moslem opinion'.[18] The offer to take the children was rejected. Robustness with regard to letting a similar number of children into Britain was paralleled by appeasement with regard to Palestine.

The Nazi propaganda machine continued to spew out its venom. 'To what extremes this campaign may go,' reported one British newspaper correspondent from Berlin on November 23, 'is shown by an article which appeared yesterday in the *Schwarze Korps*, organ of the Nazi Black Guards forecasting the physical extermination of the Jews. They must be driven into special streets, marked with a special emblem and deprived of the right to own land or a house, it says. Then, being excluded from all profitable occupations, they will soon eat up their capital and become criminals, in keeping with their hereditary instincts.'

When that stage was reached, the *Schwarze Korps* concluded, 'we would be faced with the hard necessity of exterminating the Jewish underworld by those methods which we always use in dealing with criminals, namely, fire and the sword. The result would be the final end of Jewry in Germany – its total destruction.'[19]

Addressing the world's Roman Catholics on November 21, Pope

18 Cabinet minutes, 14 December 1938: Cabinet papers, 23/96.
19 'Nazis Cry "Finish Jews"', *News Chronicle*, 23 November 1938.

Pius XI challenged the Nazi claim of Aryan racial superiority, insisting that there was only a single human race. His assertion was challenged by the German Minister of Labour, Dr Robert Ley, who declared in a speech in Vienna on November 22: 'No compassion will be tolerated for the Jews. We deny the Pope's statement that there is but one human race. The Jews are parasites.'[20]

Influenced by the strong stance of Pius XI, there had been outspoken condemnation of Kristallnacht by several leading Catholic churchmen, including Cardinal Schuster of Milan, Cardinal Van Roey of Belgium, and Cardinal Verdier of Paris. Following Kristallnacht, Pius XI, who had been Pope since 1922, wanted to break the Vatican's diplomatic ties with Germany. A sick man, he was dissuaded from doing so by his Secretary of State, Eugenio Pacelli, who had negotiated the Vatican Concordat with Hitler five years earlier.[21] Three months after Kristallnacht, Pius XI died. Pacelli succeeded him as Pope, taking the name Pius XII.

In New York on November 23 a mass demonstration organised by the Joint Boycott Council protested against the continuing anti-Jewish violence in Germany. Two days later, in Chicago, protesters burned swastika flags.[22]

No day passed without some new blow to German Jewry. On November 24 it was reported from Berlin that Jews would be forbidden to live in frontier areas, in tourist centres, or in the best residential parts of cities. That same day, all Jewish shops that

20 Reuters News Agency, reported in the *Daily Herald*, 23 November 1938.
21 Michael Phayer, *The Catholic Church and the Holocaust, 1930–1956*, page 18.
22 Associated Press photographs 50343a and 50343c, with captions.

had been repaired in the two weeks since Kristallnacht and had reopened were ordered to close. 'The Nazi appetite for victims is insatiable,' wrote the Berlin correspondent of one British newspaper. 'Plans are now being made to brand as Jews all those of mixed race who up till now have been given at least theoretical equality with Aryans.' There were also proposals for dress, 'from fantastic ideas like yellow cloaks, pointed yellow caps with embroidered Stars of David, blobs of yellow cloth fixed on breast and shoulders, down to more simple ideas like yellow armbands and badges'.[23] In the event, the 'blobs of yellow cloth', in the shape of a Star of David, were not to be introduced, except in the concentration camps, for another two years, first in German-occupied Poland, and then in Germany itself.

On November 27 the Associated Press correspondent in Vienna reported that the city authorities had removed the street signs from eighty streets that had been named after distinguished Austrians who happened to have been Jewish. Two of the names removed were those of Joseph von Sonnenfels and Siegfried Marcus. Sonnenfels was the man 'responsible for the abolition of torture as a method of police investigation'.[24] Marcus was one of the inventors of the automobile, building in the 1870s the first vehicle powered by a four-stroke engine, the first with petrol as a fuel, with a carburettor for a petrol engine, and the first magneto ignition. In the Nazi ideology such an achievement counted for nothing given his Jewishness.

German and Austrian Jews who had managed to find asylum in Italy searched for asylum again from Mussolini's anti-Jewish laws,

23 'Insatiable', *News Chronicle*, 25 November 1938.
24 'Vienna Changing Names', *New York Times*, 28 November 1938.

introduced two days before Kristallnacht, barring Jews from government or municipal employment, or from teaching in Italian schools. Many tried to cross into neutral Switzerland. On November 23 Heinrich Rothmund, head of the Police Division of the Swiss Federal Department of Justice and Police, protested to the Swiss Foreign Minister about Jewish refugees being allowed to enter the country. Rothmund had discovered that several Swiss Consulates in Italy had been 'randomly' issuing visas to Jews from Austria, allowing them to enter Switzerland. Several Swiss Cantons had complained about this influx of Jews.

Of the 2,800 visas issued by Swiss Consulates in Italy in the course of a single year, 1,600 were issued in Milan by two Swiss officials, Pio Perucchi and Candido Porta. To curb them, Heinrich Rothmund insisted that visas could only be issued if those receiving them promised not to remain in Switzerland, but to transit through it. Perucchi and Porta continued issuing visas to those they knew had no intention of abandoning the safety of Swiss neutrality.[25]

In Berlin, Captain Foley was even more active after Kristallnacht than before in helping Jews to leave Germany. Ze'ev Padan later recalled how at the time of Kristallnacht his father, Gunther Powitzer, formerly a taxi driver in pre-war Berlin, was already in Sachsenhausen. Two years earlier he had been imprisoned in Brandenburg for twenty-one months, charged with 'Race Defilement'. His girlfriend's family, who were Nazi sympathisers, had reported his relationship to the authorities, despite the fact that he and his girlfriend already had a baby son. Having served his prison term, Powitzer had been about to return home to

25 'Perucchi, Pio (1870–1945) and Porta, Candido (1892–1988)': appendix to Manli Ho, manuscript, 'Dr Feng Shan Ho, Chinese Consul General to Vienna, Austria, 1938–1940'.

Berlin when an SS man told him, 'You are not free,' and he was sent to Sachsenhausen. Captain Foley went personally to the concentration camp with a Palestine Certificate and procured his release. Within a week Powitzer and his son were on their way by train to Italy, and thence by boat to Palestine. Foley accompanied them to the railway station in Berlin to make sure they were allowed to leave Germany without further hindrance.[26]

After the war, one of those whom Foley had saved – whose name was not recorded – described his method, and his achievements in individual cases. 'As a Passport Control Officer', the man wrote, Foley 'was not subject to any personal instructions, but was free to interpret existing rules and regulations according to his discretion. In that situation he never chose the easy way out. He never tried to make himself popular with the Ambassador (Sir Nevile Henderson) nor with the Home Office by giving a strict and narrow interpretation to the rules. On the contrary, he was not above sophistic interpretations if he could help Jews to emigrate.'

An example of this was when Foley issued a Category A Palestine Certificate, granted to those with £1,000 of capital, and intended strictly for themselves alone. This particular certificate, the witness noted, was issued to a woman in possession of the required £1,000 for herself, but was granted for her 'to be "accompanied by her infirm mother" (an interpretation which contradicted both the letter and the spirit of the Palestine Migration Ordinance). And so great was his authority with the Palestine Migration Office that upon arrival in Haifa the Port Immigration Officer (an Englishman) did not question the validity of the document.'

---

26 Ze'ev Padan, conversation with the author, 13 January 2002.

In another instance, the witness recalled, Foley granted an immigration visa into a British Dominion to a young girl of nineteen, although she came to him straight from prison, having served two years for Communist activities. She did not deny having been a Communist, even though that would automatically prevent her being given the visa. Having talked to her, Foley decided: 'The girl is now nineteen. When she was a Communist she was seventeen. At that age everyone is liable to commit a youthful stupidity without being aware of the consequences.' In another instance Foley personally stamped a visa for a British Crown Colony into the passport of a Jew after his office was closed and his staff had gone home, in order to secure the man's immediate release from Sachsenhausen. After Kristallnacht, 'when crowds of thousands were besieging his office day and night', Foley increased the number of his assistants from two to six, and doubled his clerical staff, 'something quite extraordinary in peacetime Britain of those days'.[27]

Among those who saw Foley at work was the young Dutch Jew Wim van Leer. Forty-six years later he recalled Foley's 'genuine compassion for the throngs that day in, day out besieged his office with their applications, requests and enquiries as to the progress of their case'. Van Leer added: 'The winter of 1938 was a harsh one, and elderly men and women waited from six in the morning, queuing up in the snow and biting wind. Captain Foley saw to it that a uniformed commissionaire trundled a tea-urn on a trolley along the line of frozen misery, and all this despite the clientele, neurotic with frustration and cold, doing little to lighten his task.'

Van Leer took twenty-two young Jews with him to Britain.

27 'Major Francis Edward Foley'. Single-page note, no author given. March 1960. Yad Vashem Righteous Among the Nations Archive, file 8378.

Foley recommended their route, from Leipzig to Emden, near the northern tip of the German border with Holland, then across the border lagoon by boat to the Dutch village of Termunten, and on through Amsterdam. In Emden, van Leer was helped by a German Lutheran who was a descendant of refugees from religious oppression in the Spanish Netherlands three hundred years earlier. On a last journey from Leipzig to Berlin, by taxi, van Leer had all twenty-two passports stamped by Foley.[28]

No one knew how much time remained for the flow of refugees out of Germany. Foley continued his work without interruption. He was 'an active little man', noted Margaret Reid, a member of his staff. 'He appears to work fourteen hours a day and remain good-tempered.'[29] One of those who saw a great deal of him, Benno Cohn, a leader of the Berlin Jewish community and a beneficiary of one of the precious Palestine Certificates, spoke twenty years later at a ceremony just outside Jerusalem honouring Foley's work: 'He did not act in violation of his duties, but in accordance with his own judgement, and in such an open-hearted way, that many got the longed-for visa, who certainly would not have got it, had he strictly followed his regulations. Tourist visas, capitalist certificates or relationship certificates, the whole complicated alphabet of Palestine immigration was manipulated by him in such a way that precisely during those years of considerable restrictions, there was a considerable quantity of immigration.'

The 'peak' of Foley's activities, Benno Cohn recalled, was reached during the 'dark weeks' after Kristallnacht. 'Approaching the building of the Consulate in the Tiergartenstrasse, you could see women queuing up to be allowed to enter. The rooms of the

28 Wim van Leer, *Time of My Life*, pages 174–7.
29 Margaret Reid, quoted in Douglas Davis, 'The Hero Inside a Quiet Little Man', *Jerusalem Post*, 29 January 1999.

Consulate were transformed into a shelter for Jews, looking for protection from persecution. 32,000 men were in prison in concentration camps during those weeks, their wives besieging the Consul for a visa that meant liberation for their husbands. It was a question of life or death for several thousands. During those days, Captain Foley's extensive humanity became obvious. Day and night he was at the disposition of those seeking help. Generously, he distributed every kind of visa, thus helping the liberation of many thousands from the camps.'

Reflecting on Foley's motivation, Benno Cohn commented that he was 'a real Christian, for whom help to others was the first commandment. He often told us that, as a Christian, he wanted to prove how little the Christians, governing Germany then, had to do with real Christianity. We knew, however, that he did not act from mere love of Mordechai, but at the same time out of hatred against Haman. He hated the Nazis and, as he told me once in a conversation, considered them as the realm of Satan on earth. He despised their mean actions and he felt responsible to extend help to the victims.'[30] Mordechai was a Jew in ancient Persia whose niece Esther was married to King Ahasuerus. They persuaded the King not to allow the Grand Vizier, Haman, to murder the Jews.

At the end of November there was yet another exclusion of German Jews from German life. A decree issued a month earlier, before the expulsions to Poland and before Kristallnacht, came into effect on November 30. No Jew with a permit to practise as a lawyer could do so any longer. Jewish patent lawyers had also to cease their practice. Jewish lawyers in Austria would have to cease practising at the end of the year.

30 Benno Cohn, 'Address on the Occasion of the Planting of a Forest Near Harel in Remembrance and in the Name of Major Foley, 10 July 1959', Yad Vashem Righteous Among the Nations Archive, file 8378.

On November 30 a British newspaper reported a further threat against the Jews of Germany in the *Schwarze Korps*, the SS newspaper: 'On the day that a Jewish weapon or a weapon purchased with Jewish money is raised against any of the German leaders, on that day there will be no more Jews left alive in Germany.'[31]

Of the 30,000 Jewish men arrested and taken to concentration camps immediately after Kristallnacht, Walter Loeb – four of whose uncles served in the First World War, with one dying in 1923 from wounds received in action – was among the 11,000 who were sent to Dachau, just outside Munich. 'We were greeted,' he later recalled, 'by a "welcoming committee" consisting of a large body of heavily armed SS guards with helmets and riot gear, who constantly taunted us with loud insults, such as "You are all going to kick the bucket here," and other vicious slogans. Some guards went through our ranks and asked individual prisoners the asinine question: "Do you know why you are here?" Anyone who answered "No" was promptly slapped in the face. I was spared that ordeal as they passed me by.'

A guard then 'yelled for "the rabbi" to step forward. The guard became almost ecstatic when to his fiendish delight, he reaped a bonanza, as not just one but several persons who appeared to be rabbis stepped forward, and in gratitude for their obedience were beaten up.' There was no food for three days 'while we were processed into the system. We were given showers, sham medical examinations, and our heads were shaved clean. The showers became a special ordeal and the guards took fiendish delight by alternately squirting hot and cold water into the mouths of prisoners.'

31 'Germany "Will Wipe out Jews if . . ." ', *Daily Herald*, 30 November 1938.

Each prisoner was then interrogated and asked for his past political affiliation and occupation. 'They countered usually with strong sarcasm. Thus, if one was a "business man" he was called a "cheat", and if one was a skilled craftsman, such as an electrician, he was called a "liar". We were also photographed and our physical measurements were taken in a room that supposedly was doing racial research. Each prisoner was assigned a number, which we had to just sew on the uniform sleeve with a yellow star.'

Each barrack to which the new arrivals were assigned held a thousand prisoners. 'The barracks became hopelessly over-crowded, as we slept packed like sardines.' The camp rules were severe. There was an eight o'clock curfew, but the barracks were not locked. 'Anyone who would open the door after eight and stepped outside, would be shot immediately. The searchlights were constantly illuminating the barracks at night, and the guards from the machine gun towers would have little difficulty in spotting violators. A few prisoners committed suicide by touching the electrified barbed wire that surrounded the camp.'

The daily routine began at 4.30 in the morning. 'All prisoners had to parade on the Appel Platz (roll call square). The com-mander or his deputy took the roll call, by ordering all prisoners "in protective custody", as we were called, to stand at attention. This charade could take hours, especially if the counting of the prisoners yielded an incorrect result. And the guards would be-come nervous out of fear that a prisoner somehow had managed to escape.' Most of the day was occupied 'by doing military forma-tion drills, double time runs, marching, etc. Some of the older prisoners collapsed and later died, as they could not keep up this rigorous routine.'

After the second week at Dachau the Jewish prisoners were individually ordered to an office 'where we were asked to declare our personal income, bank account, and other assets'. The reason for this was the billion-mark fine imposed on the Jewish community. 'One morning, on roll call square, the order was issued for all millionaires to step forward, and a number of persons complied. Near me stood an elderly banker, presumably a millionaire who defied this order and did not budge. At that moment, one of the guards remembered this banker from the time of registration. He yelled at the man, had him pulled out and beaten severely until he was unconscious.'

After about a month the prisoners were given postcards on which to write home, 'using a prescribed text, that we were well and well treated. Our family should send us money, which we were to use to buy toothpaste and soap at the canteen run by the SS, at exorbitant prices. They also made us subscribe to the official Nazi newspaper, the *Völkischer Beobachter*. At least we learned about some of the news outside, even if much was propaganda.'

The winter was intensely cold. Due to a shortage in the camp stores, some prisoners had not received shirts. 'Some had the idea of stuffing newspapers into their uniform as insulation from the cold,' Walter Loeb remembered. 'This was reported, and the next morning an announcement was made, that anyone caught with newspapers in their uniforms would receive twenty-five lashes.'

What were known in the camp as the 'November' Jews were mostly released during the winter. This, Walter Loeb stressed, 'was the last time that inmates were released from a concentration camp. They had to pledge to leave Germany quickly. When my turn came, I had to take a medical examination. I did not pass, because I had visible frostbite on my hands, and they did not want the outside world to see scars or marks of maltreatments (such as beatings, etc.). They were still sensitive to public and foreign opinion.' Nazi propaganda had told the world that the

German people had 'spontaneously erupted' after the murder of vom Rath, and 'used this as an excuse to bring us to Dachau to protect us from the rage of the German people'.

Helped by the German prisoner in charge of his barrack, who lent him his gloves, Walter Loeb was called for another medical examination a week later. 'This time I passed the physical, and they returned my clothes and belongings. I had spent a total of two months in Dachau.' There was a final talk from the authorities. 'The Commandant told us how lucky we were, that our stay in Dachau was so short, and we were treated well. If we were to tell otherwise on the outside we would be hauled back in no time, never to be released again. And we must leave Germany within ninety days. He also admonished those planning to go to the United States or elsewhere that the same would apply, because the Gestapo has "long arms" (those were his words). I was put on a train back to Karlsruhe and reported to Gestapo headquarters, as ordered. There was a debriefing, and a Gestapo officer repeated the same threats that we heard from the camp commander before leaving.' All three Karlsruhe synagogues had been destroyed on Kristallnacht.

Walter Loeb was finally able to leave Germany for the United States in March 1940. A year later he was drafted into the United States Army, and served two and a half years in the Pacific.[32]

Gary Himler's father was fortunate in Dachau, at least when his name, so similar to that of the SS chief Himmler, seemed to act as a protection. 'Dad always felt that he was treated differently from the rest of the prisoners, with a certain respect, or distance,' his son Gary later recalled. 'As if the guards were not sure if this Himler were there to check up, to report, even to rate them.'

32 Walter Loeb, letter to the author, 11 July 2005.

Towards the end of his three months in Dachau he did experience, however, with the other prisoners, a roll call when 'the whole company was made to stand naked in the freezing weather, and the guards sprayed them with water over and over again'. As a result, he got frostbite all over his body. Shortly afterwards he was allowed to leave: his wife had been able to show the authorities an affidavit from a relative in the United States who would vouch for the whole family if they went to America. 'Dad stuffed wet toilet paper into all his frost wounds so that they would not be visible. The guards did not see them when they inspected him, and he was allowed to leave.'[33]

At Buchenwald and Sachsenhausen the scenes of torment were similar to those at Dachau. A Jew released from Buchenwald wrote of how an older prisoner had been so knocked about by the SS guards that at night, in the shed in which the men slept, 'he kept up a continuous moaning. The brute in charge of this shed hit this man in the face repeatedly, telling him to stop the noise. By morning the old man was dead.'[34]

An estimated 350 of the Jews arrested on Kristallnacht died in Buchenwald that winter.[35] At Buchenwald, Sachsenhausen and Dachau the combined death toll exceeded five thousand, of whom 2,958 were Austrian Jews.[36]

33 Gary Himler, letter to the author, 2 July 2005.
34 'Statement of a Former Prisoner at the Concentration Camp at Buchenwald', communicated to the Foreign Office, 18 February 1939: *Treatment of German Nationals in Germany, 1938–1939*, page 30.
35 Report by F. M. Shepherd, British Consul in Dresden, 2 February 1939: Foreign Office papers, FO 371/23052.
36 Gertrude Schneider, *Exile and Destruction: The Fate of Austrian Jews, 1938–1945*, page 169.

8

Escape and Rescue

On 1 December 1938 the Australian government, whose representative at Evian had adopted a negative stance towards Jewish refugees five months earlier, agreed to take 15,000 refugees over three years, although not specifically Jewish refugees.[1] In 1939 5,000 Jewish refugees were admitted, an almost fourfold increase on the previous year. That same December 1 the first train with German Jewish children on board bound for Britain reached the Hook of Holland. On board were 206 children who had left Germany at twenty-four hours' notice, each with two bags of clothing.[2]

This first children's transport – the Kindertransports as they became known – gave priority to orphans, children of one-parent families, children whose fathers had been taken off to concentration camps after Kristallnacht, and boys who had themselves been threatened with incarceration in concentration camps. Each child had been allowed to bring one small suitcase and ten reichsmarks for their future life in Britain.[3]

From the Hook of Holland the children travelled by boat across

---

1 Paul R. Bartrop, *Australia and the Holocaust, 1933–45*, page 77.
2 *The Times*, 3 December 1938.
3 Archives of the Jewish Museum, London. Ten reichsmarks was the equivalent of £1 in 1938. In the money values of 2006 it was worth £40.

the North Sea to the British port of Harwich, a journey of a hundred miles, reaching British soil at 5.30 in the morning of December 2. Among the children on this first boat was Julius Carlebach, from Hamburg, who celebrated his sixteenth birthday within a month of reaching Britain. After wartime service in the Intelligence Department of the Royal Navy, he was to become a leading British childcare specialist, criminologist and educator.[4]

While the Kindertransport children – known as the Kinder – found sanctuary in Britain, there were fewer permits or funds for the hundreds of thousands of adults, among them Julius Carlebach's father, Hamburg's leading rabbi Dr Joseph Carlebach, who was to perish in a concentration camp near Riga. 'The first effort,' noted the Provincial Council for German Jewry in Hull, 'will be to save the children.'[5] One of those children, fourteen-year-old Felix Rinde, who had been an eye-witness of Kristallnacht in Vienna, remembered: 'I left on the Kindertransport on 10 December 1938 and arrived at Harwich two days later.' In August 1940 he left England for the Dominican Republic, in the Caribbean, where he spent the rest of the war.[6] The Dominican Republic accepted six hundred refugees between 1933 and 1940.

There were strong demands in Britain, including from the Churches and Parliament, for emergency regulations to allow in as many Jews from Germany as possible. On December 8, in a public broadcast launching the Lord Mayor of London's Fund for Jewish refugees reaching Britain, Lord Baldwin, a former Prime Minister, said: 'Thousands of men, women, and children, despoiled of their goods, driven from their homes, are seeking

4 'Professor Julius Carlebach', *Jewish Chronicle* (obituary), 11 May 2001.
5 Hull Committee of the Council for German Jewry. Letter to potential supporters, 7 December 1938: archives of Hull Jewry, Jack Lennard papers.
6 Felix Rinde, letter to the author, 27 June 2005.

asylum and sanctuary on our doorsteps, a hiding place from the wind and a covert from the tempest.' Baldwin added: 'They may not be our fellow subjects, but they are our fellow men. Tonight I plead for the victims who turn to England for help ... Thousands of every degree of education, industry, wealth, position, have been made equal in misery. I shall not attempt to depict to you what it means to be scorned and branded and isolated like a leper. The honour of our country is challenged, our Christian charity is challenged, and it is up to us to meet that challenge ...'[7]

Three days after Lord Baldwin's broadcast, a second Kindertransport reached Britain, the first to leave Vienna. Among those on it was Herbert Friedman, who had witnessed Kristallnacht in Vienna and had so nearly been arrested. The train left Vienna close to midnight, just as he was about to celebrate his fourteenth birthday.

On December 14, six days after Lord Baldwin's appeal, Neville Chamberlain's Cabinet decided to allow a continuing influx of German Jewish children to enter Britain. The only provision was that the Jewish refugee organisations in Britain would guarantee to maintain them.[8] Five thousand were to receive immediate permits. There would be at least another 5,000 in the second wave. Had it not been for the outbreak of war eight months later, and the sealing of Germany's western borders, even more would have made the journey to safety. Eight thousand of the new arrivals were helped by Jewish organisations, principally the Central British Fund, the German Jewish Aid Committee, the Austrian Self-Aid Committee and the Women's International Zionist Organisation (WIZO). A further 2,000 were looked after by the

7 *The Times*, 9 December 1938.
8 Cabinet No. 59 of 1938, London, 14 December 1938, Conclusion 6: Cabinet papers, 23/96.

German and Austrian Committees of the Society of Friends (the Quakers), and the Catholic Committee for Refugees. A coordinating body was set up with the name Movement for the Care of Children from Germany. Later it became known as the Refugee Children's Movement.

A snag had arisen. According to British law, children could not be scattered in private homes all over the country unless each of them had a legal guardian. To ensure legality, Parliament passed the Guardianship (Refugee Children) Act in record time. The Chairman of the Refugee Children's Movement was a Protestant peer of the realm, Lord Gorell, who commented: 'It is simple, unusual – and also truthful – to be able to say that I have had more children, legally, than any man since Solomon.'[9]

No other country made such an effort to take in Jewish children as Britain. Those who were the beneficiaries have never forgotten. 'I left Berlin with one of the famous Kindertransports,' Serem Freier later wrote. 'From the railway journey I have retained a mental picture of a Dutch engine driver frantically polishing his engine levers. In those times, the Dutch were famous for their cleanliness. In the evening when we boarded the ferry for England I think we slept on the benches. In the morning we were offered a breakfast of insipid white bread and bananas. One of the boys of our group confided to me, very knowingly, that this was a typical English breakfast. I imagine he had never heard of bacon and sausage or of ham and eggs. Nor had I. We boarded the train in Dover and when we arrived in London, my father waited at the railway station.'[10]

On December 23, Manfred van Son, whose home in Hamburg

---

9 Quoted in Herbert Agar, *The Saving Remnant*, page 99.
10 Zerem Freier, letter to the author, 19 June 2005.

had been untouched on Kristallnacht because of the apparently aristocratic name of its occupants, reached London and safety. Five days later, Anne Lehmann, a twelve-year-old girl from Berlin, left Hamburg for Britain with a large group of German Jewish children. She later wrote: 'Foster homes were found – both Jewish and Gentile – hostels were opened, boarding schools contacted, and established summer camp facilities were readied to receive these children. It was a tremendous undertaking, and all of us owe our lives to this venture.'[11]

Anne Lehmann's parents did not survive the war. Her father Eugen, who had lost an arm fighting for Germany on the Western Front in the First World War, was to die in the Theresienstadt ghetto. Her mother Marta was deported from Theresienstadt to Auschwitz a few months later, and did not survive. The kindness of a non-Jewish English couple, Mary and Jim Mansfield, and their family lightened the burden of Anne's life as a wartime evacuee from London, in the village of Swineshead.[12]

Robert Smallbones, the British Consul General in Frankfurt, was uneasy at the restrictive implications of the Kindertransport. 'As far as it is possible to mitigate the plight of the Jews in Germany,' he wrote to the British Embassy in Berlin on December 14, 'I venture to think that the policy indicated at present is not "women and children first", but men first; they are in the concentration camps and in imminent danger of death, and they are the poten-

11 Anne L. Fox, *My Heart in a Suitcase*, page 43.
12 Anne Fox (*née* Lehmann) later published, with another Kindertransport child, Eva Abraham-Podietz, a book for children, *Ten Thousand Children: True Stories Told by Children who Escaped the Holocaust on the Kindertransport*, West Orange, New Jersey: Berman House, 1999. The book was based on testimony of former Kindertransport children at the Oral History Archives of Gratz College, Philadelphia.

tial bread-winners. If they die the problem of dealing with their families will be all the more formidable. I gather that some of the Quakers wish to put up an organisation in Germany to feed and clothe non-Aryans, and that they contemplate gradual evacuation spread over a number of years. Unless the German government agrees to such a scheme it is difficult to calculate what percentage of these people will survive their enforced stay in Germany.' Smallbones added that 'it might be useful' to bring the facts of current German persecution of the Jews to the notice of those governments outside Germany 'which contemplate doing something towards the solution of this problem'.[13]

The emigration of German Jews to Britain continued throughout December. Four-year-old Felix Seiler, from Vienna, crossed the North Sea with his family. His father was one of fifty Austrian doctors given special entry permits. 'I remember the scene at the railway station. I could not understand why everyone was crying. After all, was this not the most wonderful adventure?'[14]

Elsa Blatt was not quite nineteen when she witnessed Kristallnacht in Mainz, where her thirty-one-year-old brother Herman was so severely beaten up that he was hospitalised. She later recalled her family's struggle to leave Germany. It began when her father was released from Buchenwald. 'He had lost a lot of weight, his head was shaven and he had no coat or jacket on. He had left them behind so that others who needed them could use them. When we asked him where he was or what happened he told us that he would not tell us anything unless we were out of the country. He had been warned that if he told a single word about

---

13 Enclosure No. 8, Command Paper 6120, Germany No. 2 (1939), *Papers Concerning the Treatment of German Nationals in Germany, 1938–1939.* London: His Majesty's Stationery Office, 1939, pages 20–4.
14 Felix Seiler, letter to the author, 6 June 2005.

what he saw we would all be taken back to the camp.' The family priority was to secure a visa 'to get my brother out of the country. Some friends sent us a letter from the Consulate of the Dominican Republic in France saying that if he would get there they would give him a visa.'

The family had to find a time when Herman Blatt would not be seen when he left the hospital and took a train to France. 'We decided that on Christmas Eve when everyone would be celebrating their peace on earth they would be too busy to bother about this Jew. We did not want him to take any money because we were afraid he might be stopped. My father took off his wedding ring and gave it to him, saying, "I know I am married, you sell it in France so that you have a few pennies." I brought my brother that evening to the train. We waited all night at the phone till we got a collect call from France. He had made it. Soon after, I got a nursing visa to go to Britain ... My parents were able to smuggle themselves to Belgium. Soon after, my sister also arrived in Belgium with a broken ankle, which she suffered during the smuggling.'[15] Later all three made their way across the Pyrenees to Portugal.

On December 21 the British Crown Colony of Northern Rhodesia, which had given haven to more than two hundred Jewish refugees, closed its doors to any more. That day the Governor, Sir John Maybin, wrote to the Colonial Secretary in London that he had instructed the colony's Chief Immigration Officer 'not to reply to any further inquiries on behalf of German Jewish refugees'.[16]

*   *   *

15 Elsa Kissel (née Blatt), letter to the author, 18 July 2005.
16 Letter of 21 December 1939: Frank Shapiro, *Haven in Africa*, page 68.

1. Polish-born Jews at Zbaszyn railway station, late October 1938.

2. *Right* Herschel Grynszpan, whose parents and sister were deported from Hanover to Zbaszyn. In Paris on 6 November 1938 he carried out a terrible act of revenge.

3. The synagogue in Baden Baden burns on Kristallnacht.

4. The furnishings of a looted synagogue being taken away by truck.

5. *Above* Local residents pass a Jewish shop window in Berlin, 10 November 1938.

6. *Left* Jewish shop-owners sweep up broken glass.

7. Jewish men being marched through Regensburg after Kristallnacht. The slogan reads: 'The removal of the Jews'.

8. A snapshot of Jewish men being taken from Regensburg to Dachau by truck after Kristallnacht.

9. Registration of Jewish prisoners at Dachau after Kristallnacht.

10. Roll call of Jewish prisoners at Buchenwald after Kristallnacht.

11. The first Kindertransport: German Jewish boys on the train from Berlin to the Hook of Holland, en route to Britain, 1 December 1939.

12. Chava Reichnitz (later Chava Cohn): a photograph taken when she was fifteen, shortly before she left Berlin for Britain, 1 December 1939.

13. Inge Neuberger (later Janet Ettelman): a passport photograph taken when she was ten, shortly before she left Germany for the United States in March 1940.

14. *Left* Adina Koor from Mannheim, a month and a half after her arrival in Britain, on the day of her evacuation from London. Her gas mask is in a box hanging around her neck.

15. *Above* Miriam Walk (later Miriam Spira) from Berlin, in London during the Second World War at Nurses' Training School, St Mary's Hospital, Paddington.

16. The last deportation from Regensburg, 2 April 1942. All the men, women and children lined up here were deported to the death camp at Belzec. There were no survivors.

17. *Left* Theresienstadt, late summer 1944: a frame from a Nazi film aimed at portraying Theresienstadt as a model ghetto. When the film was completed, those who had appeared in it were deported to Auschwitz.

18. German and Austrian Jews in the Hongkew district of Shanghai; a photograph taken in 1940. In 1942 the area was turned into a ghetto by the Japanese.

19. Else Wachsner's tombstone, Shanghai. She and her husband left Breslau in 1939. She died in Shanghai during the war. Her tombstone was among hundreds thrown out of the cemetery during the Cultural Revolution. It was recovered in 2002, in a village twelve miles from Shanghai.

The year 1939 opened with more children arriving in Britain. On January 3, Ruth Herskovits, who had witnessed Kristallnacht in Hanover, and her twin sister Eva were taken by their parents to Hanover railway station, where they boarded a children's transport from Berlin. 'This was nothing like the vacation trips we used to take with our parents,' she remembered. 'The railroad station had lost its air of pleasurable anticipation. It was merely grimy and deserted that morning.'[17]

Among those who showed goodwill and breadth of spirit in Britain were two teachers in the West of England, James and Kathleen Crossfield. They took in Pauline Makowski, a ten-year-old Jewish girl from Stuttgart. 'I was fostered by a Christian family from 16 January 1939 until I left their home in 1947 to train as a nurse,' she writes. 'Their home was always regarded as my home and their children still regard me as their sister. They were exceptional people and their generosity of spirit should be acknowledged.'[18] Pauline's parents did not survive the war: in her words, they were 'part of the lost six million'.[19]

Richard Attenborough was fifteen years old when his mother travelled to London from their home in Leicester to bring back with her two Jewish girls, Irene, aged twelve, and Helga, nine. Attenborough later reflected: 'My parents' generosity represents only one of many acts of kindness of the British people in those dark days.' He added: 'My parents' attitude to life was always that there is such a thing as "society", and that it involves obligations of concern, tolerance and compassion for those less fortunate than we are. But taking Helga and Irene into our family as sisters

---

17 Ruth Gutmann (*née* Herskovits), letter to the author, 28 June 2005.
18 Pauline Worner (*née* Makowski), letter to the author, 7 March 2002.
19 Pauline Worner, letter to the author, 19 February 2002.

wasn't theory. It was first-hand experience. These were human beings whom we came to love.'[20]

Reiner Auman and his older brother George, both of whom had witnessed Kristallnacht in Frankfurt-on-Main, spent many weeks acquiring the documents needed for emigration. Their father had been released from Buchenwald after four weeks. When he came back to Frankfurt, Reiner Auman remembered, 'he was like a changed person. He was now fearful, defensive and confused. While emigration had hitherto been haphazardly talked about, he had to face the fact that it would have to happen quickly. The seriousness of the situation had sunk in on him, and he seemed overwhelmed.'

The sixteen-and-a-half-year-old Reiner felt, in those few weeks, transformed 'from a typical teenager to a grown-up, decisive and energetic young man'. On January 15 he and his brother, equipped with German passports and British visas, left Germany for Britain. Their parents followed in August 1939, on the eve of war. George later served with distinction in the United States Army both in the invasion of German-dominated Europe and in the liberation of the concentration camps. Reiner fought in the Pacific, at Okinawa.[21]

Also that January, Lutz Wachsner, the partner in a textile firm who had been with his family in Breslau on Kristallnacht, saw his plans for emigration begin to come to fruition when his older son Frank left for the Far East from Hamburg on a Danish ship.

20 Lord Attenborough, Preface to Mark Jonathan Harris and Deborah Oppenheimer, *Into the Arms of Strangers: Stories of the Kindertransport*, page xii. Deborah Oppenheimer, whose mother came to England on the Kindertransport, produced a feature-length documentary film on the Kindertransport, issued by Warner Brothers Pictures in 2000. It won an Academy Award.
21 Reiner Auman, letter to the author, 2 August 2005.

His younger son Egon was eligible, at the age of fifteen, to go to England on a Kindertransport, and did so that spring, later serving in the British Army. Lutz Wachsner and his wife Else left for Shanghai later that summer. Else Wachsner, who was not well, died in Shanghai: her tombstone, damaged but readable, survived the ravages of the Chinese Cultural Revolution. Only Lutz Wachsner's elderly mother, Rosa, remained in Germany; she was later to be deported to Theresienstadt and did not survive the war.[22]

On January 15 two groups of German Jewish refugees reached Shanghai. Two hundred of them arrived by boat via the Suez Canal. Forty-four arrived by train via the Trans-Siberian and Trans-Manchurian railways, many becoming ill 'from the severe cold'.[23] They were the fortunate ones. On January 30 the Canadian Prime Minister, William Mackenzie King, told the Parliament in Ottawa 'that Canada would not throw her doors wide open to political refugees, but would deal with special cases on their merits'. A Jewish Member of Parliament, the Labour leader Abraham Heaps, protested.[24] Canada had already taken 6,000 German Jewish refugees since 1933, but pressure, especially from the Province of Quebec, prevented the numbers being higher.

Czechoslovakia had given sanctuary to 25,000 Jewish refugees from Germany and Austria, but how long it could preserve its own territorial integrity, having lost the Sudetenland to Germany, was a matter of much debate.

*   *   *

22 Frank Wachsner, letter to the author, 11 September 2005.
23 '244 More Reich Jews Arrive at Shanghai', *New York Times*, 16 January 1939.
24 'Ottawa Cautious on Refugee Issue', *New York Times*, 30 January 1939.

Speaking in Berlin on January 30, Hitler declared publicly that in the event of war, 'The result will not be the Bolshevisation of the earth, and thus the victory of Jewry, but the annihilation of the Jewish race in Europe.'[25] Six days before Hitler's speech, Field Marshal Goering had secretly instructed Reinhard Heydrich, deputy head of the SS and Gestapo, to 'solve' the so-called Jewish problem 'by emigration and evacuation'.[26] Heydrich did his utmost to accelerate the departure of Jews from Germany and Austria. His aim was to stimulate the 'mass exodus' of German Jewry. In this he succeeded. Emigration figures for 1938 from the Altreich (Germany, without Austria) were 40,000. For the first nine months of 1939 they rose to 78,000.

As 1939 began, those seeking to emigrate continued their searches for visas. The problem was not on the part of Germany, for whom Jewish emigration was an imperative, but on the part of the nations reluctant to take in the immigrants. In Berlin, Captain Foley opposed British government pressure against continuing Jewish emigration to Shanghai. 'It might be considered humane on our part not to interfere officially to prevent the Jews from choosing their own graveyards,' he wrote to his superiors. 'They would rather die as free men in Shanghai than slaves in Dachau.'[27]

In England, a disused army camp at Richborough in Kent was opened in February for adult arrivals from Germany. It could hold 3,000 people at a time. Individual visas were not required by those who arrived: only a single collective permit. Within twelve months, 8,000 Jews had passed through this camp to homes

25 Norman H. Baynes (editor), *The Speeches of Adolf Hitler, April 1922–August 1939*, Volume 1, page 741.
26 Quoted by Goering in his letter to Heydrich of 31 July 1941: International Military Tribunal, Nuremberg, Document PS–710.
27 Captain Foley to Sir George Ogilvie Forbes, 17 January 1939: Foreign Office papers, FO 371/24079.

in Britain, most of them young men who had been sent to Dachau, Sachsenhausen and other concentration camps after Kristallnacht, and had later been released.[28]

On February 2 another Kindertransport left Germany. 'My mother took me to the station,' recalled fourteen-year-old Laurie Lowenthal, who had been in Aschaffenburg during Kristallnacht, 'and, as the train slowly pulled out, my mother became smaller and smaller. I never saw my parents again.'[29] On February 19, in Vienna's Western Station, two third-class railway carriages were attached to the Hook of Holland Express. In them were 130 Jewish boys and girls for whom temporary homes had been arranged in Britain by the Quakers.[30] The children reached Britain safely two days later.

Among those German Jewish youngsters who travelled to Britain on a Kindertransport early in 1939 was Eric Lucas, who on Kristallnacht had watched in horror the destruction of the synagogue in the village of Hoengen. 'It was a cold, dark February morning,' he later wrote of his departure. 'The train which was to carry me to safety waited on the platform. I had hoped that in a few days, that train would carry my sister, and perhaps in a few months, my parents, to safety. When I was at last allowed to board the train, I rushed to the window to look for my parents, whom I could not see until I had left the customs shed. They stood there, in the distance, but they did not come to the train. I waved timidly, and yet full of fear, after the control I had just passed; but even that was too much. A man in a black uniform rushed

28 Judith Tydor-Baumel, 'The Kitchener Transmigration Camp at Richborough', in Livia Rothkirchen (editor), *Yad Vashem Studies, XIV*, pages 233–46.
29 Laurie Lowenthal, 'My Childhood in Germany', sent to the author 4 June 2005.
30 'Children Leave Vienna', *New York Times*, 20 February 1939.

towards me. "You Jewish swine – one more sign or word from you and we shall keep you here. You have passed the customs." And so I stood at the window of the train. In the distance stood a silent and ageing couple, to whom I dared neither speak nor wave a last farewell; but I could see their faces very distinctly in the light of the oncoming morning.'

Lucas remembered how, a few hours previously, 'first my father and then my mother had laid their hands gently on my bowed head to bless me . . . Standing at the window of the train, I was suddenly overcome with a maiming certainty that I would never see my father and mother again. There they stood, lonely, and with the sadness of death. Cruel hands kept us apart in that last intimate moment. A passionate, rebellious cry stuck in my throat against all that senseless brutality and inhuman cruelty. Why, O God, had it all to be like that?'

Like so many Kinder, Lucas never forgot that terrible, final moment. 'There stood my father and my mother. An old man, leaning heavily on his stick and holding his wife's hand. It was the first and the last time in my life that I had seen them both weep. Now and then my mother would stretch her hand out, as if to grasp mine – but the hand fell back, knowing it could never reach. Can the world ever justify the pain that burned in my father's eyes? My father's eyes were gentle and soft, but filled with tears of loneliness and fear. They were the eyes of a child that seeks the kindness of its mother's face, and the protection of its father. As the train pulled out of the station to wheel me to safety, I leant my face against the cold glass of the window, and wept bitterly. Those who have crossed the Channel, escaping from fear of death to safety, can understand what it means to wait for those who are still beyond it, longing to cross it, but who will never reach these white cliffs, towering over the water.'

A month after his arrival in Britain, Eric Lucas was trying to find a foreign embassy in London willing to give his parents a visa for some distant destination.

'Have you sufficient money for your parents to live there without working?'

'A small sum could be got together.'

'Have your parents a valid passport?'

'No, because they can only apply for a passport to leave the country if they have a visa and permission to proceed to the country to which they want to go.'

'Yes, I see, but they cannot get a visa until they have a valid passport.'

'Months passed,' Lucas noted, 'and hope vanished.' Unable to obtain the necessary papers and permits, the teenage Lucas was distraught. His parents perished three years later.[31]

At the Austrian–Swiss border, where hundreds of Jews were trying to cross each day to escape Nazi rule, the compassionate Swiss police officer Paul Grüninger was again in trouble. On February 11 the Swiss police chief wrote to Grüninger's immediate superior: 'You have assured me that the responsibility for immigrant control will be taken away from Police Captain Grüninger . . . Nevertheless, it appears that this civil servant and officer sanctioned or even provoked illegal immigrations off his own bat.'[32]

Grüninger was suspended from his duties on April 3. Two days later he wrote in defence of his actions: 'I am going to explain why, in one single case, I offended against the instructions of the department. I acted as a human being and an officer out of

31 Eric Lucas, manuscript, 'The Sovereigns', pages 187–90.
32 Meir Wagner, *The Righteous of Switzerland*, page 39.

commendable motives. One of the most valuable rights of sovereignty is the right of asylum.' Switzerland always honoured this. 'During our entire history we have opened our doors in a liberal manner to political refugees, not because of sympathy for their person or their ideology, but on purely humanitarian grounds.'[33]

Grüninger was fined for breaching the regulations, and then dismissed from the police force.

Charlotte Neumann's father Yehuda had been taken from Würzburg to Dachau after Kristallnacht. In the First World War, while serving in the German army, he was wounded, contracted tuberculosis, and was taken prisoner by the Russians. After seven weeks in Dachau he was a broken man.

Helped by Robert Smallbones, the British Consul General in Frankfurt, Yehuda Neumann's daughter received a visa to go to Britain as a household help. On February 17, after three months 'dealing with chicanery and harassment', she received her German passport. Ten days later she left by train for England, to work in the northern city of Salford. Her parents were later deported from Würzburg to Auschwitz. They did not survive the war. Nor did her younger brother Itzhak Yona, then aged seventeen, who died during the war at Majdanek concentration camp, in German-occupied Poland.[34]

On February 23, in a further turn of the screw, Goering announced in Berlin that all German Jews must, within two weeks, surrender 'all jewels and other objects of gold, silver or platinum as well as all diamonds, pearls and other precious stones'. Silver knives,

---

33 Meir Wagner, *The Righteous of Switzerland*, page 42.
34 Charlotte Lapian (*née* Neumann), letter to the author, 17 August 2005.

forks and spoons must also be given up. Local public pawnshops would offer 'compensation'. Not to comply would result in a fine, or imprisonment with hard labour for up to ten years.[35]

Two days later, on February 25, as Goering's harsh decree was being implemented, the Gestapo ordered the Jewish community in Berlin to produce each day the names of a hundred Jews – 3,000 a month – who would then be obliged to leave Germany within two weeks of their names being put forward. This was exactly the number of emigration permits that the whole German Jewish community was able to obtain from foreign countries. But those 3,000 permits had also to include Jews from Vienna, Breslau, Frankfurt, Stuttgart, Dresden, Cologne and Hamburg, the main centres from which emigration was being organised.

Distressing news reached the Jews of Germany on February 25. In Montevideo, the government of Uruguay had refused entry to sixty-eight German Jewish refugees on board the Italian liner *Conte Grande*. Argentina also refused them entry. And in Georgetown, British Guiana, 165 German Jewish refugees who had arrived on a German ship, the *Koenigstein*, were refused permission to land. In Budapest, a Hungarian Foreign Office official stated that no German Jews forced from Germany by the newly announced policy of daily expulsions would be allowed into Hungary.[36] Three days later, Argentina refused to allow another group of German Jews to land, twenty-eight in all, who had reached Buenos Aires from Hamburg on board the German liner *General San Martin*. They had to return to Germany.[37]

In Hamburg, the chocolate manufacturer Josef Gold had been arrested a few months after Kristallnacht and sent to prison for

---

35 'Reich Orders Jews to Cede Valuables', *New York Times*, 24 February 1939.
36 '100 Jews Each Day Must Leave Reich', *New York Times*, 26 February 1939.
37 '68 Jews Forced Back', *New York Times*, 1 March 1939.

his involvement in socialist politics and anti-Nazi activities. Two years earlier he had fought in Spain on the Republican side. Released from prison, he stowed away on a Swedish ship in Hamburg and landed in New York. He had no immigrant visa. Held on Ellis Island, he was deported back to Germany on a German ship.

On landing in Hamburg, Josef Gold was sent back to prison. Later he had to work as a forced labourer – building the Hamburg U-boat bunkers – until he was sent to Theresienstadt with most of the remaining Hamburg Jews. Subsequently deported to Auschwitz, Mauthausen and Ebensee, he survived the war. His young son Edgar survived the war in the village of Reinfeld, in hiding with German friends of his family. His mother was sent to a slave labour camp near Stuttgart. She too survived.[38]

The search for havens of refuge was continuous. On March 1, Chile accepted the sixty-eight refugees on board the *Conte Grande* who had been rejected by both Uruguay and Argentina.[39] That day, Guatemala said it would take in any Jews who already had relatives there, on condition 'that they engage in agriculture and refrain from business'. In 1938, on that basis, Guatemala had given refuge to 232 Jews.[40]

On March 4 the local German police in the Free City of Danzig supervised the emigration of five hundred Jews within a few hours. Starting at 3.30 in the morning, while it was still dark, the men, women and children were ordered to the quayside. The British Consul General, Gerald Shepherd, saw them 'with heavy rucksacks, bundles and small hand luggage' as they arrived. From

38 Edgar Gold, letter to the author, 9 September 2005.
39 '68 Get Haven in Chile', *New York Times*, 2 March 1939.
40 'Guatemala Limits Entry', *New York Times*, 2 March 1939.

the quayside, starting at 4.30 a.m., they were taken off in trucks.[41] Their destination was the main railway station, from where they began the long train journey southward through Central Europe to the Romanian Black Sea port of Constantsa, where they took ship to Palestine.

During March and April, four trains left Danzig for Berlin with a total of 124 Jewish children. From Berlin the children went on by train to the Hook of Holland, where they joined the Kindertransport to cross the North Sea to Harwich. On March 24, on board the German liner *Deutschland*, 125 German Jewish refugees reached New York, and with their valid permits were allowed entry. Also on board was Dr Julius Dorpmueller, Vice-President of the German State Railways, who had come 'to study American railway operations'.[42] Within three years, as Director General of the German State Railways, Dr Dorpmueller was to be a central figure in the mass deportation of Jews – including more than 150,000 German Jews – by rail, to the death camps and mass murder sites.

A week later, on April 1, Esther Ascher, who had witnessed Kristallnacht in Breslau, left her home town by train for Berlin, Munich and south through Italy to Trieste. There she took ship for Haifa, the fortunate holder of a Palestine Certificate for Youth Aliyah – young Zionist immigration.[43]

Some avenues of hope were closed before they could open. In January 1939 Winston Churchill, who was then without political office but still a Member of Parliament, had met an Albanian diplomat, Chatin Sarachi, a member of one of Albania's leading

41 Letter of 6 March 1939: Foreign Office papers, FO 371/24085,
42 '125 German Refugees Arrive', *New York Times*, 25 March 1939.
43 Esther Adler (*née* Ascher), conversation with the author, 7 August 2005.

Roman Catholic families. For the previous five years, Sarachi had been First Secretary at the Albanian Embassy in London. Churchill raised with him the possibility of allowing German and Austrian Jews to enter Albania. Six weeks later, after returning to Albania, Sarachi wrote to Churchill that he had been 'authorised to negotiate in case the question still exists'.[44] Sarachi's hopeful letter was written on March 13. Within six weeks, Mussolini had invaded and conquered Albania, ending its independence and the possibility of any such rescue scheme.

To help Jewish children in Czechoslovakia, the Children's Section of the British Committee for Refugees from Czechoslovakia had been formed immediately after the German annexation of the Sudetenland. Although these children were not then in danger, it was felt that their situation inside independent Czechoslovakia was precarious enough to warrant a rescue effort. Some were refugees from the Sudetenland. Many were orphans. In mid-October 1938 the Children's Section had set up an office in Prague, headed by a British woman, Doreen Warriner. On December 20 a master from Westminster School, Martin Blake, travelled to Prague to help her. He persuaded a twenty-nine-year-old stockbroker, Nicholas Winton, the Christian scion of a distinguished German Jewish family, to go with him.

Winton returned to Britain at the end of January 1939 to take charge of the London office. On March 7 a British schoolteacher, Trevor Chadwick, flew to Prague to expedite the rescue efforts; a week later, on March 14, he accompanied the first group of Jewish children, twenty in all, to Britain, by air. 'They were all cheerfully sick,' he later recalled, being enticed by the little paper bags,

---

44 Chatin Sarachi to Winston S. Churchill, 13 March 1939: Foreign Office papers, FO 371/24081.

'except a baby of one who slept peacefully in my lap the whole time.'[45] On the following day, German forces entered Prague.

Czechoslovakia's independence had been guaranteed by Britain, France, Italy and Germany at the Munich Conference six months earlier. But on March 15, as German troops overran the country and raised the swastika flag in the capital, Britain and France took no action. Slovakia declared its independence. The Czechoslovak provinces of Bohemia and Moravia became a German Protectorate, and that night Hitler entered Prague as a conqueror. In Prague lived 56,000 Jews, of whom 25,000 were refugees from Germany, Austria and the Sudetenland provinces of Czechoslovakia. Some of Prague's Jews were able to flee northwards to Poland, or southwards to Hungary. Others went to France, a few to Britain. A few, in desperation, flew to Britain without permits. They were put on the next day's plane back to Prague.

On March 16, the day after the German occupation of Prague, several hundred German Jewish children and adults reached Harwich from the Hook of Holland. One of the children was Susanne Hatschek, who had been in Vienna during Kristallnacht. She and her parents were given a place to live by Earl de la Warr and his wife Diana at Fisher's Gate, Withyham, in Sussex. Also on the March 16 boat were twelve Jewish children who went to a hostel that had just been opened in Highgate, North London, by a prominent paediatrician, Dr Bernard Schlesinger, and his wife Winifred. The Schlesingers already had five refugee children living in their own home. It had taken them several months to get permission to use the Highgate house as a hostel. In addition to the children, they obtained emigration permits for four German

---

45 Quoted in Barry Turner, . . . *And the Policeman Smiled: 10,000 Children Escape from Nazi Europe*, page 93.

Jewish adults: a matron and three young women to take care of the children. Most of the children came from Berlin and Leipzig, the matron from Liegnitz.[46] The synagogue in Liegnitz was among those destroyed on Kristallnacht.

Reaching Prague within a few days of the German occupation was Adolf Eichmann, who had been put in charge of Jewish emigration from the Protectorate, as earlier he had been in charge of emigration from Austria. Eichmann's orders were to carry out Heydrich's instructions, via Goering, to accelerate Jewish emigration. In the six months that were to be at his disposal before the outbreak of war, Eichmann secured the emigration of 30,000 Jews: Czech Jews, and German, Austrian and Sudeten Jews who had found refuge in Prague.

Among those in Britain who took immediate action to try to help the Jews of Prague was a non-Jew, Robert Auty, who had earlier made several journeys to Germany to try to help Jews leave. He took the first night train possible to the newly occupied Czech capital. A friend wrote: 'I myself got to know about Robert Auty's activities some years ago, by chance, through meeting somebody whose parents had been saved by him.' Being 'such a modest man', Auty had asked his friend 'not to tell anybody else'.[47]

The Hook of Holland to Harwich boats continued to bring their human cargo of children from fear to safety. At the Jawne Jewish school in Cologne, the head teacher, Dr Erich Klibansky,

---

46 Ilse Eden and Ilse Henry, 'The Schlesingers' Hostel at 26 Shepherd's Hill, London N6, March–September 1939'.
47 Professor Richard Griffiths, letter to the author, 20 November 1978. Professor Griffiths had just written the obituary of Auty in the *Jewish Chronicle*.

arranged for four groups of his pupils to be transferred to British schools. One of those pupils, Rolf Schild, was later a successful British medical engineer and healthcare pioneer. His parents, and Dr Klibansky, were among those Cologne Jews later deported to their deaths.[48] Among those on the boat that docked in Harwich on March 18 was Ernst Gerstenfeld, the young Viennese Jew who had been taken to Dachau after Kristallnacht.

The actions of those in Britain who opened their homes to Jewish youngsters made a strong impression on those they welcomed. Margit Diamond wrote of the woman with whom she was lodged in Britain: 'When I arrived in England from Berlin as an eleven-year-old Kindertransport child in May 1939, it was Miss Elsie M. Lobb, Headmistress of Trinity Hall School for Girls – All Methodist ministers' daughters – who took me in. This excellent boarding school was located in Southport, Lancashire, and since I was an "Enemy Alien", Miss Lobb had to make special arrangements for me to be there lest, in the event of a German invasion by sea, I should aid the enemy!'

Margit Diamond remembered that at Trinity Hall 'we went to church twice every Sunday and also had Sunday School. When I demonstrated reluctance at having to kneel in church, this dear lady called me into her office and said most kindly: "Margit, children can be quite cruel if they think you're very different from them. Going to church and Sunday School will never make you Methodist – you will always be Jewish" – and she made arrangements for the local rabbi to come and visit me regularly several times a month! NEVER, at any time, was any attempt made to convert me!' Margit Diamond added that one of her deepest regrets was that Miss Lobb died 'before I was in a position to

48 Rolf Schild, OBE, obituary, *Jewish Chronicle*, 2 May 2003.

repay in some small measure (I could NEVER actually repay what she did for me, of course) what she had done for me'.[49]

Otto Hutter was one of two Jewish refugee boys from Germany who were given a place at Bishop's Stortford School in Hertfordshire. The Old Boys of the school raised the money needed for their schooling. In a special appeal letter, J. F. Attenborough, the President of the Old Stortfordian Club, had written: 'From one country after another in Europe today men and women, who have been guilty of no offence, are being driven out as penniless refugees. To their distress none of us can be indifferent, but few of us can, out of our own resources, offer any effective assistance. What, then, can Stortford do?'[50]

Finding this letter sixty-one years after the school had given him a place, Otto Hutter wrote: 'It may serve as a fine example of how compassionate people in England joined together in those dark days "to make a lasting contribution", in this case by affording two refugee boys a fine education. True, the cry "What, then, can Stortford do?" did not reverberate across the country, but for that it is surely the more worthy of record.'[51]

Leaving Berlin on May 10 and reaching the British port of Liverpool the following day, Chava Rechnitz – with her memories of Kristallnacht in both Berlin and Ratibor – recalled 'sitting with maybe eighty other children in a large hall, and being amongst the last ones claimed by my foster parents'. These were Captain and Mrs Edwards, of Wheldrake, Yorkshire. For a year she looked after their two-year-old-daughter, until, on 26 May 1940, she left

49 Margit A. Diamond, letter to the author, 2 May 2001.
50 Printed circular letter, headed 'Old Stortfordians' Club', dated 22 February 1939.
51 Professor Otto Hutter, letter to the author, 17 February 2000.

Britain on a Japanese ship bound for Shanghai, which she reached, via the Cape of Good Hope, almost three months later. Her exit permit was stamped 'No return to United Kingdom'.[52]

The British government was afraid, one Cabinet Minister, Lord Winterton, told a deputation of German Jews on May 18, that there were limits, occasioned by 'anti-Semitism and anti-alienism' beyond which 'it was dangerous to go' in taking in Jewish refugees.[53] Nevertheless, the effort was made. Stoatley Rough School, which had been started for German Jewish refugees in 1934, received 150 letters a week from Germany seeking places. As a result of the school's efforts after March 1939, thirty to forty children arrived before the outbreak of war made it impossible for any more to leave Germany for Britain. The bureaucracy could be complex, stifling and frustrating. 'In one case,' wrote the historians of the school, 'they were desperately trying to get out a young girl, which resulted in correspondence between New York, Stuttgart, Stoatley Rough and London, and comprises thirty-two letters. The girl never made it to Britain.'[54]

Following the German occupation of Prague in March 1939, the Children's Section of the British Committee for Refugees from Czechoslovakia had redoubled its efforts. Trevor Chadwick, returning to Prague, worked extraordinarily hard to collect the children and send them to Britain by train. When it emerged that some of the children did not have the proper travel documents, he provided counterfeit papers, and persuaded the German authorities to allow the children to continue to Britain.[55]

---

52 Chava Cohn (*née* Rechnitz), letter to the author, 4 July 2005.
53 Deputation of 18 May 1939: Foreign Office papers, FO 371/24983.
54 Katherine Whitaker and Michael Johnson, *Stoatley Rough School, 1934–1960*.
55 Archives of the Jewish Museum, London.

Chadwick's office in Prague, helped by the Children's Section in London headed by Nicholas Winton, brought a total of 654 children from German-occupied Prague to Britain, in eight separate journeys. The first group after the occupation left Prague on April 19, with thirty-six children.[56] Some children were able to travel privately. Fourteen-year-old Rudolph Wessely's father was, until the German occupation, the Secretary of the Prague Produce Exchange, and a judge at the Arbitration Court. On March 21 he appealed to friends in Britain to guarantee his son, who was found a home in Britain, arriving in London on July 1. But despite the offers of the judge and his wife 'to do any work' in Britain, even to take domestic posts despite their 'former social standing', no places could be found for them.[57]

On April 15, Hannelore Heinemann, then just three years old – whose father and grandfather had been saved from possible deportation to concentration camp after Kristallnacht by the non-Jewish caretaker of their Berlin apartment – boarded ship at Genoa with her parents for the voyage to Shanghai. That same day, in New York, five hundred German Jewish refugees disembarked from the ocean liner *Washington*. In Europe, Holland, France, Belgium, Luxembourg, Sweden, Finland, Norway and Denmark continued to accept Jewish refugees from Germany. During May, 3,000 German and Austrian Jewish refugees reached Shanghai, more than doubling the number already there. But places of refuge became fewer with each month. Anti-Jewish legislation was also spreading in Europe. On May 3 a Hungarian law forbade any Hungarian Jew from becoming a judge, a lawyer, a

---

56 'Appendix', Muriel Emanuel and Vera Gissing, *Nicholas Winton and the Rescued Generation*, page 127.

57 Letters of 11 March 1939 and 13 May 1939: archives of the Hull Committee of the Council for German Jewry: Jack Lennard papers.

schoolteacher or a member of the Hungarian Parliament. The Republic of Ireland set its face against admitting Jewish refugees, even rejecting a Vatican request for the entry of a small number of German doctors who were Jewish converts to Catholicism.[58]

In Aachen that May, Vera Dahl's brother Rudi celebrated his Barmitzvah. The ceremony, marking his thirteenth birthday and reaching manhood, was held in a small prayer room across the courtyard from the burned-out synagogue. 'There were charred pieces of prayer books blowing all over the place,' Vera Dahl remembered. 'The service was terribly sad for poor Rudi, who did his part very well ... Afterwards we all walked home very quietly – the important thing was not to be seen "congregating" or "celebrating", and of course no one wore anything new. The gentlemen had always worn top hats to synagogue, but that was of course no longer done.'[59]

A week later Vera Dahl left for Britain, having received a permit as a domestic servant. During the Blitz she worked at the Whittington Hospital in London. Her brother Rudi and her parents Adolf and Olga were deported from Aachen in 1942 on one of the transports to the East, almost certainly to the death camp at Belzec. Two of her mother's six brothers had been killed in action fighting for Germany in the First World War.

Would-be refugees, scanning the newspapers, were tossed between hope and despair. On May 16 the Colombian government announced that no more Jewish refugees would be admitted,

58 Dermot Keogh, 'The Irish Free State and the Refugee Crisis, 1933–45', in Paul R. Bartrop (editor), *False Havens: The British Empire and the Holocaust*.
59 Vera Bier (*née* Dahl), recollections set down on 12 November 1988; sent to the author by her son David Bier, 1 September 2005.

pending agreement on a 'definite, comprehensive immigration policy'. Even the 1,500 applications from Jews who had parents, wives or children already in Colombia would be put in abeyance.[60] On the following day, May 17, the British government issued its 1939 Palestine White Paper, fixing an upper limit of 20,000 Jews a year to be admitted to Palestine over the next five years. Of these, 5,000 a year could be refugees.

With more than 250,000 Jews still trapped in Greater Germany, the Palestine White Paper was an even more severe curb on immigration than the United States' quota system of 27,000 a year. A British Member of Parliament, Alfred Duff Cooper, who had earlier resigned from the government in protest at the Munich Agreement, spoke against the new restrictions, telling his fellow parliamentarians: 'It is the strong arm of the British Empire that has opened the door to them when all other doors are shut. Shall we now replace that hope – that we have revived – by despair, and shall we slam the door in the face of the long-wandering Jew?'[61]

To enforce the new restrictions the British government put diplomatic pressure on the governments of Yugoslavia, Romania, Turkey and Greece not to allow boats with 'illegal' immigrants on board to proceed towards Palestine. On May 26 a British government inter-departmental conference in London discussed the possibility of paying money to the Romanian government for fifteen days' worth of food for each 'illegal' refugee, in order to encourage the Romanians to detain them and then send them back to Poland, Central Europe and Germany.[62]

60 'Colombia Bars Refugees', New York Times, 17 May 1939.
61 Hansard, Parliamentary Debates.
62 Inter-departmental conference, 26 May 1939: Foreign Office papers, FO 371/24090.

The Jews of Palestine found one unexpected means to circumvent these pressures and restrictions. In March, Pino Ginsberg, the Mossad agent who had Gestapo permission to reside in Berlin, was summoned to Gestapo headquarters and ordered, by Heydrich himself, to organise the departure of four hundred German Jews a week to Palestine. The Gestapo imperative was Jewish emigration, whether legal or illegal from the British perspective. The Gestapo demanded, however, enormous sums of money that neither the Jewish community nor the Mossad could easily raise. Under the Gestapo–Mossad scheme, the first 280 Jews left Berlin later that month. The train took them to Vienna, where 120 Austrian Jews collected by the Mossad representative there, Moshe Bar-Gilad, were to join them.

Another Mossad operative then in Vienna, the Austrian-born Ehud Uberall, later recalled how at dawn the 120 Austrian Jews, whose night had been spent in the Jewish Agency building opposite Gestapo headquarters in the Hotel Metropole, 'were awakened and formed a column that marched down the street to catch the early tram to the southern station. The train from Berlin carrying the 280 passengers had arrived exactly on time . . . I came along with them and sensed the extreme tension as we approached the station and saw the four hundred passengers that were to leave in a few minutes – and to be saved.'[63] The four hundred German and Austrian Jews went by train to Susak, a Yugoslav port on the Adriatic, and were taken from there by sea to Palestine, where they landed at night on deserted beaches even as British warships offshore were attempting to intercept them.

A new group left each month, by different routes. Some were intercepted by the Royal Navy and interned in Palestine, others

63 Ehud Avriel (Uberall), *Open the Gates!*, pages 54–5.

made their way ashore unmolested. In August 1939 five small boats with a total of 297 German refugees, and a larger boat with eight hundred on board, were all intercepted and their passengers interned in Palestine. They were allowed to stay, their numbers being deducted by the British from the annual Palestine quota. For the October 1939 emigrants from Germany, Heydrich personally approved their direct departure from two German ports, Hamburg and Emden, to avoid the problem of transit visas through other countries. The Mossad had already chartered the ships when the outbreak of war put an end to this ongoing rescue activity.[64]

Across the Atlantic lay another, vaster potential haven: the United States. In Washington, Senator Robert F. Wagner Sr (Democrat, New York) had introduced a Senate Joint Resolution on February 9 to bring 20,000 German Jewish refugee children of fourteen and under into the United States. In the House of Representatives, Congresswoman Edith Rogers (Republican, Massachusetts) had introduced an identical resolution four days later. Both were referred to the respective Senate and House Subcommittees on Immigration, where they were discussed on eight separate days, starting in the Senate subcommittee on April 20 and in the House of Representatives subcommittee on May 24.

One argument raised against the Bill was that the admission of 20,000 refugee children to the United States from Germany, and the refusal to admit their parents, would be against the laws of God, and therefore would open a wedge for a later request for the admission of 40,000 adults – the parents of the children in question. The main objections, repeated many times, were the fear of 'flooding' the already overburdened orphanages, future

64 Jon and David Kimche, *The Secret Roads, The 'Illegal' Migration of a People, 1938–1948*, pages 33–4, 43.

competition for jobs during a period of high unemployment, and neglecting American children who were already in need of assistance in order to help foreign children instead. One newspaper report read out to the committee declared: 'America is failing to take care of its own children.'

Another objection raised was that the Bill would allow Nazi or Communist children into the country, and indeed other children who were not being victimised. There was a fear of creating a precedent for similar situations in many other countries – China and Spain were mentioned – which would result in the wholesale breakdown of the existing immigration statutes.[65] The last discussion was on June 1. Both Bills 'died in committee' and no further action was taken.

On May 13, in the interval between the Senate and House of Representatives hearings, an ocean liner, the *St Louis*, left Hamburg with 927 German Jewish refugees on board. All had immigration quota numbers, issued by the American Consulates in Germany, entitling them to enter the United States not that year, 1939, but in 1940 and 1941. On May 27 the *St Louis* reached Cuba and anchored in Havana harbour. There, only twenty-two of the refugees were allowed to land. Cuba, which had already taken in 5,000 German Jewish refugees since 1933, wanted no more. The *New York Times* correspondent in Havana explained that 'growing sentiment against the entrance of Jewish refugees, fanned by campaigns through the press and radio' in Cuba, 'is held responsible for the increasingly strict regulations being imposed by the government'.[66]

65 United States Congress, Senate Joint Resolution 64; and United States Congress, Senate Committee on Immigration. Admission of German Refugee Children, Hearing, 20–22 April 1939. 76th Congress, 1st Session. Microfiche (CIS-No: 76 H852-2) Washington: Government Printing Office, 1939.
66 '700 Jewish Refugees Await Fate off Cuba', *New York Times*, 27 May 1939.

Despite frantic appeals from those on board the *St Louis*, which had steamed more than 4,000 miles, seven Latin American countries – Argentina, Brazil, Chile, Colombia, Panama, Paraguay and Uruguay – refused to take a single one of the refugees. Leaving Havana on June 2, cleared for the journey back to Hamburg, the *St Louis* steamed slowly between Havana and Miami. On June 4 it passed Miami going north, and on the following day passed Miami again going south. When, the next day, Henry Morgenthau Jr, Secretary of the Treasury and a Jew, suggested that the refugees be given tourist visas to enter the United States, the Secretary of State Cordell Hull explained that this could not be done. The United States, he told Morgenthau on the telephone on the afternoon of June 5, could not issue the refugees with tourist visas 'unless they had a definite home where they were coming from and were in a situation to return to it'.[67]

On June 6, as the *St Louis* was still steaming between Miami and Havana, and the House subcommittee on immigration had resumed its deliberations in Washington, Morgenthau asked Coast Guard Headquarters to locate the ship, but to keep news of the search out of the newspapers. A direct appeal that day from those on board the *St Louis* to President Roosevelt received no reply.

An appeal sent to the Canadian government on behalf of the refugees by several leading Canadians was likewise unsuccessful. On June 8, Frederick Blair, the Director of the Immigration Branch of the Canadian government, wrote that no country could 'open its doors wide enough to take in hundreds of thousands of Jewish people who want to leave Europe: the line must

67 Telephone conversation of 5 June 1939: United States National Archives, Franklin Delano Roosevelt Presidential Library, Papers of Henry Morgenthau Jr, Volume 194.

be drawn somewhere.' A day later the politically powerful French-Canadian Minister of Justice, Ernest Lapointe, wrote that he was 'emphatically opposed' to admitting any of the refugees into Canada.[68]

The *St Louis* had originally been meant, after disembarking its refugees in Havana, to go to New York to take on cruise passengers. Instead, at 11.46 p.m. on June 10, it set sail from the Caribbean to Europe with the refugees still on board. A week later it docked at Antwerp.

Once the *St Louis* was in Antwerp, and following a promise by the New York-based American Jewish Joint Distribution Committee (the Joint) to help bear the cost, four nations made a humanitarian gesture to take the returnees. France took 244, Belgium 214 and Holland 181. Britain took the largest number, 288. Britain also took, in similar proportions, the largest group from the ninety-six refugees on the *Flandres* and the forty on board the *Orduna*, two other ships that had crossed the Atlantic but had likewise been unable to land their refugees in the Americas.

Within a year, all those from the three ships taken back to countries on the European mainland came under German rule. Those in Britain were safe. More than two hundred of those who were given haven by France, Belgium and Holland were killed after being deported to the death camps together with French, Belgian and Dutch Jews. The writers Gordon Thomas and Max Morgan-Witts have commented on the voyage of the *St Louis*: 'What is certain is that if Cuba or the United States had opened their doors, almost no one from the ship need have died.'[69]

Even as the *St Louis* was still in the Caribbean, other German

---

68 Irving Abella and Harold Tropper, *None is Too Many*, page 38.
69 Gordon Thomas and Max Morgan-Witts, *Voyage of the Damned: The Voyage of the St Louis*, pages 302–3.

refugees, more than three hundred in all, on board other ships were being refused entry by Paraguay, Argentina and Mexico. At the same time, Costa Rica, which had allowed in twenty refugees on ninety-day permits, ordered all of them to leave.[70] On June 24 Brazil announced that, as a result of representations from the new Pope, Pius XII, it was lifting its immigration barriers to allow in 3,000 'German Catholics of Jewish ancestry' who were then in German concentration camps. But there was to be no relaxation of the rules preventing German Jews from entry.[71] Three days later, Bolivia announced that it would admit 250 German Jewish refugees each month. It could not know that time was running out. Meanwhile, fifteen of the refugees on the *St Louis* who had received permits to enter Shanghai were allowed to land in France, at Boulogne, and to go by train through France, Switzerland and Italy to Trieste, to board ship for the Orient.

Many of those in Britain who took in Jewish children after Kristallnacht hardly had the resources to do so, but wanted to help, and willingly accepted the hardships involved. In Archway, North London, Miss Harder, who ran a sweet and tobacconist shop, and lived in a two-room flat, took in three sisters who reached London from Prague on June 2. Six months after taking them in, she died of tuberculosis. But during the short time she looked after them, she took them on a holiday on the Isle of Wight, at her own expense, and tried – in vain – to get their mother out of Czechoslovakia.[72]

From Berlin, Captain Foley continued to try to get as many Jews

70 '304 Jews Ordered Back: Argentina and Paraguay Bar 200 – Mexico Shuts Doors to 104', *New York Times*, 3 June 1939.
71 'Brazil will Admit German Refugees', *New York Times*, 25 June 1939.
72 Wiener Library Archive.

as possible into Palestine. When Dr Dagobert Arian, a German Jew already living in Palestine, applied for permission for his mother to join him, Foley supported this application. On April 19 Dr Arian was informed by the Commissioner for Migration and Statistics in Jerusalem that Foley had nominated his mother for one of the immigration certificates put at his disposal in Berlin 'for persons living in circumstances of exceptional hardship'.

As soon as his mother reached Palestine, Dr Arian wrote from Tel Aviv direct to Foley: 'Having brought my mother home from the boat, I feel like writing to you these few lines. Destiny has placed you in a position where you daily come in touch with sorrow and despair, and where a man like you always feels the restrictions of power to help those who suffer. However, I know that whenever you find a possibility to assist the oppressed you do all you can to help them and by doing so you find happiness and satisfaction. My thanks, which I hereby express for the help given to my mother, is surely but a small portion of your own heart's satisfaction. It may also please you to hear that wherever your name is mentioned "From Dan to Beer Sheva" – you are talked of with the greatest respect and devotion and that you and a few other persons serve as a counterweight where the evils of everyday politics suppress and destroy the faith in honesty and humanity.'[73]

Foley's work was unceasing. Peter Weiss recalled a visit his mother Ida had made from her home town in Germany to Berlin: 'When I asked her the purpose of her visit she told me that she had heard that visas were being arranged at the British Passport Office in Berlin. She did not give me any great detail, but said

73 Dr Arian to Captain Foley, undated letter: Yad Vashem Righteous Among the Nations Archive, file 8378.

that she had met an Englishman to whom "we should be ever grateful". She remembered the man as a Mr Foley, but did not mention (or perhaps she never knew) his first name.' Ida Weiss told her son that she had virtually no money, and was quite ill: 'Mr Foley let me stay at his house for a few days and then he came home late one night with the necessary exit visas and papers. I left for Belgium and then onward to England on the early train the next morning. The last time I saw Mr Foley was at the station.'

Ida Weiss arrived in Britain in June 1939. To her son's comment: 'This man Foley seems to have saved your life and I suppose, my own?' she replied: 'His name will always be close to my heart.' Most of her large family died in concentration camps.[74]

In India, a committee of the Indian National Congress, made up of Hindus and Muslims, discussed a draft resolution, put forward by Jawaharlal Nehru, stating that 'The Committee sees no objection to the employment in India of such Jewish refugees as are experts and specialists and who can fit in with the new order in India and accept Indian standards.' On April 3, however, Subhas Chandra Bose, the Congress President, learned that the resolution had not been accepted. Bose himself had been a leading opponent.

In vain, Nehru tried to explain to Bose why he wanted Jews to be allowed into India. The cruelties and destruction of Kristallnacht had made a powerful impact on him. 'I felt that we must express our opinion in regard to it,' Nehru wrote. 'You say that you were "astounded when I produced a resolution seeking to

74 Peter P. W. Weiss, letter to Yad Vashem, 4 January 1999. Yad Vashem Righteous Among the Nations Archive, file 8378. Ida Weiss died in Birmingham, England, in 1995.

make India an asylum for the Jews". I am surprised to learn that you felt so strongly about this as, so far as I remember, you did not express yourself definitely at the time. But is it fair to characterise my resolution as one seeking to establish an asylum for the Jews in India? It was not from the point of view of helping Jews that I considered this question, though such help was desirable where possible without detriment to our country, but from the point of view of helping ourselves by getting first-rate men of science, industry, etc., on very moderate payment.'[75]

Nehru did succeed in persuading the Indian Medical Council to recognise European medical qualifications, so that Jewish refugee doctors could practise in India. A few hundred other Jewish refugees were also able to find homes in India. The Czech Jewish composer Walter Kaufmann founded the Bombay Chamber Orchestra and became a director of All-India Radio. Another German Jewish refugee, Margarete Spiegel, became Mahatma Gandhi's secretary and friend.[76] Hungarian-born Fori Nehru, who was married to Nehru's cousin Brij Kumar Nehru, later remembered a German Jewish refugee in Bombay who 'became a famous producer of chocolates, which we never had before in India'.[77]

Turkey also continued to provide a safe haven to German Jewish refugees who could make a contribution to Turkish arts, medicine and science. Those given asylum there included Ernest Hirsch, who served on the Law Faculty at the universities of both Istanbul and Ankara, Carl Ebert, who founded the Ankara State Opera,

75 P. R. Kumaraswamy, 'India and the Holocaust: Perceptions of the Indian National Congress', *Journal of Indo-Judaic Studies*, Volume 3, April 2000.
76 Yosef Yaakov, 'An Overlooked Experience', *Jerusalem Post*, 10 September 1999, reviewing Anil Bhatti (editor), *Jewish Exile in India*. New Delhi: Manohar Publishers, 1999.
77 Fori Nehru, letter to the author, 25 August 2005.

and Dr Erich Frank, who became Professor of Internal Diseases at Istanbul University.[78]

Inside Germany, dissent was swiftly punished. Otto Gref, a schoolteacher in Freiburg – whose synagogue had been destroyed on Kristallnacht – was reported for teaching that 'in fundamental characteristics all men are alike', and are also 'likeable and honourable'. This, he said, also applied to Jews. On June 21, Gref, who was also a chaplain, was deprived of his right to teach in State schools.[79]

In June 1939, six-year-old Joseph Wohlfarth was among the Jewish children from Frankfurt who set off for Britain. His mother took him to the main station, put him on the train, and waved goodbye as the train pulled out. 'This vision of the train pulling out and my mother waving goodbye haunts me to this day,' he wrote more than half a century later. 'What must she have felt at that time knowing that she may never see me again. And so it was! I never saw my mother or brothers again. They perished in concentration camps. I remember being violently seasick on the boat. We arrived in Harwich from the Hook of Holland and were taken to Barham House in East Suffolk. It was a sort of Collection Centre for Refugees of all ages from abroad before they were allocated to either private families or hostels.' His father, who was already in Britain, visited him a few days later, 'and that was a great comfort to me'.[80]

On June 27, Rita Braumann, who at the age of twelve had been

78 List (of eleven Jewish refugees in all) on display at the Zulfaris Museum, Istanbul.
79 German Ministry of Education, letter of 21 June 1939: Foreign Office papers, FO 371/23052.
80 Joseph Wohlfarth, 'A Snapshot of the Events as I Remember Them'.

a witness of Kristallnacht in Cologne, and had reached Holland in November, also crossed the North Sea to Britain. There, 'I lived first with a Gentile family, that of William Slack, in Chesterfield, then in Sheffield with a rabbi, Solomon Fisch, and his family, and finally when I reached the ripe old age of sixteen, I was allowed to move to London where I lived in a Girls' Hostel.'[81]

That summer, Stefanie Bamberger, who had witnessed Kristallnacht in Leipzig, left Germany for England. Her parents told her that in three months' time 'they would come and join me'. Her mother travelled with her in the Kindertransport train as far as Utrecht in Holland, and then returned to Germany. Her older brother was already in Switzerland. Stefanie went to a Jewish family in Liverpool with whom her parents had been in correspondence. 'They of course did not join me in England after three months as hoped.' In 1941 they were taken to Theresienstadt 'and in 1942 we heard through the Red Cross that my father had "died", and in 1944, my mother.'[82]

Those who had to determine the British government's policy towards Jewish refugees who had managed to reach Poland from the Protectorate were not convinced that these refugees were in any real danger. 'A great many of these,' wrote one official, Patrick Reilly, on July 24, 'are not in any sense political refugees, but Jews who panicked unnecessarily and need not have left.' Many of them, he added, 'are quite unsuitable as emigrants and would be a very difficult problem if brought here'.[83]

On July 30, six days after Reilly's disparaging comment, the

81 Rita Newell (*née* Braumann), recollections entitled '10 November 1938'. Sent to the author, 28 June 2005.
82 Stefanie Segerman (*née* Bamberger), letter to the author, 9 August 2005.
83 Note by Patrick Reilly, 24 July 1939: Foreign Office papers, FO 371/24100.

British Prime Minister, Neville Chamberlain, wrote in a private letter about Kristallnacht: 'I believe the persecution arose out of two motives; A desire to rob the Jews of their money and a jealousy of their superior cleverness.' Chamberlain continued: 'No doubt Jews aren't a lovable people; I don't care about them myself;– but that is not sufficient to explain the Pogrom.'[84]

Shortly before a meeting of the British Cabinet on August 4, the Colonial Secretary, Malcolm MacDonald, reported that the British High Commissioner in Palestine had been authorised to announce that 'no immigration quota would be issued for the next six-monthly period October 1939–March 1940', to punish those 'illegals' who were making their way to Palestine without visas or Palestine Certificates. MacDonald explained that, in another effort to stop the illegal traffic, the Foreign Office was making 'strong representations' to certain governments about their 'laxity' in discouraging the would-be immigrants. Mac-Donald added: 'Very strong representations had been made in particular to Romania, Poland and Greece, and the first results of this action had been good. Romania and Greece had taken action which should secure much stricter surveillance, and while the good effect of our representations might not last, since the power of Jewish money was great, for the present at any rate the results were good.'[85]

MacDonald's reference to what he called 'the power of Jewish money' was ill chosen. In reality, the funds of the Jewish organisations and charitable institutions were almost exhausted.

With Palestine effectively barred, sanctuary in Britain was the main hope for the Jews still trapped in Germany, Austria and the

84 Letter of 30 July 1939: Neville Chamberlain papers.
85 Cabinet Committee minutes, 7 August 1939: Cabinet papers, 27/651.

Protectorate. Alfred Dubs, aged six, came with his parents. As a Labour Member of Parliament from 1979 to 1987, he served as a member of a Parliamentary Committee on Race Relations and Immigration. In 1994 he entered the House of Lords, and in 1997 was appointed Under Secretary of State for Northern Ireland. The last train from Prague with Jewish children left on August 2, with sixty-eight children on board.

On August 8, Fred Garfunkel, who had witnessed Kristallnacht in Vienna, left the city with his parents and sister by train to Ostend, and then by ferry to Dover. His father, who had been taken to Buchenwald in May 1938 during the first Nazi mass action against Jews in Austria, had been released in June 1939. Cousins in the United States had given the family the necessary affidavits. After one night in London they took the train to Liverpool, where they boarded the Cunard liner *Laconia* for New York, reaching the United States on August 22.[86]

Miriam Litke, who had witnessed Kristallnacht in Berlin, was on a Kindertransport that left the German capital on August 13: 'the last but one'.[87]

Some Czech Jews escaped through Poland. These included Karel and Anna Seifter, who reached Britain with their one-year-old son Pavel. Returning to Communist-ruled Czechoslovakia after the war, Pavel Seifter was for twenty years the editor of several dissident publications in Prague. Forced by the regime to give up his university lectureship in history, he became a window cleaner. Sixty years after reaching the safety of Britain, he returned to London as Ambassador of the newly created Czech Republic.[88]

86 Fred Garfunkel, conversation with the author, 21 August 2005.
87 Miriam Litke, letter to the author, 20 July 2005.
88 Pavel Seifter, conversation with the author, 19 March 2001.

On July 30 it was announced from El Salvador that fifty German Jewish refugees who were approaching the capital, San Salvador, would not be allowed to land, as the country was 'determined not to admit any Jewish refugees to this already most densely populated country of Latin America'.[89] On August 14 there was a further blow to German Jewish hopes when both the International Settlement and the French Concession Councils in Shanghai, acting separately, announced that 'from today no further landings in Shanghai of Jewish refugees will be allowed'. Only those already on the high seas would be permitted to land. There were already 8,000 German and almost 4,000 Austrian Jewish refugees in Shanghai.

By the end of August 1939 Britain had become a haven for almost 10 per cent of Jews who had succeeded in escaping Germany. Including those from Austria and the Protectorate, there were between 63,000 and 65,000 Jewish refugees in Britain. Of these, 9,354 were children. The Palestine Mandate, for all its restrictions, accepted a further 51,700 German and 7,100 Austrian Jewish refugees between Hitler's coming to power and the outbreak of war. Britain's colonial territories were less generous. Official Colonial Office figures show that in the six-month period up to March 1939 – after which immigration was almost everywhere more rigorously curtailed – Cyprus took in 744 Jews, Kenya 650 and Trinidad 359. Malta would only agree to take eighteen, and Aden five. In the West Indies, St Vincent accepted twenty Jews, British Honduras twelve, Grenada five, and Barbados two. Not a single Jewish refugee was allowed into the Bahamas, Bermuda, the Leeward Islands or the Windward Islands.

89 'Salvador Bars Refugees', *New York Times*, 31 July 1939.

Despite government restrictions, fuelled by popular prejudice and official hostility in so many of the lands to which Jews turned, more than half of Germany's Jews had left the country before the outbreak of war. Almost 200,000 had been given refuge in the United States. 'This number,' comment the first writers to assemble Jewish refugee statistics, 'is larger than the total of Jewish refugees resettled in any other country.'[90]

In Berlin, two members of the United States Embassy, Dr Raymond Geist, the Consul General, and William Russell, one of his deputies, were active throughout the summer of 1939 in issuing visas for Jews to leave. The post-war German Jewish magazine *Aufbau* described how Dr Geist 'helped many who were persecuted in the National-Socialist regime regardless of social class or religious faith – Jews and non-Jews alike – in leaving Germany when they were threatened with arrest or deportation to concentration camps. His interventions with the Third Reich's highest authorities went far beyond his official duties and were done at the risk of his own personal prestige. He made use of his influence without thought to any personal disadvantages. Guided by the highest humanitarian ideals, he made himself available to the persecuted day and night and saved many of them from a terrible fate by helping them to find a new life in the United States.'[91]

On the last day of August 1939, as German threats against Poland intensified, presaging war, William Russell helped a German Jew who had just been released from Dachau, where he had been badly beaten, to obtain an American visa. He then accompanied him to Berlin airport, to ensure that he would be allowed on the plane to Holland, from where he would take

90 Arieh Tartakower and Kurt R. Grossman, *The Jewish Refugee*, page 81.
91 *Afbau*, Issue 1, 2000. In 1954 Dr Geist was awarded the Order of Merit by the German Federal Republic.

ship to the United States. 'Why are you here?' a stormtrooper demanded of Russell. 'I'm from the American Embassy,' he answered. 'This man has a visa for the United States. I would like to see that he gets aboard this plane for Rotterdam. His boat sails the day after tomorrow.' The Jew was allowed to leave.[92]

That evening, 31 August 1939, as German Radio poured out a stream of venom against the Polish Republic, sixty German Jewish children were travelling with their adult escorts in a train crowded with German soldiers from Cologne to Cleve – whose 1821 synagogue had been destroyed on Kristallnacht. Cleve was the only point on the Dutch frontier to which trains were still running. Crossing the frontier, the train proceeded to the Hook of Holland. Overnight, the children crossed the North Sea to the British port of Harwich. There, at dawn on September 1, those who had just reached safety learned that Germany had invaded Poland.[93]

Germany invaded Poland on 1 September 1939. Two days later, Britain and France declared war on Germany. The Second World War had begun.

In the six years since Hitler had come to power, 200,000 German Jews, almost two-thirds of the German Jewish population in January 1933, had emigrated. In the year and a half since the German annexation of Austria, almost 130,000 Austrian Jews – 70 per cent of Austria's 185,246 Jewish population in March 1938 – had emigrated, most of them to other European countries, or to Britain, the United States, Palestine and Shanghai.

By the outbreak of war, 330,000 German and Austrian Jews were beyond the confines of the Reich. But 175,000 remained

92 William Russell, *Berlin Embassy*, pages 6–8, 26–8.
93 Eva Michaelis, 'Youth Aliyah Report, August 25th–September 7th 1939': Central Zionist Archives, Jerusalem, file S 75/746.

behind the almost totally sealed borders of a nation at war. They would suffer the consequences of the sealed borders of total war, wartime secrecy and draconian, calculating plans of destruction. Manfred Steinfeld's sister Irma had recently received her visa to go to England, 'but unfortunately the war started the week she was to leave and she was unable to get out of Germany'.[94] Similar blows were struck for several hundred other German and Austrian Jews whose visas were ready for their imminent departure when war began.

There were also Jews who chose to remain in Germany, in order to do what they could to help their fellow Jews. Four of the leaders of German Jewry who had done their utmost to maintain sanity and morale since 1933 – Otto Hirsch, Julius Seligsohn, Hannah Karminski and Cora Berliner – saw it as their task to stay on and give whatever help they could to their threatened flock. All four were later killed by the Nazis. Their leader, Rabbi Leo Baeck, also chose to remain in Germany. He was fortunate to survive deportation to Theresienstadt, where he was liberated on 3 May 1945, five days before the end of the war in Europe.

In the nine months between 2 December 1938 and 31 August 1939 the organisations involved in the Kindertransport, both Jewish and Christian, brought 9,354 refugee children to Britain; of these, 7,482 were Jewish. A further 1,350 Jewish youngsters were admitted to Britain as part of the ongoing agricultural training programmes for future emigration to Palestine; two hundred of these youngsters, both boys and girls, were sent to a training farm at Gwrych Castle in North Wales. Another seven hundred Jewish children

94 Manfred Steinfeld recollections, in Philip K. Jason and Iris Posner, *Don't Wave Goodbye: The Children's Flight from Nazi Persecution to American Freedom*, page 41.

reached Britain under the auspices of the Zionist Youth Aliyah movement. A further 650 were brought over by the Children's Section of the British Committee for Refugees from Czechoslovakia. A hundred Orthodox Jewish children were brought over by the Union of Orthodox Hebrew Congregations.

On the outbreak of war, another 180 children were ready to leave Prague for the Hook of Holland and Harwich. War ended all chance of their crossing the German border with Britain as their destination. 'What those children must feel like,' the sponsors wrote, 'having packed all their clothes, having sold everything that could not be removed, having said goodbye to their friends, can readily be understood.'[95]

A new, terrible era was about to begin.

---

95 Quoted in Barry Turner, . . . And the Policeman Smiled: 10,000 Children Escape from Nazi Europe, page 96.

9

Last Steps to Destruction

On 9 September 1939, six days after Britain and France declared war on Germany, all three hundred Jewish men in the Ruhr industrial city of Gelsenkirchen were deported to Sachsen-hausen. The women and children were left to fend for themselves. Of the 1,400-strong Jewish community in Gelsenkirchen in 1933 – whose synagogue had been destroyed on Kristallnacht – almost half had emigrated. Hardly any of the rest survived the war.

On September 21, with the German army still advancing through Poland, all Jewish communities in Germany with fewer than five hundred members were dissolved. All Jews were forced to leave their villages and towns for larger Jewish communities. A week later Poland was partitioned between Germany and the Soviet Union.

Another deportation of German Jews took place in October: several hundred would-be emigrants who, on the day war was declared, were waiting in Hamburg for the next ship to the United States, for which they had valid visas. On October 21 they were taken by train from Hamburg to a desolate area near the Polish city of Lublin. There they had to find refuge with Polish Jewish villagers in a poor region, amid near-starvation and with no possibility of returning to their homes. Many were sent to a forced labour camp established that November by the SS at Zarzecze, where a large number of them were killed by the savagery of the SS guards.

A day before the Hamburg deportations, several hundred Jews from Vienna had also been deported to this 'Lublinland', as the Germans derisively called it. Eichmann, who had hitherto been in charge of the emigration of Jews from Vienna and Prague, was given the task of coordinating deportation.

One fortunate group of 340 German Jews were already in neutral Holland that winter. Sailing from Rotterdam on board the Holland–America liner *Veendam*, they arrived in New York on December 22.[1] They were part of the United States' annual German and Austrian quota of 27,000 for 1939, their permits were in order and they were allowed to land. Five weeks later, on 1 February 1940, the Italian liner *Conte di Savoia* reached New York with a further 550 German Jewish refugees among its 960 passengers. Among the other passengers were the baritone Giuseppe de Luca, the actress Joan Gardner and the Hindu boy film star Sabu. Among the Jewish refugees were twelve children aged between three and fourteen, whose parents had been unable to obtain visas to enter the United States.[2]

In Poland, Ruth Goldfein, a witness of Kristallnacht in Danzig, had enrolled early in 1939 in a Zionist youth farm at Grochow, south of Warsaw, training for emigration to Palestine. On August 27, five days before the German invasion of Poland, her parents, Miriam and Sender Goldfein, who had found refuge in the Polish city of Lodz, travelled to Grochow to see her. 'That was the last time I saw my dearest parents. My dear, dear mother and father. May they rest in peace. Where?!'[3]

From the farm, Ruth Goldfein and her twenty-two fellow

---

1 'Refugees on Liner', *New York Times*, 23 December 1939.
2 'Among Yesterday's Arrivals from Europe . . .', *New York Times*, 2 February 1940.
3 Ruth Fluss (*née* Goldfein), typescript: letter to the author, 1 August 2005.

Zionist pioneers saw Warsaw burning as the Germans bombed it from the air. They managed to make their way eastward, to Vilna, which had just come under Soviet rule. Good fortune was with them. On 18 March 1940 they left Vilna by train for the Latvian capital, Riga, then flew – thanks to the generosity of Eva Warburg, of the Warburg banking family – to Stockholm, then on by train to Malmo, then by air to Amsterdam and Paris, then by train to Marseille where they took ship to Haifa. The whole journey to safety took only eleven days. Their destination was Kibbutz Ayelet Hashahar in the Galilee, where they resumed their farming tasks.[4]

On 15 February 1940, a thousand Jews were deported to Lublinland from the Baltic port of Stettin, and several hundred from the Baltic port of Stralsund. On March 12, a further 160 Jews were deported to Lublinland from Schneidemühl.[5] The synagogues in both towns had been destroyed on Kristallnacht.

Some Jews managed to leave Germany in the early months of 1940. Inge Neuberger, an eye-witness of Kristallnacht in Mannheim, left Germany with her father at the end of March. One of her uncles in the United States had sent the necessary affidavits and dollars. Her mother and brother followed six weeks later. They were part of a United States scheme to take a thousand Jewish children and their escorts, provided the children had relatives in the United States to take them in. One of these children was Pesach Schindler, who had witnessed Kristallnacht in Munich, and whose father was already in the United States. Taken by train

4 Ruth Fluss (*née* Goldfein), conversation with the author, 4 September 2005.
5 *Trial of the Major War Criminals Before the International Military Tribunal, Nuremberg, 14 November 1945–1 October, 1946*, Document NG-2490.

across the German border into neutral Holland, he and the group of youngsters with him continued by ship from Rotterdam to the United States. Among those on board his ship, the *Volendam*, was a twelve-year-old boy from Berlin, Max Frankel, later, for twenty years (1974–94) the executive editor of the *New York Times*.

On 9 April 1940 the German army invaded Denmark and Norway. A month later, on May 10, German troops struck at four more countries: Belgium, Holland, Luxembourg and France. Even as these violent conflicts ruled, the instinct to help did not die. On May 13, as German troops drew close to Amsterdam, a Dutch woman, Geertruida Wijsmuller-Meijer, who had been looking after Jewish refugees from Germany, assembled half a dozen motor coaches, gathered two hundred Jewish refugees, among them eighty children, and drove with them from Amsterdam to the port of Ijmuiden, where British troops were still landing in a last-minute attempt to bolster the Dutch defences.

On reaching Ijmuiden, Geertruida Wijsmuller persuaded the captain of a Dutch freighter to take the Jews on board, and to set course for England. 'At 7 p.m. we sailed,' one of the youngsters, Harry Jacobi from Berlin, later recalled. 'Far away from the shore we looked back and saw a huge column of black smoke from the oil storage tanks that had been set on fire to prevent the Germans having them. At 9 p.m. news came through, picked up by the ship's radio: the Dutch government had capitulated.'

Harry Jacobi and the two hundred Jewish refugees with him reached Britain and safety. Neither his parents, who were still in Berlin, nor his grandparents, then refugees in Holland, survived the war. There had been no room for his grandparents on the crowded coaches. Geertruida Wijsmuller-Meijer remained in Holland, where she helped to smuggle hundreds of Jews, many of them from Germany, into neutral Spain and Switzerland.[6]

Captain Foley, who had enabled so many Jews to leave Germany while serving as Passport Control Officer in Berlin, was briefly at Bordeaux in mid-June 1940, amid a mass of retreating soldiers and civilians desperate to escape the advancing German army. He continued to issue visas to German Jewish refugees.[7] On June 17, as German troops advanced rapidly through France, the Portuguese Consul General in Bordeaux, Dr Aristides de Sousa Mendes, a devout Catholic, announced that he would provide Portuguese visas free of charge. Only with such visas would the Spanish border officials let Jews into Spain. Throughout that day and the two following days, as the German army drew ever nearer to Bordeaux, de Sousa Mendes issued several thousand visas, stamping and signing them around the clock. The Foreign Ministry in Lisbon ordered him to stop, but he refused to do so. On June 20 the British Embassy in Lisbon sent a letter to the Portuguese Ministry of Foreign Affairs complaining that de Sousa Mendes was 'working outside normal hours'.[8]

As the German army prepared to enter Bordeaux, de Sousa Mendes drove south towards Spain. Stopping at Bayonne, he discovered that the Portuguese Consul there had obeyed the Portuguese government's orders and was refusing to give entry visas to Jews. De Sousa Mendes spent the day in Bayonne issuing visas, defying instructions to stop. Then, with German heavy artillery sounding to the north, he drove to the Spanish border at

---

6 Recollections of Rabbi Harry M. Jacobi, *Jewish Chronicle*, 29 September 1978; Harry Jacobi, conversation with the author, London, 21 February 1985.

7 Yad Vashem Righteous Among the Nations Archive, file 8378.

8 Ben Macintyre, 'Revealed: Aristocrat who Helped 30,000 Escape from the Nazis', *The Times*, 14 October 1998.

Hendaye. Even there he handed out several hundred visas – mere scraps of paper, but stamped with his official seal and signed with his name – stating that the bearer had the right to enter Portugal, and requesting Spain to grant the holder unimpeded passage. The scraps of paper were honoured.[9]

France signed an armistice with Germany on June 22. On the following day the Portuguese Ambassador to France arrived in Hendaye, on his way to safety, and declared de Sousa Mendes's visas null and void. Ignoring this, de Sousa Mendes, himself about to cross the border, handed his scrap-of-paper visas to a group of Jews desperate to get across, and then, in the words of the writer Eric Silver, 'instructed them to walk behind his car through a rarely used crossing point, where the single guard had no telephone and no way of checking with his superiors. The bluff worked. The refugees shuffled to safety.'[10]

Not every instinct was to help those in danger. On June 26, three days after de Sousa Mendes's act of defiant compassion, the United States Assistant Secretary of State, Breckinridge Long, outlined ways in which American Consulates in Europe, including those in Germany – for the United States was still neutral – could indefinitely postpone granting visas. As Long explained: 'We can delay and effectively stop for a temporary period of indefinite length the number of immigrants into the United States. We could do this by simply advising our consuls to put every obstacle in the way and to require additional evidence and to resort to various administrative devices which would postpone and postpone and postpone the granting of the visas.'[11]

These instructions were carried out. Two months later Ludwig

9 Mordecai Paldiel, *The Path of the Righteous*, pages 59–62.
10 Eric Silver, *The Book of the Just*, pages 50–5.
11 Library of Congress: the Papers of Breckinridge Long, Box 211.

Klein, a sixty-three-year-old hop merchant, wrote to his children in the United States from the town of Walldorf – whose seventy-eight-year-old synagogue had been destroyed on Kristallnacht – that he had just received a notice from the American Vice-Consul in Stuttgart that stated: 'Due to a change of circumstances, it is now necessary to reassess those immigration applications that had already been approved, as being insufficient. In many cases, this approval will, undoubtedly, have to be rescinded. We are therefore advising you not to make any preparations for such a trip or, if you have already made such steamship reservations, to cancel them until you hear from this consulate again. That should avoid financial losses for you or your guarantors.'

'As you can see,' Ludwig Klein wrote despondently, 'our emigration will not go as fast as imagined and we regret you will be disappointed. In any case, the journey via Russia–Japan will no longer be possible. It is totally uncertain whether or when such a possibility will exist again. The steamship lines via Lisbon or Piraeus are no longer open from here, inasmuch as there are no transit visas through Switzerland and Italy at the moment . . .'[12]

Unlike Breckinridge Long, another American citizen, Varian Fry, chose the path of rescue. On 14 August 1940, less than a month after the Franco-German armistice, he reached Marseille from the United States as the representative of a private American relief organisation, the American Emergency Rescue Committee. The area in which he worked was Vichy France. The chief beneficiaries of his efforts were German and Austrian refugees who had found sanctuary in France since 1933.

Fry's original mission was meant to last for three weeks. He stayed for more than twelve months. Among those who were able

12 Letter of 25 August 1940. Klein family archive.

to leave Europe for the United States because of his efforts were Franz Werfel, an Austrian Jew whose novel *The Forty Days of Musa Dagh* portrayed Armenian resistance at the time of the massacres after the First World War, and Lion Feuchtwanger, a German Jew living in exile in the South of France since 1933, whose novel *Jew Suss* had enjoyed enormous popularity. Both books had been banned by Hitler. Fry was supported in his work by Hiram Bingham, the United States Vice-Consul in Marseille. In defiance of State Department regulations, Bingham had already issued United States visas above the quota limits, and had even falsified documents to provide cover for individual refugees.

Some German Jews managed to escape across the southern border of Austria into Yugoslavia. One of these was Recha Freier, a former board member of the Jewish Youth Support Committee in Germany, whose son was already in Britain. On Kristallnacht she had been in London, but she hurried back to Berlin to help accelerate the emigration of Jewish children to Palestine, if necessary by illegal means. For this she had been expelled from the board and denounced by her colleagues for anti-Nazi agitation. On her journey across the Austro–Yugoslav border she took fifty German Jewish teenagers with her. Seven months later they reached Palestine.

Inge and Bertha Engelhard's parents also made that southward journey, their daughters having earlier reached Britain on a Kindertransport. From Munich, Inge Engelhard later wrote, they made their way to the Austrian city of Graz, 'where they were put up by a people smuggler named Joseph Schleich, until he had enough people to make a group to send with various guides over the border', to Zagreb in Yugoslavia. After the German invasion of Yugoslavia in April 1941 they managed to make their way to Italy, and from there to Spain and Portugal, 'before finally arriving in England on Christmas Day 1943, via Yankee Clipper flying boat!'[13]

In the autumn of 1940 the government of Haiti offered to take in a hundred German Jewish refugee families. This plan was stamped on by the State Department in Washington, the Secretary of State himself, Cordell Hull, instructing the American Chargé d'Affaires in Haiti to make clear to the President of Haiti that the United States would 'deplore' any further Haitian offers to take in refugees, 'among whose numbers will doubtless be found elements prejudicial to the safety of the Republic of Haiti and this country'.

This telegram was dated September 30. Two days later the American Chargé d'Affaires telegraphed to Washington that he had explained to the Haitian government that because the refugees were 'at most only anti-Hitler, we regard these refugees as suspect and cannot view with approval their migration from place to place'. The United States, he explained, was spending more than $12 billion in defence of the United States and the Western Hemisphere, and 'it would be unreasonable to expect that we would view without concern the uncontrolled movement of alien suspects'.[14]

Britain, too, had taken the stand that, with Britain at war with Germany, all Germans, whether Jews or not, were 'enemy aliens' and could not be granted visas.

On 22 October 1940 the Nazi planners, with Adolf Eichmann as their expert organiser, deported 15,000 Jewish men, women and children from the western German provinces of Rhineland-

---

13 Inge M. Sadan (*née* Englehard), letter to the author, 22 June 2005.
14 *Foreign Relations of the United States, Diplomatic Papers, 1940*, Volume II, pages 241, 242.

Palatinate, Saar and Baden to four camps in South-West France under Vichy French control: Gurs, Noé, Récébédou and Rivesaltes. Conditions were harsh. Almost 2,000 of the deportees, many of them elderly, died in these camps of the severe conditions. Among the 1,260 deaths at Gurs were thirty-four-year-old Vera Meyer from Halberstadt, sixty-year-old Emma Weil from Lörrach, and sixty-one-year-old Melanie Wertheimer from Bühl, each of whose synagogues had been destroyed on Kristallnacht.[15]

Among those deported to Gurs were Ludwig and Alice Klein, who had learned only two months earlier that their application to go to the United States to join their children, having been approved, would have to be reassessed. Together with Ludwig's brother Heinrich and his wife Melanie, the Kleins survived two years in Gurs, before being sent to Auschwitz and their deaths.[16]

On 14 February 1941 a German Jew, Gerhard Neumann, wrote from Gurs on behalf of himself and six others to Robert M. Lovett, the Acting Governor of the United States Virgin Islands, asking if the islands 'could improve our actual situation by giving us permission to stay in your territory until we can immigrate to the USA. We are aware, that we do an extraordinary step in applying to you. But this is our last chance.' On March 15 the Acting Governor replied: 'I regret to inform you that a procedure for giving effect to the plan of affording temporary refuge in the Islands has not been worked out by the State Department and the Department of the Interior.'

Walter Bruehl, one of the returnees from the *St Louis*, who was also in Gurs, wrote to the Acting Governor of the Virgin Islands in April, receiving a reply on May 20: 'I regret to inform you that

15 'Gurs', Serge Klarsfeld, *Le Mémorial de la Déportation des Juifs de France*, pages 582–994.
16 Klein family archive.

the State Department has refused permission to put into effect the plan proposed for the reception of the refugees . . .'[17]

Neither Neumann nor Bruehl survived the war.

In Marseille, where the neutral United States still had its official representation, Hiram Bingham provided documents that enabled Varian Fry's committee to procure the release of several hundred of those held in the Vichy camps. In cases where no visas or passports were available for those released, Bingham issued signed affidavits that enabled them to leave Europe. Unfortunately for those seeking safe havens, Bingham was not supported in his rescue activities by his immediate superior, the American Consul General, Hugh Fullerton, and was reassigned to Lisbon.[18]

Within eight months, Fry lost his base of rescue. On 13 May 1941 President Roosevelt's wife Eleanor wrote to Fry's wife Eileen: 'I think he will have to come home because he has done things which the government does not feel it can stand behind.'[19] Fry returned to the United States. Bitterly, he wrote in his memoirs: 'When I arrived in New York, I learned that the State Department had devised a new and cruelly difficult form of visa application, which made it almost impossible for refugees to enter this country.'[20]

For the Jews in Germany the year 1941 saw an intensification of discrimination and terror. As the year began, all Jews who had

17 'Chronological Account of Inter-Departmental Negotiations on Admission of Alien Visitors into Virgin Islands', United States National Archives, Record Group 126. Quoted in William R. Perl, 'The Holocaust and the Lost Caribbean Paradise', *The Freeman*, The Foundation for Economic Education, Volume 4, Number 1, January 1992.
18 Material in Eric Saul, 'Visas for Life' exhibition, 2000.
19 Quoted in Varian Fry, *Surrender on Demand*, page 251.
20 Varian Fry, *Surrender on Demand*, page 236.

not already done so were forced to leave their homes and to crowd into special 'Judenhaüser' (Jewish houses), houses owned by Jews who had to fit in as many as six people to a room, sometimes more. In German-occupied Poland the enforced overcrowding and privation were even more harsh: ghettos had been established, often in the poorest quarter of the town, to which the Jews were deported and confined, and where many died each month of starvation and disease.

To the largest of those ghettos, that of Warsaw, 10,000 German Jews were deported, including several hundred from Bremen. In the first six months of 1941, 13,000 Jews died of starvation in the Warsaw ghetto, including many of the deportees from Germany. Starting on 15 February 1941, and continuing for four weeks, 5,000 Austrian Jews were deported from Vienna to the ghettos of Lublin and Kielce, as well as to slave labour camps in German-occupied Poland. There, along the German–Soviet border, they were forced, in the harshest of conditions, to drain marshes and build border fortifications.

On 19 September 1941 all Jews in Germany over the age of six were ordered to wear a yellow star. Beginning that October, more than a third of them – 50,000 in all – were sent eastward. The first set of these deportation trains went to Minsk, whose ghetto, since the German invasion of the Soviet Union that June, had become a centre of incarceration, slave labour and execution.

The first train from Germany reached Minsk on November 10 with a thousand Jews from Hamburg. They were taken to a large apartment block complex that was designated 'Ghetto Hamburg'. The Hamburg deportees were followed within a week by more than 6,000 Jews from Frankfurt, Bremen and the Rhineland. On November 18 a train arrived from Berlin. On it was twenty-two-year-old Haim Berendt, who recalled twenty years later how his fellow deportees 'felt themselves as pioneers who were brought to settle the East'.[21] The new arrivals became part of the slave labour force in Minsk, and in due course shared the fate of the Jews of Minsk: destruction.

Seventeen thousand German Jews were deported to the Lodz ghetto that November. They made an immediate impact on the ghetto dwellers. 'From the very beginning,' wrote one of the ghetto chroniclers, 'these newcomers have been a great attraction for music lovers.' One result of the resettlements was that 'the ghetto has acquired an array of talented performers – pianists and singers. The piano performances by maestro Birkenfeld of Vienna deserve special mention.' Each of Leopold Birkenfeld's concerts 'is truly a feast for the ghetto's music lovers'. Within two weeks, thirty musicians, actors, singers and painters had been registered. A leading Viennese attorney, Dr Meir Kitz, was appointed a judge of the Jewish ghetto court. Four rabbis from Germany were co-opted onto the ghetto's rabbinical court. Karol Rozencwajg, a travelling salesman from Vienna, became the popular guitar and zither accompanist to a local singer.

The severity of life in the Lodz ghetto was ever-present. The ghetto chroniclers recorded several deaths among the newcomers, including thirty-year-old Lili Walder from Vienna on November 29, who went to the barbed wire at a forbidden point and was shot dead. 'The victim had been suffering from nervous depression.'

On December 3, Leopold Birkenfeld's performances of Schubert's *Unfinished Symphony*, Beethoven's *Moonlight Sonata*, Liszt's *Rhapsody No. 2* and a few works by Mendelssohn 'literally

21 Testimony of Haim Berendt, Eichmann trial, 5 May 1961, session 29.

enchanted the audience'. Eight days later the ghetto chroniclers reported the death, at the age of seventy-four, of Dr Ernst Sandheim, one of the 'grand old men' of medicine in Berlin.[22]

On 15 November 1941 the first of five deportations took place from Germany to the Lithuanian city of Kovno, which had been under German occupation since June. The first thousand deportees were from Munich. Their journey took ten days. Within two weeks 15,000 Jews had arrived: from Berlin, Munich, Vienna, Breslau and Frankfurt. They were not taken to the ghetto, but to the nearby Ninth Fort. A Kovno Jew, Dr Aharon Peretz, later described how, as the deportees were being led along the road to the Ninth Fort, which ran near the ghetto perimeter, 'they could be heard asking the guards, "Is the camp still far?"' They had been told they were being sent to a work camp. But, Peretz added, 'We know where that road led. It led to the Ninth Fort, to the prepared pits.'[23]

On reaching the Ninth Fort, the deportees were kept for three days in underground cellars, freezing, without any form of heating, denied either food or drink. Only then, frozen and starving, were they ordered to undress, taken to the pits at the edge of the fort, and shot.

Such was the terrible fate of those who had survived almost nine years of Nazi rule, who had witnessed Kristallnacht, and who had been trapped by the outbreak of war inside the sealed confines of the German Reich. In the suitcases of the murdered deportees at the Ninth Fort were found printed pamphlets urging them to prepare for a difficult winter. For this reason, some had brought

---

22 Lucjan Dobroszycki (editor), *The Chronicle of the Lodz Ghetto*, pages 83–94.
23 Dr Aharon Peretz, Eichmann trial, 4 May 1961, session 28.

small heating stoves with them. On being ordered to undress, they had struggled against the Germans. It was a hopeless struggle. The SS killing squad that carried out the executions recorded on November 25, with its customary precision, that on one occasion at the Ninth Fort, 1,159 Jewish men, 1,600 Jewish women and 175 Jewish children, described as 'settlers from Berlin, Munich and Frankfurt-am-Main', had been killed.

Four days later it was 693 Jewish men, 1,155 Jewish women and 152 Jewish children, 'settlers from Vienna and Breslau'.[24] They too were killed within a few hours.

Three years after Kristallnacht, its cruel aftermath was unfolding with ruthless and relentless efficiency.

On November 27 the first of nineteen trains left Germany for Riga, the former Latvian capital, another German eastern conquest. The train came from Berlin. On reaching Riga almost all the thousand Jews on board were taken to specially dug pits in the nearby Rumbula forest – where more than 10,000 Riga Jews had been massacred in the previous week – and machine-gunned to death.

The next deportees from Germany were sent into the Riga ghetto, from which a further 25,000 Riga Jews had been taken to Rumbula and murdered even as the trains were on their way. On November 29 a train reached Riga with 714 Jews from Nuremberg, Würzburg, Furth and smaller towns around them. On December 1 a further 1,200 Jews arrived from Stuttgart.

On December 3, just over a thousand Jews reached Riga from Vienna, and on the following day more than eight hundred from

---

24 *Trial of the Major War Criminals Before the International Military Tribunal, Nuremberg, 14 November 1945–1 October, 1946*, Document PS-2283 (the Jaeger Report).

Hamburg. All four thousand on these four transports were sent to Jungfernhof, a former Latvian army barracks that had been converted into an SS-run concentration camp. Within two months at least five hundred were dead.

Among those imprisoned in Jungfernhof was Dr Joseph Carlebach, the Chief Rabbi of Hamburg and Altona. 'He saw to it,' writes Gertrude Schneider – the historian of the German and Austrian Jews deported to Latvia, and herself a deportee from Vienna – that the Jewish holidays were observed and that the prayer in memory of the dead was recited: 'he consoled the bereaved when loved ones died, and raised the morale of all those around him. He and part of his family were exterminated in March 1942. After he was gone, there was little left of organised religious life, but people somehow knew the correct dates of the Jewish holidays and tried to observe them.'[25]

On December 7 – the day of Pearl Harbor – yet another train left Germany for Riga, with a thousand Jews from Cologne. Reaching Riga on December 10, the deportees were not sent to Jungfernhof concentration camp, as had the previous four trains, but to the Riga ghetto, where a special 'German' section had been set aside for them, once part of the Latvian Jewish ghetto but separated from it. Gertrude Schneider writes: 'Often, the newcomers discovered frozen corpses, which had been overlooked by the clean-up details and which they later had to bury themselves. It took them months to scrub off the many bloodstains they saw on the walls, the floors and the steps of their new homes.'[26]

Within two months, more than 15,000 German and Austrian Jews had been deported into this 'German' ghetto, each train –

25 Gertrude Schneider, *Journey into Terror*, page 33.
26 Gertrude Schneider, *Journey into Terror*, page 37.

made up of regular third-class passenger carriages – with a thousand deportees. In addition to the Jews from Cologne, the deportees came from many towns and the smaller communities around them: from Kassel, Fulda and Eschwege on December 9; from Duisburg, Krefeld and Düsseldorf on December 11; from Bielefeld – whose synagogue had been burned out on Kristallnacht – on December 12; and from Hanover on December 15. Then, after a three-week break, from Theresienstadt on 9 January 1942, Vienna on January 11, Berlin on January 13, Theresienstadt again on January 15, Berlin on January 19, Leipzig and Dresden on January 21, Berlin again on January 25, Vienna on January 26, and Dortmund on January 27.

On the train on December 9 was Martin Lowenberg, who had witnessed Kristallnacht in Fulda. All six members of his family were taken to a single room in the 'German' ghetto, with one other couple. There was no running water and no toilet. 'Since the previous occupants of the room had left food uncovered when they were suddenly rounded up, the room was full of rats, bedbugs, fleas and cockroaches.'

In 1935 Martin Lowenberg's older sister and brother had gone to Palestine. In 1937 his next oldest sister had emigrated to the United States. They survived the war. His parents, younger sister and twin brothers who had been sent to Riga did not.[27]

On February 5, 1,100 Jews from Berlin and four hundred from Vienna were taken out of the ghetto and shot. Four days later a thousand German and Austrian Jews were taken from Jungfernhof and likewise executed.

A final train had left Vienna for Riga on February 6. In one of the carriages was a well-known Viennese Jewish financier,

27 Martin Lowenberg, letter to the author, 25 September 2005.

Siegmund Bosel. Extremely ill, he had been brought to the station from hospital, by ambulance, in his pyjamas. During the journey the transport commander chained him to the floor and taunted him about his former riches, until tiring of this cruel game he shot him dead.

This last Vienna deportation to Riga arrived on February 10. It was forty-two degrees below zero. Those who could not face the seven-kilometre walk from the station to the ghetto were told that they could go by truck. People were desperate to join the trucks: a majority was allowed to do so. These innocuous-looking vehicles had been manufactured at the Saurer Works at Steyr, in Austria, to a special specification: they were sealed vans into which the exhaust pipe was turned. All those on the truck were dead within half an hour of it setting off.

There was a further deportation from Vienna on February 19. It went not to Riga but to the town of Kielce in German-occupied Poland. All 1,003 deportees were sent to live with the local Polish Jews; a month later they had to take their place in the newly established Kielce ghetto. Of the 1,003 deportees, only eighteen survived the war.

One of the deportees from Vienna to Kielce was fifty-two-year-old Gertrude Zeisler. Her letters to cousins in Switzerland give a glimpse of the worsening situation for the Jews of Vienna in the ghetto: 'I count myself amongst those lucky enough to have a few articles of clothing, which I am now forced to sell' (10 October 1941); '. . . those who have died before these times need not be pitied' (6 March 1942); '. . . how I already wish that I could talk about the days in Kielce as a memory of the dim past' (5 June 1942); '. . . you would not recognise the old, ugly woman I have become' (3 July 1942); and, in her final letter, 'I seem to lose my reason in this atmosphere of doom and idleness. Maybe if I return to normal surroundings I will once again become a thinking human being' (13 August 1942).

Seven days after writing this letter Gertrude Zeisler was deported with the other Viennese Jews, and the Jews of Kielce, to Treblinka. There were no survivors. The last letter written to her from her cousins in Switzerland was returned, marked 'Left the district'.[28]

An SS report from the police captain in charge of the 11 December 1941 deportation from Vienna to Riga, a journey that took sixty-one hours, criticised the stationmaster at Konitz, one of the many stations where the train stopped on its thousand-mile journey, for being 'one of those citizens who still talk about "poor Jews" and to whom the true concept of "Jew" was unknown'. The captain had no complaints about the guards who travelled with him, 'except perhaps for the fact that I had to remind some of them to treat the Jews in a sharper manner whenever they disobeyed my orders'.[29]

In the German ghetto in Riga, under the watchful, often vengeful eye of the SS, forty German Jews served as policemen. Others served as street cleaners. Thus order was preserved and cleanliness maintained. Gertrude Schneider, who had been on the last transport from Vienna, later described how the ghetto 'was a tiny German hamlet, scrupulously clean, complete with German street names, German police, German street cleaners, even German schools and occasional strains of German music. One could hear the impeccable

28 Gerda Hoffer (editor), *I Did Not Survive: Letters from the Kielce Ghetto*, pages 4–26.
29 Report by Captain of Police Salitter: Gertrude Schneider, *Journey into Terror*, pages 197–211.

speech of people from Hanover, the flat twang of the Berliners, the broad dialect of people from Leipzig and Dresden, the soft, lilting speech of Bavarians and Viennese, and the hard, but correct German spoken by Czechs. All those proper, middle-class people had one thing in common: they were Jews who had been deported to the East for liquidation, but had been spared temporarily because their labour was needed.'[30] There were even Catholic church services held in the ghetto for practising Catholics of Jewish descent, deported because they were 'Jews by race'.

A third destination for German Jews deported to Riga was the nearby slave labour camp at Salaspils. Conditions there were so harsh that few inmates survived. One who perished, a Hebrew teacher from Stuttgart named Jaffee, tried to ensure that, despite a Nazi prohibition, prayers for the dead were recited at the mass burial site there.

On 15 March 1942 a further 1,900 German and Austrian Jews were taken from the Riga ghetto to their deaths – having been told they were going to a work camp with lighter work and more food. The resilience of the surviving German and Austrian Jews was not weakened. Distinguished physicians maintained a small hospital. Mary Korwill, who had run the Tante Mary's Children's Camp in Austria, set up a school – until she was found wearing a gold wristwatch, and shot. Lesson plans were devised by a Vienna high school teacher, Alfred Lemberger. Adults attended lectures, including a series on Goethe's *Faust* by Dr Weil, who had been a professor of German literature at the University of Vienna. Neither Lemberger nor Weil survived the war. Nor did Grete Picker, a talented young woman who entertained the ghetto inmates with her singing.

30 Gertrude Schneider, *Journey into Terror*, page vii.

Among the plays put on by the ghetto inmates were Lessing's *Nathan the Wise*, Goethe's *Faust* and Stefan Zweig's *Jeremias*. Erich Eichenbaum, a concert violinist from Vienna who had managed to keep his violin, gave concerts, accompanied by an orchestra whose programmes included works by Brahms, Haydn, Mozart and Beethoven. Eichenbaum was not among the survivors. Nor was the owner of a cello who had been murdered at Salaspils, and whose name was unknown, but whose instrument became part of the ghetto orchestral endeavour.[31]

Amid the executions and the hunger in the ghetto, the German and Austrian Jews clung to the hope that they would survive. But of 20,000 deportees, there were only eight hundred survivors.

The suffering of the German Jews deported to Riga who remained in the ghetto was terrible. Lore Pels, who was deported from Hanover, later recalled the fate of Rolf Becher, who was caught bringing food into the ghetto. 'He had to pay for his life on the gallows. We had to watch when they hanged him.'[32] Ruben Moller, deported from Bochum to the Riga ghetto, later wrote: 'We were intermittently exposed to selection processes by which the old, sick, disabled and children were singled out for extermination ... I was selected, but managed to get away from the doomed group.' Those selected were killed in gas vans. 'When Latvian Jewish ghetto police were suspected of having weapons, the entire police force of about thirty men was assembled in an open area of the ghetto and machine-gunned. Yet, in spite of everything, I celebrated my Bar Mitzvah in the Riga ghetto.'[33]

---

31 Gertrude Schneider, *Journey into Terror*, pages 37–9, 49–51, 58–9, 75 and 81–4.
32 Lore Oppenheimer (*née* Pels), letter to the author, 4 July 2005.
33 Ruben Moller, 'A Brief History of the Moller Family', typescript sent to the author, 29 June 2005.

In Germany that November, Jews had to hand over all bicycles, typewriters, cameras and binoculars. At the same time, throughout Germany, the surviving Jewish communities were being selected for deportation to the East. In December the 403 surviving Jews of Munster, as well as 131 Jews from Fulda and six from Warendorf – whose synagogue survived Kristallnacht – were among the deportees to Riga.[34] From his pulpit in Berlin, the courageous Pastor Lichtenberg offered a public prayer for the Jews who were being deported to the East, and urged his congregants to observe the Biblical commandment 'Love thy neighbour.'[35] He was denounced to the Gestapo, arrested, and sentenced to two years in prison. He was sent to Dachau, but in the words of the official announcement, died 'on the way'.[36]

As 1941 drew to an end, a new technique of killing was being devised. In November, from among the German Jewish prisoners at Buchenwald, 1,200 were taken to the euthanasia institute at Bernberg, and murdered by gas.[37] The experiment was judged a success. The new method was first put into effect on December 8 – the day after Pearl Harbor – near Chelmno, a remote village in German-occupied Poland, where, at the rate of a thousand a day, Jews from nine surrounding towns and villages were brought and killed.

That Christmas, special Christian religious services were held in the Lodz ghetto for the many hundreds of deportees from

34 'Munster', 'Fulda' and 'Warendorf' entries: *Pinkas Hakellilot Encyclopaedia of Jewish Communities.*
35 H. D. Leuner, *When Compassion was a Crime*, page 10.
36 Zvi Bacharach, 'Lichtenberg, Bernhard (1875–1943)', *Encyclopedia of the Holocaust*, Volume 3, page 868.
37 *Trial of the Major War Criminals Before the International Military Tribunal, Nuremberg, 14 November 1945–1 October, 1946*, Document NO-907.

Germany who, while born Jewish, were practising Catholics and Protestants – in the Lodz ghetto they formed an 'Association of Christians'. The Catholic service was conducted by Sister Maria (Regina) Fuhrmann, a Master of Theology from Vienna. Two Catholic priests from among the newcomers attended the service.[38] For the Nazi deportation machine it was their Jewish origins that mattered, not their lifelong religious convictions.

On 11 December 1941, four days after Japan attacked the American fleet at Pearl Harbor, Germany declared war on the United States. That week Japanese forces occupied the International Settlements area of Shanghai, and confined the 18,000 German and Austrian German Jews who had found refuge there to a ghetto. Life was cramped and hard, but there were no executions or deportations as in the German-ruled ghettos. The Jews of the Shanghai ghetto survived the war: a fortunate remnant of German and Austrian Jewry.

Those who died in Shanghai during the war were buried in the local Baikal Road Jewish cemetery. Many years later, during the turmoil of the Chinese Communist Cultural Revolution, their gravestones were dug up and dumped in fields many miles away. Several of these have recently come to light. They include those of Anita Goldschmidt from Hamburg, whose tombstone was being used as part of a wall limiting access to a river; Dr Otto Hess from Dessau, whose stone was being used as a stepping stone across a village stream; Hirsch Robert Powizer from Berlin; Elisabeth Sametz from Holleschau in the Sudetenland; Else Rivka Wachsner from Breslau; and Gisela Natowicz from Vienna.[39]

*   *   *

38 Lucjan Dobroszycki (editor), *The Chronicle of the Lodz Ghetto*, page 100.
39 Material and photographs sent to the author from Shanghai by Dvir Bar-Gal, 2 September 2005.

On 20 January 1942 a group of senior German government officials gathered at a villa on the Wannsee, just outside Berlin, to discuss the role each of their departments would play in the 'Final Solution of the Jewish Question': the hoped-for elimination of all Jewish life in Europe. Six months earlier, Field Marshal Goering had entrusted the implementation of this task to Reinhard Heydrich, one of the masterminds of Kristallnacht. During the meeting, the man who had earlier been in charge of Jewish emigration, Adolf Eichmann, presented the bureaucrats, and also Heydrich, his ultimate superior, with a list he had compiled of Jews throughout Europe, country by country – whose arrest and deportation to death was about to become a Nazi priority. The number for Germany was 131,800, for Austria, 43,700.[40] These surviving witnesses of Kristallnacht were doomed.

On January 28, eight days after the Wannsee meeting, the Swedish explorer Sven Hedin appealed to Eichmann to prevent the deportation of an elderly German Jewish colleague who was living in Bonn – both of whose synagogues had been destroyed on Kristallnacht. Eichmann declined to help, instructing his subordinates: 'It cannot be agreed that he stays in Bonn until he dies, because when we deal with a final solution of the Jewish problem, the plan is that Jews above the age of sixty-five will be put in a special ghetto for the aged.'[41]

This 'special ghetto' was the Theresienstadt ghetto, established two months earlier in the former Czech garrison town of Terezin, a hundred miles north-west of Prague, in German-annexed

---

40 *Trial of the Major War Criminals Before the International Military Tribunal, Nuremberg, 14 November 1945–1 October, 1946*, Document NG-2586.

41 Letter of 28 January 1942 to the Foreign Ministry, Berlin: Eichmann trial, 17 May 1961, session 43, Exhibit T.728.

Czechoslovakia. Within two years 44,900 German Jews and 15,226 Austrian Jews were among the 150,000 Jews deported there. Of that total number, 33,000 died in Thersesienstadt of starvation and disease. A further 81,000 were deported to the East and murdered there: most of them at Auschwitz, and 23,503 at the death camp of Maly Trostenets, just outside Minsk.

Among those German Jews deported to Theresienstadt were Laurie Lowenthal's parents, Adolf and Sophie Lowenthal, who had last seen him when he left Aschaffenburg on a Kindertransport in February 1939. In Aschaffenburg his father had become a street sweeper in order to earn enough money to buy food. 'What humiliation,' his son writes, 'for a man who had fought for Germany in the First World War and won the Iron Cross.' After the war, 'I heard the following news. My father died of starvation in Theresienstadt in June 1943 and my mother was deported to the extermination camp at Auschwitz on 23 October 1944 (my birthday) and killed the next day in the gas chambers.' She had been transported on the last train from Theresienstadt to Auschwitz.[42]

No German Jewish community escaped deportation. Baruch Freier had been sent after Kristallnacht to Buchenwald, with his two sons. After all three were released, the two young men obtained visas and went to Britain. Their parents had obtained visas on 1 September 1939, the day Germany invaded Poland. Britain's declaration of war on Germany two days later made emigration impossible. But, asks their nephew Serem Freier, 'Did they really want to leave?' They had visited Palestine several years earlier and decided they did not want to live in a Jewish State that did not observe the Sabbath as a collective duty. Later they

---

42 Laurie Lowenthal, 'My Childhood in Germany', sent to the author 4 June 2005.

received visas for Shanghai but did not make use of them. 'My uncle was in the habit of saying that he would leave Germany in the last carriage of the last train,' Serem Freier commented. 'Instead, he was in the first train to leave for Buchenwald. That shows the genuine psychological difficulty of leaving a country that you were brought up in and that you had fought for in the First World War. I genuinely believe that he found it emotionally impossible to leave. In 1942 my uncle and aunt were again taken to a concentration camp, never to return.'[43]

The 131,800 German Jews and 43,700 Austrian Jews listed for death by Eichmann were systematically rounded up and deported throughout 1942 and 1943. On 24 March 1942 the first such deportation took place to a newly established death camp at Belzec, in German-occupied Poland. The 692 deportees were from Würzburg, Bad Kissingen, Jülich and Fürth, and the villages around them. Not a single one of these deportees survived. A further deportation to Belzec took place on April 3, from Bavaria, including 650 Jews from Nuremberg, 213 from Regensburg and 129 from Augsburg, both of whose synagogues were destroyed on Kristallnacht. With that deportation from Augsburg, the once one-thousand-strong Jewish community came to an end. It had been founded more than seven hundred years earlier, in 1212, and in the fifteenth century had been a centre of Jewish culture.

On 27 March 1942 the first deportation took place of Jews who had been rounded up in Paris. Their destination was Auschwitz. They included several German Jews who had found refuge in France before the outbreak of war, among them Bruno Goldschmidt from Nuremberg, Siegfried Erschon from Berlin, Ernest

43 Serem Freier, letter to the author, 19 June 2005.

Mayer from Mannheim and Rudi Nissenbaum from Leipzig.[44] These deportations from France continued for two and a half years. German Jews appear in each list of deportees, their name, date of birth, and place of birth diligently recorded: in all 6,222 German Jews and 2,127 Austrian Jews appear in the lists of deportees from France. There were at least five hundred more Jews who, although listed as 'stateless', had been born in Austria. A further four thousand Austrian, and many thousand German, Jews were deported to Auschwitz from Belgium and Holland. Among them, from Holland, was Anne Frank, a German Jewish girl born in Frankfurt-on-Main whose parents had emigrated to Holland shortly after Hitler came to power, when she was four.

Inside Germany, small communities as well as large were wiped out. Among those who were deported from Würzburg on April 25 – when 852 Jews were sent to Belzec – were the last sixteen Jews from the small town of Goldbach, in which Jews had lived for 250 years, and whose synagogue had been destroyed on Kristallnacht. Among those deported from Goldbach and killed were five members of the Brandstädter family and seven Oppenheimers. From the nearby town of Hössbach, Steffi Löwenthal, aged eleven, and her brother Henri, aged three, were among the deportees.[45] Henri Löwenthal had been five months old at the time of Kristallnacht. On May 10 a deportation train from Leipzig carried 369 Jews to Belzec. There were no survivors.

In the Lodz ghetto, Bronia Schwebel, one of the deportees from Vienna, recalled her father telling his family: 'Hang on, there will

44 'Convoi No. 1', Serge Klarsfeld, *Le Mémorial de la Déportation des Juifs de France*, pages 24–37.
45 Ingrid Heeg-Engelhart, *Die jüdische Gemeinde in Goldbach von ihren Anfängen bis 1942*, page 30 (facsimile deportation list, privately printed).

come a time when there won't be any borders, food will be on the table and we will be free.' She added: 'He never saw the day.'[46] On April 29 a proclamation, No. 380, was posted on walls throughout the Lodz ghetto. All 'unemployed' newcomers from Germany – except for holders of the Iron Cross or medals for wounds incurred in the First World War while fighting in the German or Austrian armies – were to be 'resettled', starting on May 4. Of the 17,000 newcomers only 3,000 had employment.[47]

The deportees were told that they could take twelve and a half kilograms of luggage with them. Starting on May 4, and continuing with a thousand a day, they were brought during the afternoon to the Central Prison and several nearby buildings, where they were kept overnight. There they were given bread, ersatz coffee and soup. They were also given a loaf of bread for the journey – free of charge. At four o'clock the next morning they were taken by tram to the suburban railway station of Radogoszcz.

On reaching the platform the deportees were arranged in groups of ten at each compartment door. Then they were ordered to step five paces back and throw all their baggage to the ground: suitcases, knapsacks, blankets and hand-held parcels. They were only allowed to keep the bread. Then they boarded the train, which consisted of regular third class carriages. Every person was given a seat. The sick and the elderly – some brought to the station from hospital – were carried on board by porters.

From Radogoszcz, the train left punctually at seven. Its destination lay fifty miles to the north-west, at a wayside halt near the village of Chelmno. From the halt the deportees were marched a few hundred yards to a brick mill on the right bank of the River

46 Bronia Sonnenschein (*née* Schwebel), letter to the author, 21 July 2005.
47 Lucjan Dobroszycki (editor), *The Chronicle of the Lodz Ghetto*, 29 and 30 April 1942.

Warta. From there they were taken in small groups by van into the Chelmno woods. The van was a sealed gas van. There were no survivors. The train returned to Lodz, empty, at eight that same evening.

In the words of one Lodz ghetto diarist: 'People from Vienna, Berlin, Cologne are the first sacrifice.' One of those in the first 'transport' of a thousand was the pianist Leopold Birkenfeld, from Vienna, 'skin and bones, starved, ripped out of his hospital bed in the night'.[48]

A thousand German Jews were assembled each day for deportation. The second thousand were deported on May 5. All were murdered on reaching Chelmno, as were the third thousand on May 6. On May 7 the Lodz ghetto chronicle wrote of the arrival of the newcomers from Germany scarcely six months earlier, comparing the smart clothes, ample food provisions and self-confidence of the new arrivals at the end of 1941 with the same men and women six months later: 'The soups they had scorned became the height of their dreams ... Some of the metamorphoses could not be imagined, even in a dream ... Ghosts, skeletons with swollen faces and extremities, ragged and impoverished, they now left for a further journey on which they were not even allowed to take a knapsack. They had been stripped of all their European finery, and only the Eternal Jew was left . . .'[49]

On the second day of the deportations, Professor Jakob Edmund Speyer died in the ghetto of exhaustion and weakening of the heart. He was sixty-three years old. Originally from

48 Oskar Rosenfeld's notebooks, May 1942, in Alan Adelson and Robert Lapides (editors), *Lodz Ghetto: Inside a Community Under Siege*, pages 208–9.
49 Jozef Klementynowski's diary, in Alan Adelson and Robert Lapides (editors), *Lodz Ghetto: Inside a Community Under Siege*, pages 213–14.

Frankfurt-on-Main, he was one of the great inventors of modern medical chemistry, the discoverer of Eudokal, a painkiller that improved on morphine, and a pioneer in the nutritional benefits of the use of vitamins.

The daily deportations from the Lodz ghetto were organised according to the place of origin of the deportees: first Vienna, Berlin and Cologne, then Hamburg and Düsseldorf, then more from Berlin, followed on a continuing daily basis by Jews from Hamburg, Vienna, Prague, Prague again, Vienna, Frankfurt, Cologne and, finally, Luxembourg. A group of 260 members of the Association of Christians was allowed to travel together. They were put with the deportees of May 9. A few days later, three hundred German Jews in a shelter for old people were ordered to leave. The tenth and final transport left on May 15. The precise figures compiled in the Lodz ghetto show that 10,915 German Jews were deported in the course of eleven days. There was not a single survivor from any of these deportations.

Six thousand German Jews remained in the ghetto, to share the fate of all the ghetto inmates. There were to be no further exemptions for holders of the Iron Cross or medals for wounds incurred in the First World War. All the 'newcomers' who did not starve in the ghetto joined the deportations to Auschwitz two years later.

In May 1942 yet another destination was chosen by the SS for the mass murder of German and Austrian Jews. It was Maly Trostenets, previously a Soviet collective farm on the outskirts of Minsk, former capital of the Belorussian Soviet Socialist Republic. The first train, with 998 Austrian Jews – men, women and children – left Vienna for Minsk on May 6. All those on board were taken from the Minsk freight station by truck to a wood on the outskirts of the farm and shot.

Between May and October 1942, sixteen trains left Vienna, Cologne, Königsberg and Theresienstadt for Maly Trostenets. A total of 15,000 deportees – half of them Viennese Jews – were murdered there. Fewer than two dozen of the deportees survived, the remnant of five or six hundred who were taken to another part of the farm and used as slave labourers.[50]

Among the thousand Jews deported from Vienna to Maly Trostenets on May 20, and killed on arrival, was Ernst Fleischer, born in Traunkirchen, who as a fifteen-year-old, a year before Kristallnacht, helped save a young non-Jewish woman from drowning in the Danube, an act that won him much praise in the Viennese newspapers at the time. He was deported with his younger sister Ruth. His fellow rescuer, thirteen-year-old Herbert Friedman, had been fortunate to leave Vienna on the first Kinder-transport, a month after Kristallnacht.[51]

In June 1942 one train of deportees from Germany, with a thousand Jews from Dortmund and the smaller towns of West-phalia, was sent to the ghetto of Zamosc, in south central Poland. Among the deportees was Alwin Lippman, a First World War German air ace and friend of Goering. Lippmann's exploits as a pilot had won him much acclaim in interwar Germany. Neither he nor his wife and daughter, who were deported to Zamosc with him, survived the war.

Throughout the summer of 1942, from all the main German cities, Jews were deported to Auschwitz. On June 8 it was the last Jews of Hassfurt and the surrounding villages who were deported. Their synagogue, built in 1888, had been burned out but not

50 Documentation Centre of Austrian Resistance, Vienna.
51 Herbert Friedman, letter to the author, 8 August 2005.

demolished on Kristallnacht: restored after the war, today it is a suite of medical offices.[52] On July 13, fifty-seven children were deported from Leipzig to Auschwitz. The official SS transport list gives their names, dates of birth and places of birth. Cila Zellner from Leipzig was two years old. Joel Zernik from Berlin was seven months old. Dewora Krauthammer from Leipzig was four months old.[53] All fifty-seven were murdered on their arrival in Auschwitz.

On September 12, in one of the deportations from Vienna to Theresienstadt, Lucie Draschler was among the deportees, with her mother and sister. In May 1944 her mother and sister were deported to Auschwitz. Both perished. Nor did she ever see her father again: he had earlier escaped to the Soviet Union after being deported to Poland in 1939. 'I am the sole survivor of my family.'[54]

Those who had earlier witnessed Kristallnacht also filled the slave labour camps of the Third Reich. On 17 October 1942 the first four hundred of 10,000 German Jews then in Buchenwald were deported to Auschwitz. Several thousand more were deported to Auschwitz from Sachsenhausen. Most were sent to the nearby Monowitz slave labour camp (known as Auschwitz III), to work in the Buna synthetic oil factory there.

On October 29 there was a deportation from Berlin to Riga. The parents of Max Kopfstein – who had gone to England on a

52 Sheldon Kirshner, 'German Woman Preserves Jewish History', *Canadian Jewish News*, 14 July 2005.
53 'Kinder und Schüler der Transport-Liste vom 13.7.1942 nach Auschwitz', in Adolf Diamant, *Deportationsbuch in den Jahren 1942 bis 1945 von Leipzig aus gewaltsam verschickten Juden*, page 215.
54 Lucy Mandelstam (*née* Lucie Draschler), 'Memoirs', enclosed with letter to the author, 24 July 2005.

Kindertransport in February 1939 – were among those in that deportation. His mother worked as a nurse in Berlin's Jewish hospital, the staff of which the Germans had ordered to be reduced. 'Father was as yet under no such obligation, but volunteered to accompany her.'[55] All 798 deportees were killed on arrival.

Four years after Kristallnacht, the murder of those Jews who had witnessed it was at its most intense. On November 1 a train with 1,014 Jewish women and old people reached Auschwitz from Berlin. During the selection, thirty-seven women were admitted to the barracks and given tattoo numbers. The remaining 977 deportees were killed in the gas chambers.[56]

At the end of November 1942 almost all the few surviving Jews from Pomerania, most of them from Stettin and Stolp, 179 in all, were rounded up and deported to Auschwitz. The synagogues in Stolp and Stettin had both been destroyed on Kristallnacht.

On 12 January 1943 the first deportation took place of Berlin Jews direct to Auschwitz. Of the thousand deportees who reached Auschwitz on the following day, 127 men were admitted to the camp and tattooed. The other 873 were killed in the gas chambers.[57] There were also deportations from Berlin to Theresienstadt. On January 28 three leaders of the German Jewish community, Rabbi Leo Baeck, Dr Paul Eppstein and Philip Kusover, were deported to Theresienstadt. Three of Leo Baeck's sisters had already died there. A fourth sister died shortly after his arrival.

On February 3 the so-called 'Factory Action' was launched throughout Germany. All Jews working at hitherto protected jobs in German war industries were to be deported. In three

55 Max Kopfstein, letter to the author, 6 June 2005.
56 Danuta Czech, *Auschwitz Chronicle, 1939–1945*, page 262.
57 Danuta Czech, *Auschwitz Chronicle, 1939–1945*, page 305.

deportations that month almost 3,000 Jews were killed at Auschwitz. A thousand Jewish men, women and children reached Auschwitz on February 4. Of them, 181 men and 106 women were taken to the barracks and tattooed. The remaining 713 were killed in the gas chambers.

Among the German Jews who reached Auschwitz on February 4 was thirty-five-year-old Feliks Hofstaetter, from Duisburg, all three synagogues of which had been destroyed on Kristallnacht. Two days after reaching the camp he escaped. Gestapo telegrams alerted the German police throughout the region. Four days later he was captured and brought back to Auschwitz. Sent to the notorious penal bunker of Block 11, he died that same day.

A further 3,000 German Jews were deported to Auschwitz in February: two more trains with a thousand each from Berlin, and a thousand from Breslau, of whom 994 were sent straight to the gas chambers.[58] Those who had not been able to leave Germany after Kristallnacht were being murdered without compunction and at incredible speed.

On February 27, the day after the third Factory Action deportation, the Berlin Gestapo rounded up 4,700 German Jews who were married to non-Jews. They were taken to a detention centre in the Rosenstrasse – a former Jewish community centre – from which they were to be deported to Auschwitz. In a gesture of defiance, 3,000 of their non-Jewish wives gathered in front of the building and demanded their husbands' release. The protesters stayed in the street for a week, refusing to leave until their husbands were freed. Then, on March 6, Josef Goebbels announced that the Jews who had been about to be deported were 'privileged

58 Danuta Czech, *Auschwitz Chronicle, 1939–1945*, pages 322, 324, 327, 334, 336.

persons': free men, he explained, who 'are to be incorporated in the national community'.[59] The 4,700 Jewish husbands thereby survived the war, living in Berlin.

On 2 March 1943 one of the largest single deportations to Auschwitz took place: 1,500 Jewish men, women and children from Berlin. Of them, 1,350 were sent to the gas chambers on arrival.[60] 'We are now definitely pushing the Jews out of Berlin,' Goebbels wrote in his diary on the day of the deportation. 'They were rounded up last Saturday and are to be carted off to the East as quickly as possible. Unfortunately our better circles, especially the intellectuals, once again have failed to understand our policy about the Jews and in some cases have even taken their part. As a result, our plans were disclosed prematurely, and a lot of Jews slipped through our hands. But we will still catch them.' Goebbels added: 'I certainly won't rest until the capital of the Reich, at least, has become free of Jews.'[61]

Six days after this deportation, Goebbels expressed his indignation when, as the deportation began of Berlin Jews from an old-age home, there were what he called 'regrettable scenes . . . when a large number of people gathered and some of them even sided with the Jews'. Three days later he confided to his diary: 'The scheduled arrest of Jews on one day failed because of the short-sighted behaviour of industrialists who warned the Jews in time. We therefore failed to lay our hands on about 4,000. They are now wandering about Berlin without homes, are not registered with the police and are naturally quite a public danger.' He had

59 Nathan Stolzfus, *Resistance of the Heart: Intermarriage and the Rosenstrasse Protest in Nazi Germany*, pages 207–57.
60 Danuta Czech, *Auschwitz Chronicle, 1939–1945*, page 342.
61 Diary entry, 2 March 1943: Louis P. Lochner (editor), *The Goebbels Diaries, 1942–1943*.

given orders for them to be rounded up 'as quickly as possible'.

On March 15, at Hitler's headquarters at Vinnitsa, deep in German-occupied Russia, Goebbels told Hitler 'that I deemed it essential to force the Jews out of the entire Reich as soon as possible. He approved, and ordered me not to cease or pause until not a single Jew is left anywhere in Germany.'[62]

Mass deportations to Auschwitz took place in the last two weeks of March 1943 from Berlin, Breslau, Munich and Hamburg. Also starting that March, the remnant of Rhineland Jewry who were still being held in the Vichy camps, principally Gurs, were deported to their deaths at Auschwitz. All had been witnesses of Kristallnacht.

On 20 April 1943 one of the last deportations of Jews from Germany took place. It was of 150 Jewish youngsters – about a hundred boys and fifty girls – who had been living since 1940 on a farm near Furstenwalde, Zionist pioneers being trained for work in Palestine in anticipation of receiving their Palestine Certificates. For almost three and a half years their life on Neuendorf farm had been that of cultivators of the soil and chicken farmers. But no corner of Germany, no enterprise however worthy, no scheme however rooted in past example, could avert the destructive eye of the Gestapo.

That April 20 almost all the youngsters were deported to Auschwitz. The few who were allowed to remain, including Gerd Bocian, because they had the expertise to complete the factory work needed for the laying of 30,000 eggs, were then sent to various slave labour camps.[63]

*　　*　　*

62 Diary entries, 11 and 15 March 1943: Louis P. Lochner (editor), *The Goebbels Diaries, 1942–1943*.
63 Jerry (Gerd) Bocian, conversation with the author, 14 September 2005.

On November 2 more than 2,000 German and Austrian Jews were deported to Auschwitz from the 'German' ghetto in Riga. There were almost no survivors.

On November 22 the patients at the Jewish mental home in Berlin, more than a hundred mostly elderly Jews, were deported to Auschwitz and murdered on arrival. German Jews were also among the French resistance fighters murdered by the Gestapo after being captured. Among those executed in France on 12 August 1944 were fifty-one-year-old Oscar Roskann from Berlin and twenty-one-year-old Isaac Rudecki from Aachen.[64] Also executed in 1944 was Willi Szapiro: he was one of eighteen Austrian Jews shot for their part in resistance activities in France. Writes Gertrude Schneider: 'there has never been a ceremony to honour this courageous Jew from Austria'.[65]

Of the 131,800 German Jews whom Eichmann had listed for death, fewer than 10,000 survived the war, 4,700 as a result of the Rosenstrasse protest, some five thousand others in hiding, their lives saved by German non-Jews who often had to pass them from family to family to escape Gestapo searches and the ever-present possibility of betrayal. Every non-Jewish attempt at rescue was fraught with danger. Emmy Erdmann, a non-Jewish German woman from Trier – the synagogue of which was destroyed on Kristallnacht – gave her identity card to a Jewish friend, who thereby survived the war. She also helped other Jews escape across the border into Holland. She was executed for these humane acts.[66]

64 'Juifs fusillés ou exécutés sommairement en France', Serge Klarsfeld, *Le Mémorial de la Déportation des Juifs de France*, pages 607–18.
65 Gertrude Schneider, *Exile and Destruction: The Fate of Austrian Jews, 1938–1945*, page 43.
66 United States Holocaust Memorial Museum, Photo Archive, Worksheet 05772.

In the autumn of 1944, more than six hundred German, Austrian and Czech Jewish refugees were rescued in one of the partisan-controlled areas of Yugoslavia. Their rescue was the result of a suggestion made by Winston Churchill's son Randolph, then serving with the Yugoslav partisans behind German lines, that these refugees be evacuated by air to Allied-controlled southern Italy. The first twenty-nine Jews were airlifted out on September 18, flown across the Adriatic Sea and reaching safety two hours later.[67]

In Kaiserwald concentration camp, to which many of the surviving Jews from the 'German' ghetto in Riga had been sent in the summer of 1943, the instinct to escape was heightened in September 1944, as Soviet troops drew near. Three Jews from Cologne managed to get away: Dr Rolf Bischofswerder, a young physician who had advised on contraception and treated venereal disease in the ghetto, his wife Ruth and their fellow-escapee, Lotte Adler. They were found by the Germans, brought back to Kaiserwald, and executed.[68]

On 28 April 1945, 3,000 Jewish women in Ravensbrück concentration camp, north of Berlin, were taken from the camp in Red Cross buses to Sweden. In the list of those who reached Sweden but were too weak to survive even with the care and attention of Swedish nurses, and died soon after their arrival, was Helena Hausmann, born in Dresden. She had been fourteen at the time of Kristallnacht.

Many witnesses of Kristallnacht had been caught up in the ever-widening grip of tyranny and destruction. Hans Biglajzer, one of the eye-witnesses in Bonn, both of whose synagogues

67 List of Jews to be evacuated from Topusko (Yugoslavia) to Bari (Italy),
    3 September 1944: War Office papers, 202/293.
68 Gertrude Schneider, *Journey into Terror*, page 90.

were destroyed that night, and whose sister had been able to get a permit to Britain, writes: 'All other members of my family, parents, grandparents, uncles, aunts, and my brother, perished. I spent the war in the Lodz ghetto and Auschwitz.'[69] He was being marched away from Dachau, in the direction of Innsbruck, when, on 2 May 1945, near the town of Bad Tölz, the marchers were overtaken by soldiers of the United States Seventh Army – their liberators.[70]

Ruben Moller, from Bochum, was nine years old during Kristallnacht. He survived deportation to the Riga ghetto, and seven further ghettos and slave labour camps. When he was at Kaufering – a subcamp of Dachau – in the last months of the war, he overheard a fragment of conversation between a German mother and her six- or seven-year-old daughter, who were walking past outside the camp only a few feet from the perimeter, wearing their Sunday best. The child asked: '*Mutti, was für Menschen sind die?*' 'Mother, what kind of people are they?' to which the mother replied: '*Das sind keine Menschen, das sind Juden.*' 'These are not people, they are Jews.'[71]

Kristallnacht taught several lessons.

It taught those who were the source of prejudice that a whole people can be demonised; that a whole nation can be turned totally and obscenely against a decent, hard-working, creative, loyal and integral part of its own society. This point was made on 19 August 2005 when Pope Benedict XVI, on his first visit to his native Germany after becoming Pope, went to the Roonstrasse

69 Hans Biglajzer, letter to the author, 6 June 2005.
70 Hans Biglajzer, letter to the author, 29 July 2005.
71 'A Brief History of the Moller Family', typescript sent to the author, 29 June 2005.

synagogue in Cologne, which had been destroyed on Kristallnacht and rebuilt after the war, and denounced the rise in anti-Semitism in the twenty-first century.

Kristallnacht taught those German Jews who still retained hope that Nazism would modify its anti-Jewish stance that the time had come to leave, except those who still clung, as some did, to the belief that the norms of civilised behaviour could not be totally breached or abandoned, and that, for example, war service for one's country must be more meaningful than a stirred-up racial animosity.

During the ten months between Kristallnacht and the outbreak of war nearly as many German Jews left (120,000) as in the five and a half years before then (150,000). The Austrian emigration figures for the ten months were about 140,000. Thus more than a quarter of a million people left their homes and their homeland in the wake of that one night and day of violence.

Kristallnacht taught several overseas governments that the time had come to open their gates to the growing tide of refugees. Britain was among those countries that opened their gates widely, although still retaining, as did all countries except, for a while at least, the International Settlements of Shanghai, restrictions and barriers to unrestricted immigration.

Kristallnacht taught the Nazi administrators and planners that they must in future act with silence and secrecy, hiding what they were doing to the Jews from the eyes of world indignation. The less the outside world knew or saw, the more efficient would be whatever policy they chose, and the less liable to outside concern or interference.

Kristallnacht taught, in hindsight, a historical lesson, that what begins as something finite in destruction and limited in time can quickly develop into a monster of mass murder; that evil has gradations, but is also a process, and can move smoothly, effort-lessly forward to greater evil.

Six years of legalised anti-Jewish discrimination, isolating the Jews from their fellow Germans and depriving them of the rights of full citizenship, were replaced on Kristallnacht by the first manifestations of direct, nationwide, physical violence, combined with arson, the destruction of property, the theft of property, the impoverishment of a whole community, physical assault, deport-ation, and mass murder. It was a brutal, hysterical, uninhibited assault on everything Jewish, on a far wider scale than hitherto, and yet only a prelude to something far larger still.

As they were taking place, the events of Kristallnacht shocked sensitive, humane men and women everywhere. First when emi-gration was still possible, and then when the Nazi regime turned from extrusion to extermination, there were always those who made every effort to take in refugees, and to save those who could be saved. Such generous souls were few in number, but large in spirit. Thanks to them, amid the collapse of morality, morality survived. Amid the ruins of civilisation, civilisation was reborn. But the losses are irreplaceable.

MAPS

1. (*Top*) Places mentioned in the text whose synagogues were destroyed on Kristallnacht
2. (*Above left*) Places mentioned in the text between Hesse and Baden whose synagogues were destroyed on Kristallnacht
3. (*Above right*) Places mentioned in the text between Bremen and the Ruhr whose synagogues were destroyed on Kristallnacht

4. Places in Germany and Austria mentioned in the text, with the Greater German borders at the time of Kristallnacht

5. Places in Europe mentioned in the text; and an escape route from Warsaw to Palestine

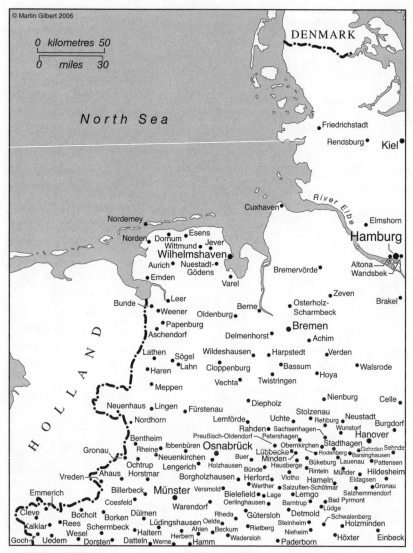

6. Places whose synagogues were destroyed on Kristallnacht: north-western Germany

7. Places whose synagogues were destroyed on Kristallnacht: from the Baltic to Leipzig

B a l t i c   S e a

Lauenburg

Stolp

Zoppot

Rügenwalde

Danzig
FREE
CITY

Tiegenhof

Bütow

Köslin

EAST
PRUSSIA
SEE
MAP 8

Kolberg

Rummelsburg

Treptow

Belgard

Cammin

Baldenburg

Greifenberg

Wollin

Regenwalde

Polzin

Hammerstein

Schivelbein

Neustettin

Schlochau

Naugard

Labes

Templeburg

Ratzebuhr

Preußisch-
Friedland

Gollnow

Jastrow

Stettin

Nörenberg

Flatow

Altdamm

Stargard

Kallies

Deutsch-
Krone

Krojanke

Woldenberg

Neuwedell

Tutz

Pyritz

Arnswalde

Schneidemuhl

Schönlanke

Lippehne

Bernstein

Soldin

Friedeberg

Groß-Strehlitz

Landsberg

Vietz

Schwerin

Drossen

Meseritz

Zielenzig

Frankfurt-Oder

Ziebingen

Schwiebus

Crossen

Züllichau

Grünberg

Fraustadt

Sommerfeld

P O L A N D

Glogau

Guhrau

Sorau

Sagan

Sprottau

Trachenberg

Milicz

Festenberg

Groß-
Wartenberg

Freienwalde

Lüben

Trebnitz

Bunzlau

Haynau

Neumarkt

Oels

Bautzen

Liegnitz

Breslau

Landsberg

0 kilometres 50

0 miles 30

8. Places whose synagogues were destroyed on Kristallnacht: Baltic–Stettin–Breslau region

9. Places whose synagogues were destroyed on Kristallnacht: East Prussia

10. Places whose synagogues were destroyed on Kristallnacht: Silesia

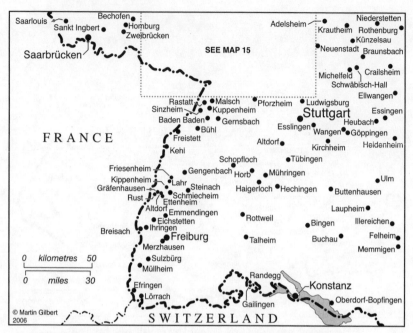

Saarlouis
Sankt Ingbert
Saarbrücken

Bechofen
Homburg
Zweibrücken

SEE MAP 15

Adelsheim
Krautheim
Neuenstadt

Niederstetten
Rothenburg
Künzelsau
Braunsbach

FRANCE

Michelfeld
Schwäbisch-Hall

Crailsheim

Rastatt
Sinzheim
Baden Baden
Bühl
Freistett
Kehl

Malsch
Kuppenheim
Gernsbach

Pforzheim
Ludwigsburg
Stuttgart
Esslingen
Altdorf

Ellwangen
Essingen
Heubach
Wangen
Göppingen
Kirchheim
Heidenheim

Friesenheim
Kippenheim
Gräfenhausen
Rust
Altdorf
Breisach

Gengenbach
Lahr
Steinach
Schmiecheim
Ettenheim
Emmendingen
Eichstetten
Ihringen
Freiburg
Merzhausen

Schopfloch
Horb
Haigerloch

Tübingen
Mühringen
Hechingen

Rottweil
Talheim

Bingen
Buchau

Ulm
Buttenhausen
Laupheim
Illereichen
Felheim
Memmigen

0 kilometres 50
0 miles 30

© Martin Gilbert
2006

Sulzbürg
Müllheim
Efringen
Lörrach

Randegg

Gailingen

Konstanz
Oberdorf-Bopfingen

SWITZERLAND

11. Places whose synagogues were destroyed on Kristallnacht: south-western Germany

Bibra
Weißenfels
Naumberg
Bautzen
Frankenthal
Erfurt
Gotha
Arnstadt Dornheim
Bürgel
Altenburg
Dresden
Rudolstadt
Zwickau
Chemnitz
Suhl
Reichenbach
Kirchberg
SEE
MAP 14
Lengfeld
Schleusingen
Annaberg
Themar
Plauen
Hof
Adorf
Ermershausen
Coburg
Kronach
Maroldweisach
Burgreppach
Hochstadt
Burgkunstadt
Lichtenfels
Altenkunstadt
Reckendorf
CZECHOSLOVAKIA
Ebelsbach
Memmelsdorf
Bamberg
Aufseß
Bayruth
Hirschaid
Buttenheim
Burghaslach
Forcheim
Floss
Uehlfeld
Baiersdorf
Auerbach
Heßdorf
Hüttenbach
Neustadt
Erlangen
Schnaittach
Wilhelmsdorf
Fürth
Ottensoos
Niederstetten
Eschenau
Amberg
Rothenburg
Zirndorf
Nuremberg
Ansbach
Schwabach
Leuterhausen
Lichtenau
Roth
Neumarkt
Feuchtwangen
Windsbach
Sulzbürg
Cham
Georgensgmünd
Crailsheim
Gunzenhausen
0 kilometres 50
Wittelshofen
Ellingen
Thalmässing
Regensburg
Mönchsroth
Markt Berolzheim
0 miles 30
Wassertrüdingen
Treuchtlingen
Ellwangen
Pappenheim
Aufhausen
Wallerstein
Hainsfarth
Straubing
Offenburg
Essingen
Nördlingen
Heubach
Harburg
Ingolstadt
Heidenheim
Buttenwiesen
Holzheim
Vilshofen
Binswangen
Ulm
Ichenhausen
Augsburg
Linz
Krumbach
Fischach
Wörth
Illereichen
Graben
AUSTRIA
Felheim
Munich
Memmigen
Altenstadt
Salzburg
© Martin Gilbert 2006

12. Places whose synagogues were destroyed on Kristallnacht: south-eastern Germany

13. Places whose synagogues were destroyed on Kristallnacht: from the Ruhr to the Rhineland

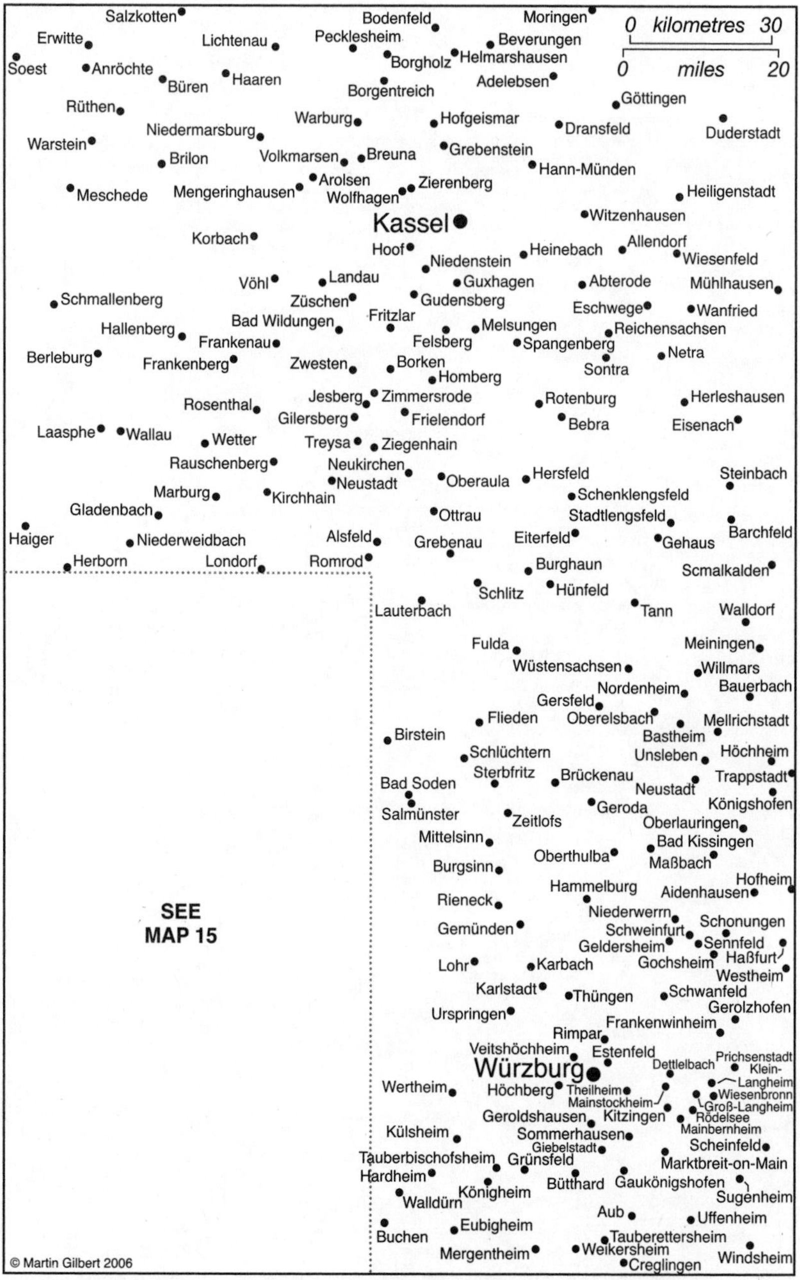

Salzkotten
Erwitte
Lichtenau
Pecklesheim
Bodenfeld
Moringen
Beverungen

Soest
Anröchte
Büren
Haaren
Borgholz
Helmarshausen
Borgentreich
Adelebsen
Göttingen

Rüthen
Warstein
Niedermarsburg
Brilon
Warburg
Hofgeismar
Dransfeld
Duderstadt

Volkmarsen
Breuna
Grebenstein
Hann-Münden

Meschede
Mengeringhausen
Arolsen
Wolfhagen
Zierenberg
Heiligenstadt

Korbach
Witzenhausen

Kassel

Hoof
Niedenstein
Heinebach
Allendorf
Wiesenfeld

Vöhl
Landau
Züschen
Guxagen
Abterode
Mühlhausen

Schmallenberg
Gudensberg
Eschwege
Wanfried

Hallenberg
Bad Wildungen
Fritzlar
Melsungen
Reichensachsen

Frankenau
Felsberg
Spangenberg
Netra

Berleburg
Frankenberg
Zwesten
Borken
Homberg
Sontra

Rosenthal
Jesberg
Zimmersrode
Rotenburg
Herleshausen

Gilersberg
Frielendorf
Bebra
Eisenach

Laasphe
Wallau
Wetter
Treysa
Ziegenhain

Rauschenberg
Neukirchen
Neustadt
Oberaula
Hersfeld
Steinbach

Marburg
Kirchhain
Schenklengsfeld

Gladenbach
Ottrau
Stadtlengsfeld

Haiger
Niederweidbach
Alsfeld
Grebenau
Eiterfeld
Gehaus
Barchfeld

Herborn
Londorf
Romrod
Burghaun
Scmalkalden

Schlitz
Hünfeld
Tann
Walldorf

Lauterbach

Fulda
Meiningen

Wüstensachsen
Willmars

Nordenheim
Bauerbach

Gersfeld

Flieden
Oberelsbach
Mellrichstadt

Birstein
Bastheim
Höchheim

Schlüchtern
Unsleben

Sterbfritz
Brückenau
Trappstadt

Bad Soden
Neustadt
Königshofen

Salmünster
Zeitlofs
Geroda
Oberlauringen

Mittelsinn
Bad Kissingen

Burgsinn
Oberthulba
Maßbach

Hammelburg
Hofheim

Rieneck
Aidenhausen

Niederwerrn

Gemünden
Schweinfurt
Schonungen

Geldersheim
Sennfeld

Lohr
Karbach
Gochsheim
Haßfurt

Westheim

Karlstadt
Thüngen
Schwanfeld

Gerolzhofen

Urspringen
Frankenwinheim

Rimpar

Veitshöchheim
Estenfeld
Prichsenstadt

Würzburg
Dettelbach
Klein-Langheim

Wertheim
Höchberg
Theilheim
Wiesenbronn

Mainstockheim
Groß-Langheim

Geroldshausen
Kitzingen
Rödelsee

Külsheim
Sommerhausen
Mainbernheim

Giebelstadt
Scheinfeld

Tauberbischofsheim
Grünsfeld
Marktbreit-on-Main

Hardheim

Königheim
Bütthard
Gaukönigshofen
Sugenheim

Walldürn
Aub
Uffenheim

Eubigheim

Buchen
Tauberettersheim
Windsheim

Mergentheim
Weikersheim
Creglingen

SEE
MAP 15

© Martin Gilbert 2006

14. Places whose synagogues were destroyed on Kristallnacht: central Germany

15. Places whose synagogues were destroyed on Kristallnacht: Rhine–Main area

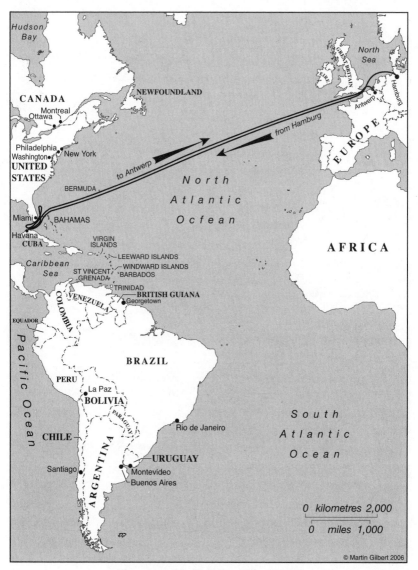

16. The voyage of the *St Louis*, and the Americas

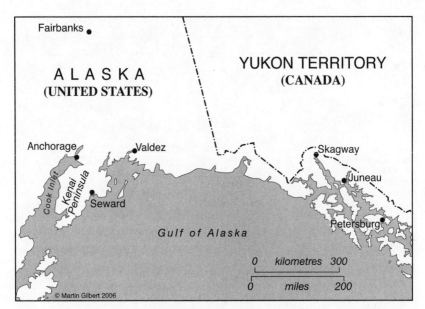

Fairbanks .

A L A S K A
(UNITED STATES)

YUKON TERRITORY
(CANADA)

Anchorage • •Valdez   •Skagway

Cook Inlet

Kenai Peninsula   •Juneau

•Seward

Gulf of Alaska   Petersburg•

0   kilometres   300

0   miles   200

© Martin Gilbert 2006

17. Alaska: the haven that never was

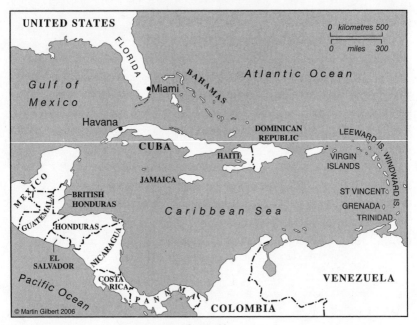

UNITED STATES

0   kilometres 500

0   miles   300

FLORIDA

Gulf of
Mexico

BAHAMAS

Atlantic Ocean

•Miami

Havana•

DOMINICAN
REPUBLIC

LEEWARD IS

CUBA

HAITI

VIRGIN
ISLANDS

WINDWARD IS.

JAMAICA

ST VINCENT•

MEXICO

Caribbean Sea

GRENADA•

•BRITISH
HONDURAS

TRINIDAD

GUATEMALA

HONDURAS

EL
SALVADOR

NICARAGUA

Pacific Ocean

COSTA
RICA

P A N A M A

VENEZUELA

© Martin Gilbert 2006

COLOMBIA

18. The Caribbean

19. Britain: places mentioned in the text

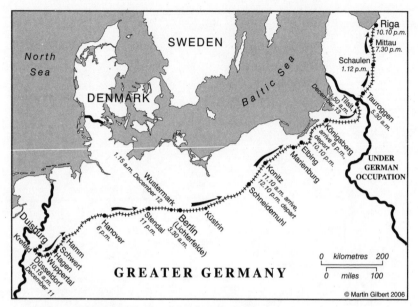

20. A deportation journey from the Ruhr to Riga, 11–13 December 1941,
with the train timetable

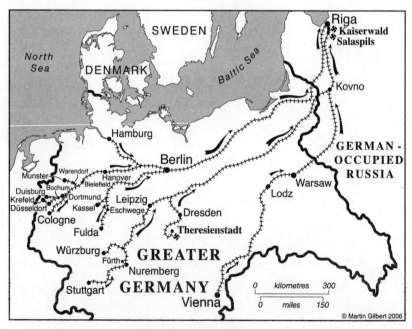

21. Deportation routes to Riga, 1941–42

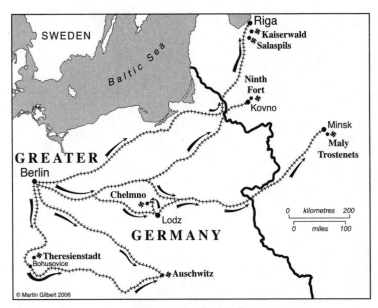

22. Deportations from Berlin, 1941–44

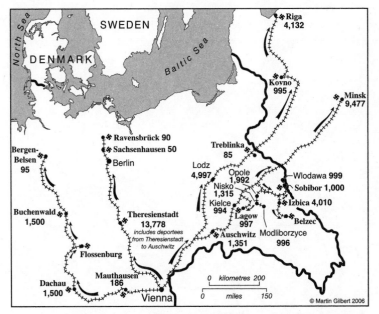

23. Deportations from Vienna, 1941–44, with the number of Jews murdered at each destination

24. Deportations to Auschwitz, 1942–44

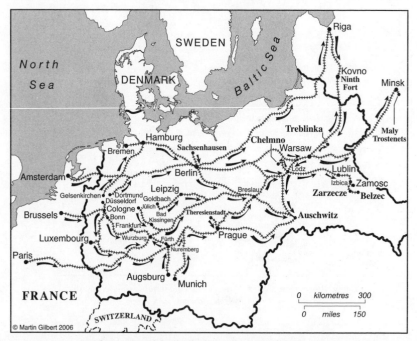

25. The pattern of the deportation of German Jews, 1940–44

SOURCES AND BIBLIOGRAPHY
OF WORKS CITED

Archival Collections

Central Zionist Archives, Jerusalem
Jewish Museum Collection, London
Klein family archive
Library of Congress
National Archives (formerly Public Record Office), London
National Archives and Records Administration, Washington DC
Orianenburger Strasse Synagogue Museum, Berlin
Sydney Jewish Museum
Wiener Library Archive, London
Yad Vashem Archives, Jerusalem
Zulfaris Synagogue Museum, Istanbul

Individual Recollections of Kristallnacht Sent to the Author

ASCHAFFENBURG: Laurie Lowenthal
BAD KREUZNACH: Marianne Geernaert
BERLIN: Jerry Bocian, Chava Cohn, Max Kopfstein, Helga Leib,
   Miriam Litke, Zerem Freier, Miriam Spira
BOCHUM: Ruben Moller
BRESLAU: Esther Adler, Frank Wachsner
COLOGNE: Hans Biglajzer, Rita Newell
DANZIG: Ruth Fluss
ELBING: Gerhard Maschkowski
FRANKFURT-ON-MAIN: Reiner Auman, Hans Benjamin Marx,
   Batya Rabin, Joseph Wohlfarth

FULDA: Naftali Kurt Wertheim, Martin Lowenberg, Margot
Wohlman-Wertheim
FURTH: Oskar Prager
GLATZ: Ruth Lewin
HAMBURG: Edgar Gold, Adina Koor
HANOVER: Ruth Gutmann, Lore Oppenheimer
HOENGEN: Eric Lucas
HORB: Margot Wilde
KARLSRUHE: Walter Loeb
LEIPZIG: Esther Reisz, Joseph Schwarzberg, Stephanie Segerman
MAINZ: Elsa Kissel
MANNHEIM: Janet Ettelman
MARKTBREIT-ON-MAIN: Lassar Bruekheimer
MUNICH: Inge Sadan, Pesach Schindler
RATIBOR: Chava Cohn
SIEGBURG: Fred Gottlieb
STUTTGART: Edith Rogers, Henry Stern
VIENNA: Susan Ben Yosef, Gertrude Bibring, Fred Garfunkel, Gary
Himler, Ilse Loeb, Lucy Mandelstam, Helga Milberg, Felix Rinde,
Felix Seiler, Bronia Sonnenschein, Hans Waizner
WUPPERTAL: Renie Inow
WÜRZBURG: Charlotte Lapian

Typescripts and Manuscripts Sent to the Author

Professor Arthur Freud, 'Looking Back'
Ruth Gutmann, 'The Nazi Noose Tightens'
Laurie Lowenthal, 'My Childhood in Germany'
Eric Lucas, 'The Sovereigns' (Kibbutz Kfar Blum, Palestine, 1945)
Manli Ho, 'Dr Feng Shan Ho, Chinese Consul General to Vienna,
Austria, 1938–1940' (San Francisco, February 2000)
Ruben Moller, 'A Brief History of the Moller Family'
Stephen Nicholls, 'A Heroic Stand During the Night of 9th/
10th November 1938' (Wichard von Bredow)
Batya Rabin, 'Friendly Aliens, or Uprooted but not Rootless'
Pesach Schindler, 'A Jewish Child Growing up in Nazi Germany'
(Jerusalem, 2004)
Joseph Schwarzberg, 'My Life Story' (1990)

Joseph Wohlfarth, 'A Snapshot of the Events as I Remember Them'
Margot Wohlman-Wertheim, 'The First Day of my War'

Unpublished Typescripts

Kenneth Ambrose, 'The Suitcase in the Garage: Letters and
Photographs of a German Jewish Family, 1800–1950'
Ilse Eden and Ilse Henry, 'The Schlesingers' Hostel at 26 Shepherd's
Hill, London N6, March–September 1939'. London, June 1999

Published Documents

*The Trial of Adolf Eichmann: Record of Proceedings in the District
Court of Jerusalem*, Volume 1. Jerusalem: Yad Vashem, 1992
*Trial of the Major War Criminals Before the International Military
Tribunal, Nuremberg, 14 November 1945–1 October, 1946*, 42
volumes. Nuremberg, 1947–49
*Papers Concerning the Treatment of German Nationals in Germany,
1938–1939*. London: Command Paper 6120, Germany No. 2 (1939),
His Majesty's Stationery Office, 1939
Alan Adelson and Robert Lapides (editors), *Lodz Ghetto: Inside a
Community Under Siege*. New York: Viking, 1989
Norman H. Baynes (editor), *The Speeches of Adolf Hitler, April
1922–August 1939*, Volume 1. London: Oxford University Press,
1942
Adolf Diamant, *Zerstörte Synagogen vom November 1938*.
Frankfurt-on-Main: privately printed, 1978
Adolf Diamant, *Deportationsbuch in den Jahren 1942 bis 1945 von
Leipzig aus gewaltsam verschickten Juden*. Frankfurt-on-Main:
privately printed 1991
Lucjan Dobroszycki (editor), *The Chronicle of the Lodz Ghetto, 1941–
1944*. New Haven, Connecticut: Yale University Press, 1984
Ingrid Heeg-Engelhart, *Die jüdische Gemeinde in Goldbach von ihren
Anfängen bis 1942*. Facsimile deportation list, privately printed
Gerda Hoffer (editor), *I Did Not Survive: Letters from the Kielce
Ghetto*. Jerusalem: Gefen, 1981
Serge Klarsfeld, *Le Mémorial de la Déportation des Juifs de France*.
Paris: Beate et Serge Klarsfeld, 1978

Louis P. Lochner (editor), *The Goebbels Diaries, 1942–1943*. Westport, Connecticut: Greenwood Press Reprint, reprint edition, 1970

Encyclopaedias and Reference Works

Blackbook of Localities Whose Jewish Population was Exterminated by the Nazis. Jerusalem: Yad Vashem, 1965

Encyclopaedia Judaica, 16 volumes. Jerusalem: Keter, 1972

Foreign Relations of the United States, Diplomatic Papers, 1940, Volume II. Washington: United States Government Printing Office, 1957

Pinkas Hakellilot Encyclopaedia of Jewish Communities, 12 volumes (Hebrew). Jerusalem: Yad Vashem, 1969–99

Yitzhak Arad (editor), *A Pictorial History of the Holocaust*. New York: Macmillan, 1990

Elke Fröhlich (editor), *Die Tagebücher von Joseph Goebbels: Sämtliche Fragmente* (The Goebbels Diaries: All Entries). Munich: K. G. Saur, 1998

Israel Gutman (editor-in-chief), *Encyclopedia of the Holocaust*. New York: Macmillan, 1990

Jacob Robinson and Henry Sachs (editors), *The Holocaust: The Nuremberg Evidence*, Part 1, Documents. Jerusalem: Yad Vashem, 1976

J. Hope Simpson, *The Refugee Problem, Report of a Survey*. London: Oxford University Press and Royal Institute of International Affairs, 1939

Shmuel Spector (editor-in-chief), *The Encyclopedia of Jewish Life Before and During the Holocaust*. New York: New York University Press, 2001

Arieh Tartakower and Kurt R. Grossman, *The Jewish Refugee*. New York: The Institute of Jewish Affairs of the American Jewish Congress and the World Jewish Congress, 1944

Books

Irving Abella and Harold Troper, *None is Too Many: Canada and the Jews of Europe, 1933–1948*. Toronto: Lester and Orpen Dennys, 1982

Eva Abraham-Podietz and Anne Fox, *Ten Thousand Children: True*

Stories Told by Children who Escaped the Holocaust on the Kindertransport. West Orange, New Jersey: Berman House, 1999

Herbert Agar, *The Saving Remnant: An Account of Jewish Survival since 1914.* London: Rupert Hart-Davis, 1960

Ehud Avriel (Uberall), *Open the Gates! A Personal Story of 'Illegal' Immigration to Israel.* London: Weidenfeld and Nicolson, 1975

Leonard Baker, *Days of Sorrow and Pain: Leo Baeck and the Berlin Jews.* New York: Macmillan, 1978

Paul R. Bartrop, *Australia and the Holocaust, 1933–45.* Melbourne: Australian Scholarly Publishing, 1994

Anil Bhatti (editor), *Jewish Exile in India.* New Delhi: Manohar Publishers, 1999

Mary Bosanquet, *The Life and Death of Dietrich Bonhoeffer.* London: Hodder and Stoughton, 1968

Malcolm S. Cole and Barbara Barclay, *Armseelchen: The Life and Music of Eric Zeisl.* Westport, Connecticut: Greenwood Press, London, 1984

R. M. Cooper (editor), *Refugee Scholars: Conversations with Tess Simpson.* London: Moorland Books, 1992

Danuta Czech, *Auschwitz Chronicle, 1939–1945.* London: I. B. Tauris, 1990

Günther Deschner, *Heydrich: The Pursuit of Total Power.* London: Orbis, 1981

Muriel Emanuel and Vera Gissing, *Nicholas Winton and the Rescued Generation.* London: Vallentine Mitchell, 2002

Anne L. Fox, *Between the Lines: Letters from the Holocaust.* Margate, New Jersey: ComteQ Publishing, 2005

Saul Friedlander, *Nazi Germany and the Jews: The Years of Persecution, 1933–1939.* New York: Harper Perennial, 1998

Varian Fry, *Surrender on Demand.* New York: Random House, 1945

Ruth Gruber, *Inside of Time: My Journey from Alaska to Israel.* New York: Carroll and Graf, 2003

Mark Jonathan Harris and Deborah Oppenheimer, *Into the Arms of Strangers: Stories of the Kindertransport.* London: Bloomsbury, 2000

Hannelore Headley (*née* Heinemann), *Blond China Doll: A Shanghai Interlude, 1939–1953.* St Catherine's, Ontario: Triple H Publishing, 2004

Philip K. Jason and Iris Posner (editors), *Don't Wave Goodbye: The Children's Flight from Nazi Persecution to American Freedom.* Westport, Connecticut: Praeger, 2004

Jon and David Kimche, *The Secret Roads: The 'Illegal' Migration of a People, 1938–1948.* London: Secker and Warburg, 1954

Lionel Kochan, *Pogrom: 10 November 1938.* London: André Deutsch, 1957

Roberta Kremer (editor), *Diplomatic Rescuers and the Story of Feng Shan Ho.* Vancouver: Vancouver Holocaust Education Centre, 1999 (brochure)

H. D. Leuner, *When Compassion was a Crime: Germany's Silent Heroes.* Amherst, New York: Prometheus Books, 1978

Bertha Leverton and Shmuel Lowensohn, *I Came Alone: The Stories of the Kindertransports.* Suffolk, England: The Book Guild, 1990

Andy Marino, *A Quiet American: The Secret War of Varian Fry.* New York: St Martin's Press, 1999

Jean Medawar and David Pyke, *Hitler's Gift: Scientists Who Fled Nazi Germany.* London: Richard Cohen Books, 2000

Arthur D. Morse, *While Six Million Died: A Chronicle of American Apathy.* New York: Random House, 1968

Mordecai Paldiel, *The Path of the Righteous: Gentile Rescuers of Jews During the Holocaust.* Hoboken, New Jersey: Ktav Publishing House, 1993

Michael Phayer, *The Catholic Church and the Holocaust, 1930–1956.* Bloomington and Indianapolis: Indiana University Press, 2000

Anthony Read and David Fisher, *Kristallnacht: The Nazi Night of Terror.* London: Michael Joseph, 1989

Edith Rogers, *No Childhood.* No place given: First Books Library, 2002

William Russell, *Berlin Embassy.* New York: E. P. Dutton, 1941

Gertrude Schneider, *Journey into Terror: The Story of the Riga Ghetto.* New York: Art House, 1979

Gertrude Schneider, *Exile and Destruction: The Fate of Austrian Jews, 1938–1945.* Westport, Connecticut: Praeger, 1995

Frank Shapiro, *Haven in Africa.* Jerusalem: Gefen, 2002

Eric Silver, *The Book of the Just: The Silent Heroes Who Saved Jews from Hitler.* New York: Grove Atlantic, 1992

Michael Smith, *Foley: The Spy Who Saved 10,000 Jews.* London: Hodder and Stoughton, 1999

Leo Spitzer, *Hotel Bolivia: The Culture of Memory and a Refuge from Nazism.* New York: Hill and Wang, 1999

Nathan Stolzfus, *Resistance of the Heart: Intermarriage and the Rosenstrasse Protest in Nazi Germany.* New York: W. W. Norton, 1996

Frederick Taylor, *Dresden: Tuesday 13 February 1945.* London: Bloomsbury, 2004

Rita Thalmann and Emmanuel Feinermann, *Crystal Night: 9–10 November 1938.* London: Thames and Hudson, 1974

Margaret Thatcher, *The Path to Power.* London: HarperCollins, 1995

Gordon Thomas and Max Morgan-Witts, *Voyage of the Damned: The Voyage of the St Louis.* London: Hodder and Stoughton, 1974

Barry Turner, *. . . And the Policeman Smiled: 10,000 Children Escape from Nazi Europe.* London: Bloomsbury, 1990

Wim van Leer, *Time of My Life.* Jerusalem: Carta and the Jerusalem Post, 1984

Salomon van Son, *The van Son Family.* Jerusalem: privately printed, 1991

Ulrich von Hassell, *The von Hassell Diaries.* Boulder, Colorado: Westview Press, 1994

Meir Wagner, *The Righteous of Switzerland.* Tel Aviv: Ktav Publishing House, 2000

George Weidenfeld, *Remembering my Good Friends.* London: HarperCollins, 1995

Katherine Whitaker and Michael Johnson, *Stoatley Rough School, 1934–1960.* Privately printed, 1994

Articles

K. J. Ball-Kaduri, 'Berlin is "Purged" of Jews. The Jews in Berlin in 1943', *Yad Vashem Studies V.* Jerusalem, 1963

Paul R. Bartrop, 'The Dominions and the Evian Conference of 1938', in Paul R. Bartrop (editor), *False Havens: The British Empire and the Holocaust.* Lanham, Maryland: University Press of America, 1995

Henry Walter Brann, 'Pastor who Rescued Jews is Honoured' (Pastor Grüber), *Jewish Week.* Washington DC, 20 August 1970

Douglas Davis, 'The Hero Inside a Quiet Little Man' (Captain Foley), *Jerusalem Post*, 29 January 1999

Douglas Davis, 'Ho Fengshan: The Chinese Oskar Schindler', *Jerusalem Post*, 20 February 2000

Dr Arthur Flehinger, 'Flames of Fury', *Jewish Chronicle*, 9 November 1979

Ingrid Heeg-Engelhart, *Die jüdische Gemeinde in Goldbach von ihren Anfängen bis 1942* (pamphlet), 1998

Dermot Keogh, 'The Irish Free State and the Refugee Crisis, 1933–45', in Paul R. Bartrop (editor), *False Havens: The British Empire and the Holocaust*. Lanham, Maryland: University Press of America, 1995

Sheldon Kirshner, 'German Woman Preserves Jewish History', *Canadian Jewish News*, 14 July 2005

Tom Kizzia, 'Sanctuary: Alaska, the Nazis, and the Jews: The Forgotten Story of Alaska's Own Confrontation with the Holocaust', *Anchorage Daily News*, 16, 17, 18 and 19 May 1999

P. R. Kumaraswamy, 'India and the Holocaust: Perceptions of the Indian National Congress', *Journal of Indo-Judaic Studies*, Volume 3, April 2000

Gerald Levy, 'Kristallnacht Revisited', *Zachor*, Sydney, Australia, November 2002

William R. Perl, 'The Holocaust and the Lost Caribbean Paradise', *The Freeman*, The Foundation for Economic Education, Volume 4, Number 1, January 1992

Arthur Propp, 'November, 1938 in Königsberg', *Midstream*, February 1987

Denis Staunton, 'In Defiance of Fascism' (obituary of Countess von Maltzan), *Guardian*, 18 November 1997

Judith Tydor-Baumel, 'The Kitchener Transmigration Camp at Richborough', *Yad Vashem Studies XIV*: Jerusalem, 1981

Yosef Yaakov, 'An Overlooked Experience' (Jewish refugees in India), *Jerusalem Post*, 10 September 1999

Order of Service

A Service of Prayer and Intercession for the Jews of Germany. London: Chief Rabbi's Office, 20 November 1939

Film Transcript

Melissa Hacker, *My Knees were Jumping: Remembering Kindertransports*, Bee's Knees Productions, New York, 1996

Exhibition

Eric Saul, 'Visas for Life: The Righteous Diplomats', first exhibited at the Simon Wiesenthal Centre, Museum of Tolerance, Los Angeles, and the California State Capitol Building, Sacramento, 2000. Since then the exhibit has travelled to fifteen countries and been shown in more than 150 venues.

Newspapers

Daily Herald
Daily Telegraph
Evening News
Evening Standard
Haàretz
Manchester Guardian
New York Times
News Chronicle
Observer
Palestine Post
The Times
Washington Post

INDEX

(Compiled by the author)